MONOMANIA

MONOMANIA

*The Flight from
Everyday Life in
Literature and Art*

Marina van Zuylen

CORNELL UNIVERSITY PRESS
Ithaca and London

First published 2005 by Cornell University Press
Printed in the United States of America

Library of Congress Cataloging-in-Publication Data

van Zuylen, Marina.
    Monomania : the flight from everyday life in literature and art / Marina van Zuylen.
        p.   cm.
    Includes bibliographical references and index.
    ISBN 0-8014-4298-2 (alk. paper) — ISBN 0-8014-8986-5 (pbk. : alk. paper)
    1. Mental illness in literature.   2. Obsessive–compulsive disorder in literature.   3. European literature—19th century —History and criticism.   4. European literature—20th century—History and criticism. Art history.   I. Title.
    PN56.M45V36 2005
    809'.933561—dc22

                                    2004023886

Cloth printing   10 9 8 7 6 5 4 3 2 1
Paperback printing   10 9 8 7 6 5 4 3 2 1

To my students

Contents

—m—m—m—

Acknowledgments

—ɯ——ɯ——ɯ—

This book could not have been written without the intellectual iconoclasm and independence of spirit of my colleagues and students at Bard College. The openness I have encountered there is what enabled me to cultivate subjects well outside my own expertise and write about them. I am most indebted to Odile Chilton, Tabetha Ewing, Stephanie Kufner, Ann Lauterbach, Medrie MacPhee, Melanie Nicholson, Alice Stroup, Karen Sullivan, and Eric Trudel. I thank those anonymous colleagues who selected me for a Bard Research Grant. The students in my First-Year Seminar on Baudelaire and in my class "Doctors and Writers" inspired some of my best pages. I owe a special debt of inspiration to the much missed Bill and Annys Wilson and to the unforgettable Margaret Creal Shafer.

The yearly Nineteenth-Century French Studies Colloquium has played a great role in the conception of this project. It is there that I met exceptional colleagues and was given the chance to present talks that became the basis for many chapters in this book. Among them is Bill Paulson, whose help with the manuscript has been so precious, and his suggestions so crucial, that it made me wonder whether he had not written parts of the book himself in a previous life. Friends like Deborah Jenson, a great interlocutor throughout the years, Catherine Nesci, who helped me in many ways, and Janet Beizer, whose *Ventriloquized Bodies* has been a seminal influence, played an important role in convincing me that it was time to let monomania loose.

My time teaching at Columbia University was also a great source of inspiration. I deeply thank my former colleagues and students in the French Department and in the Core Curriculum. At Columbia I also benefited from a Lurcy Fellowship and the James A. MacDonald Faculty Development Award.

The wonderful people at Cornell University Press made the editing of this book seem effortless. Without Bernie Kendler, this project would be collecting dust in an attic somewhere. I thank him deeply. Herman Rapaport, who miraculously took time away from his own work to help with the manuscript, will never be thanked enough. I am also grateful to Teresa Jesionowski, a model of spirited efficiency, Lou Robinson, Susan Barnett, and Tonya Cook.

Without Joy Sobeck, who understands the idée fixe better than most, I would have inevitably turned into George Eliot's Casaubon and never survived my own footnotes.

I also thank Kevin Millham for his indexing genius. Nobody else could have turned chaos into form with such elegance.

Additional thanks are due to Jesse Aylen, Carol Brener, Yve-Alain Bois, Masha Belenky, Mark Caldwell, Clare Cavanagh, Eileen Gillooly, Bochko Givadinovitch, Margaret Hornick, Rachel Jacoff, Martin Kline, Philip Lavoie, Sina Najafi, Pierre Nora, Mark Petrini, James O'Shea, Michael Wachtel, and Gabrielle Wolohojian.

Sections of this book have been published in *Cabinet, Études françaises, Paragraphes,* and *Research in African Literature.* I thank their editors for permission to reprint. Emily Dickinson's poem "It might be lonelier" is reprinted in chapter 8 by permission of the publishers and the Trustees of Amherst College from *The Poems of Emily Dickinson:* Variorum Edition, Ralph W. Franklin, ed., Cambridge, Mass.: The Belknap Press of Harvard University Press, Copyright © 1998 by the President and Fellows of Harvard College. Copyright © 1951, 1955, 1979, 1983 by the President and Fellows of Harvard College.

Finally, I thank my mother and father for their eccentric but loving forms of encouragement; my nieces Sara and Jessica Watson, whose irresistible company made it almost impossible to finish this book; Iain Watson for taking seriously every idea under the sun; my beloved sisters, Chacha, Cordelia, Vanessa, and Allegra; Max and Benjamin, the latest additions to the family; my son Simon, who has endured all my strange scholarly projects with a healthy dose of skepticism; and Stephan who has made everything possible.

MARINA VAN ZUYLEN

Annandale-on-Hudson

MONOMANIA

Introduction

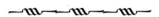

Imagine a painter who was so sickened by "the sight of lawns, trees and shrubs, [that] he would, whenever invited to tea on someone's terrace, insist on sitting with his back to the view. As a refugee in London in 1938, he rented a studio with frosted windows which prevented him from seeing out; he had the walls, floors and ceilings painted white, as he had already done in his two Paris studios."[1] The painter, who was none other than Piet Mondrian, was so allergic to "plain" nature that he fought against it with all the might of abstract art. Where his fellow-Dutchmen had repelled the sea with geometric dykes and man-made polders, he chose to strike out against the real with the absolutism of his vertical and horizontal lines. But the real always ended up resurfacing: despite the grids that framed Mondrian's monochromatic tones with ever increasing urgency, despite the "hairshirts and the self-chastisements . . . the arbitrary merely form[ed] again."[2]

This book is about the obsessive strategies people use to keep the arbitrary out of their lives; it is about the fanaticism and intolerance linked to their ideas of perfection and permanence. Mondrian rejected nature because it would never conform to his will or sit still in grid-like immutability. It was disconcertingly mobile, dangerously *itself*.[3] So instead of enduring nature's fickle instability, he devoted his life to a series of idées fixes that would offer a solid scaffolding to his ever-shifting inner

1. Frank Whitford, "Beauty and the Boogie: The Colourful Emotional Discipline in Mondrian's Neo-Plastic Technique," *Times Literary Supplement*, October 6, 1995.

2. Yves Bonnefoy, *The Lure and the Truth of Painting: Selected Essays on Art*, ed. Richard Stamelman (Chicago: University of Chicago Press, 1995), 103.

3. We are reminded of Hegel, who not only found no interest in the so-called beauty of nature, but considered any landscape boring until it had been transfigured into art. See the excellent article by Robert B. Pippin, "What Was Abstract Art? (From the Point of View of Hegel)," *Critical Inquiry* 29 (Autumn 2002): 1–24. Hegel went so far as to claim that "a landscape painting is the proper object of human attention and speculative contemplation, not a natural landscape itself" (*Aesthetics* 1:29; quoted in ibid., 9).

being. There is much to learn from individuals who have shaped their lives as Mondrian did his paintings. The protagonists of this study do everything in their power to stabilize their universes and expel indeterminacy from their worlds. They have learned that it is the fluctuating nature of phenomena that invalidates their belief in inner permanence; they seek, as a counterattack, the self-inflicted wounds of austere and codified lives. Haunted by the fear of a purposeless existence, they pledge their lives to a plan, a project, or a person who becomes their sole *raison d'être*. Guided by this creed, they turn the world into a private and sterile laboratory where they hope to do away with incoherence and chaos. In Schiller's words, such an individual strives "to destroy everything in himself which is mere world," replacing it bit by bit with a harmonious whole.[4] The world, as it stands, will never satisfy the quest for perfection; either too prosaic or too perplexing, its lines must be redrawn to fit the utopian dream of perpetual meaning. Such a dream, however, leaves nobody unscathed; while lavishing on its perpetrators a grandiose sense of purpose, it turns everyday necessities into trivial burdens and injects into ordinary emotions a bored sense of *déjà vu*.

Those who inhabit these pages are driven by the type of idée fixe immortalized by the great monomaniacs of world literature—Cervantes's Don Quixote, Melville's Ahab, or Molière's Alceste. Having been disenchanted, having seen their worlds go asunder, they turn for redemption to their impregnable obsession. Their lives are full of tell-tale symptoms—compulsive collecting, a pathological need for enclosure, a frenetic gathering of knowledge, an undivided focus on an ailing body. Without these rituals, they would not have left their mark on the strange history of obsession, though more importantly they would not have let us in on a curious phobia—that of the everyday, with its disruptive constraints, its oppressive demands, and its way of foiling the ideal.

There is no question that this book could expand infinitely and include the large body of literary texts usually associated with the topic of monomania—*Moby-Dick*, *Wuthering Heights*, *Lolita*, to name only a few. But instead, I concentrate on works that impart a veritable genealogy of obsession and that elaborate fully on the particular history and pre-history of a symptom. I juxtapose fiction and non-fiction, medical science and aesthetics, weaving together texts that single out obsession as a perverse form of therapy. Why these particular choices? Because directly or

4. Friedrich Schiller, *On the Aesthetic Education of Man*, ed. Elizabeth M. Wilkinson and L. A. Willoughby (Oxford: Clarendon Press, 1967), 187.

indirectly, and only when the compulsion is at work, do they present a comprehensive diagnosis of the curative potential of obsession. The cure, however, is usually short-lived because our protagonists, even if they come awfully close to finding a solution to their personal dramas, are usually betrayed by the very mechanism they had embraced. In the meantime, they introduce us to lives that have been radically shaped by a double project: to construct controllable spaces that protect these characters from the full range of life's shocks and disorders, and to find a set of indestructible norms that guarantee that somewhere still lies the promise of permanence.

The historical concept of monomania is central to this book, but only as a point of departure. It was disseminated by the *médecin-aliéniste* Esquirol and by the psychiatrist Etienne-Jean Georget in the first two decades of the nineteenth century. A watered-down version of their definition spread like wildfire in French society, and *monomania* became a favorite term among the intelligentsia. Every extremist was soon branded as a monomaniac, and even lawyers, jumping on the bandwagon, rescued the most unlikely delinquents by invoking the homicidal monomania that had possessed them. Monomania turned culprits into victims, eccentricities into pathologies; it became a favorite term among French novelists, eager to bolster their fictions with this new medical vocabulary. Stendhal was an avid reader of Dr. Philippe Pinel, Balzac integrated Georget's findings in his *Comédie humaine,* and Zola used Prosper Lucas's theories for his *Rougon-Macquart* series.[5] In her indispensable *Console and Classify,* Jan Goldstein notes that monomania originally "denoted an idée fixe, a single pathological preoccupation in an otherwise sound mind."[6] She traces the genealogy of a term that saw its apogee during the constitutional monarchy, but had already dwindled by the mid-fifties. Whether Géricault's portraits of monomaniacs or the colorful narratives of delusional figures who took to its limits their idée fixe—becoming Napoleon or setting off on murderous rampages—monomania took hold of the nineteenth-century literary imagination. So why bring it back and further confuse our already congested psychiatric vocabulary?

On account of the permeable quality of the word, I expect that a number of readers will take issue with my appropriation of *monomania.* This

5. For more bibliographical details, see Jan Goldstein's remarkable article, "The Uses of Male Hysteria: Medical and Literary Discourse in Nineteenth-Century France," *Representations* 34 (Spring 1991): 134–65.

6. Jan Goldstein, *Console and Classify: The French Psychiatric Profession in the Nineteenth Century* (Cambridge: Cambridge University Press, 1987), 155.

would be quite typical of what has happened in the past. When Esquirol turned *monomanie* into a fad almost two centuries ago, the venerable *Journal de la langue française* lashed back with an angry article, bemoaning that the "words of the people are abandoned today for words invented or introduced by scholars . . . One no longer says, it is his hobbyhorse (*dada*), his fancy (*marotte*). One says, like a grave physician: it is a monomania."[7] I was drawn to the term despite its linguistic obsoleteness and much for the same reason it attracted Esquirol—for "its porousness . . . to cultural values and cultural changes," its tendency to borrow "its objects from the dominant passions of the era."[8] Like Esquirol, who was frustrated by the *passe-partout* word *melancholy*, I have found that it bridges much more smoothly "the fixity and concentration of ideas" with the exaltation associated with mania; it is infinitely more evocative than "obsessive" or "compulsive," capturing an intensity of purpose, a religiosity of spirit absent from more ordinary fixations. My monomaniacs are all melancholics who can only abide the world if it is ruled by an all-consuming, highly abstract and exalted set of principles. They fit Esquirol's notion of *monomanie raisonnante*, a state in which "one's rational mind, without veering off into delusion . . . nevertheless was abnormally fixated on certain worries and concerns, to the exclusion of other symptoms (hence, mono-manie)."[9] But unlike Esquirol's patients, my subjects have managed to turn their mental prisons into sites of temporary inner liberation. Their obsession operates on several levels, doing two contradictory jobs at once: it endows their lives with a purpose, a worthy goal, while causing fatal disruptions. This book investigates the equivocal relationship between these disabling fixations and their curative powers. When closely scrutinized, these forms of extremism parrot the practice of any exacting activity—the meticulous making of art, the collector's frantic desire to possess, the mathematician's intractable desire to solve a problem. Like the Dutch, raising their dykes against the sea's predatory advances, the figures in this book use their obsessions to block out the world's dangers. But what are these dangers? The troubling answer is that they are all the more powerful in that they cannot be located. They are an inner condi-

---

7. Esquirol, "Le grammairien et le causeur," *Journal de la langue française,* 3rd ser., 2 (1839): 522; quoted in Goldstein, *Console and Classify,* 153.

8. Goldstein, *Console and Classify,* 158.

9. Michael H. Stone, "The History of Obsessive-Compulsive Disorder from the Early Period to the Turn of the Century," in *Essential Papers on Obsessive-Compulsive Disorder,* ed. Dan J. Stein and Michael H. Stone (New York: New York University Press, 1997), 19.

tion that mirrors life's constant flux; they emerge most violently out of a brutal recognition that transcendence has been lost.[10]

In the ensuing manifestations of the idée fixe (agoraphobia, misanthropy, art as substitute for life, hypochondria), the world falls into place because it seems guided by a divine plan, a firm and meaningful teleology. Freud explains these types of rituals in "Obsessive Actions and Religious Practices," in which he compares neurotic ceremonials (*Zwangsneurose*) to religious rites. While he finds the latter to be "full of significance and symbolic meaning," he sees the former, divorced from tradition and thoroughly independent from the way society is run, as "the half-comic, half-tragic travesty of a private religion." These fixations, he argues, are devices that provide the obsessive type with "emotional coherence." What seems like a paradox—how could an obsession bring anything but destruction?—is explained as follows: the obsessive has finally grasped that "what once had to be passively endured" (the behavior of others, the randomness of the world) can actually be controlled. The traumatic source from which this act of collecting originates is now "overcome through active countermeasures." Destroyed by change, disoriented by flux, these figures do everything in their power to hold on to an absolute—*their* passion will be the defining model of love, *their* illness will inspire doctors and patients, *their* research will put the final dot on every stray *i*. Their methods are often cruel and destructive, but were they to live without guidelines, their condition would worsen, resulting in serious breakdown. This book is about the fine line that separates extreme order from extreme anarchy, meticulous control from catastrophe.

While investigating different manifestations of monomania, I discovered that each one of its enactments is part of an abstract, autonomous desire to reorganize the world according to a long-lost model of wholeness. The symptoms of this longing meet with uncanny congruence in literature, religion, love, and even illness. This book is full of characters who have defected from society, retreating to a quasi-autistic realm; the French

10. Even though I discovered Elissa Marder's *Dead Time: Temporal Disorders in the Wake of Modernity* (Stanford: Stanford University Press, 2001) very late in the process of writing this book, I was so struck by her analyses that I went back and corrected some of my manuscript in light of her comments. While she speaks of Flaubert's "Art" as "a prophylactic defense against the pervasive, albeit highly ambiguous and unlocatable dangers posed by contemporary reality" (91), I would add that his is a type of art that thrives on its absolutist principles. It works precisely to give definition to the undefined quality of modernity. Its obsessive quality is a direct response to the unsettling and melancholy vagueness of the everyday.

Romantic Charles Nodier calls this affliction *monomanie réflective*, an introspective form of monomania that must turn the world into a personal absolute, an aestheticized version of itself.

Whether perceived as pathological, perverse, or poorly disguised maneuvers to counteract *horror vacui* and depression, these idiosyncratic obsessions are powerful weapons that enable individuals to resist the tyranny of the everyday, the dictatorial nature of materiality. The idée fixe is an infinite source of comfort; not only does it provide unshakable boundaries, but it lures the subject into a sense of agency. In contrast, in the confusion of everyday life, with its chance encounters and unanticipated challenges, formlessness prevails, rupturing our hold over things. No wonder, then, that whatever smacks of randomness and daydreaming becomes so menacing. One never knows what can emerge when our will is caught off-guard. This explains why obsessive natures never want to be surprised engaging in the formless or the unstructured. Karl Abraham defines this as a phobic fear of asymmetry. "Just as some neurotics count their steps in order to reach their destination with an even number of paces, so they tolerate no asymmetry in other matters. They arrange all their objects symmetrically. They divide everything with minute exactness. . . . The perpetual desire to be 'quits' with other people, i.e., to be under no obligation, however trifling, is also significant."[11]

These "neurotic" characters have such a deep fear of immediacy, of reciprocity, that they compulsively resort to the impersonal, as though it will purge them of their selfhood, evacuating whatever might place them in dialogue with others. The weight of a life lived "on its own," that is, following its own course rather than a pre-structured pattern, is intolerable to the monomaniac. Flaubert's obsessive return to the imagery of the straight line, the anti-arabesque, is symptomatic of this. So is the intensely structured quality of Mondrian's paintings, designed, in Bonnefoy's words, "to break with the existential content of visual perceptions." Whatever appears on the surface of the painting must have nothing to do with the individual's connection to experience. Art must defeat personal relationships and help "time to settle, like an impurity that has been contained, in the alembic of transparence."[12] It is not simply that time must

---

11. Karl Abraham, "Contribution to the Theory of the Anal Character" (1921), in *Selected Papers* (New York: Basic Books, 1953), 1:370–92.

12. "From 1910, the harmony Mondrian seeks in colors and forms . . . hopes to break with the existential content of visual perceptions; it expects time to settle, like an impurity that has been contained, in the alembic of transparence" (Bonnefoy, *Lure and Truth of Painting*, 102).

settle, it must also become depersonalized; it turns into Platonic time-lessness, shedding its individual and singular characteristics. In the obsessive rituals that are examined in these pages, the outside world emerges as a vast impurity, a corruption of something that used to be orderly and unequivocal. Those who suffer from such perfectionism believe that their will and dogged persistence will turn the world's frayed multiplicity back into unity and order. At the heart of their most personal idée fixe lies the hungry hankering for impersonality.

Those readers who have brushed against the dangers of the idée fixe, who have come close to surrendering to something or someone diabolically seductive or coercive, will recognize in these characters their own encounter with a dangerously systematized world. They might remember how desperately they wanted to believe in one figure, one cause, despite the cautious words of their peers; or how rigidly they embraced a line of work, fiercely rejecting a more open relationship to routine; or they might have focused all their energies on a covert disease, an ailment that gave their lives a strange intensity. What all these extremists share is a fear of freedom, of openness, and an overpowering need to surrender to something that will stand for authority. Left to their own devices, they might be ruled by a dangerous side of their personality, suddenly overwhelmed by the openness of life. This is why they would rather capitulate their free-will and follow blindly an unerring guiding hand. Under the yoke of a domineering figure or routine, they hope to shut out any problematic inner voices, basking rather in the loud injunctions of a confident leader.

The monomaniacal mindset is uncannily close to that of the fanatic. It is no coincidence that Isaiah Berlin, in an article on tolerance, chose the term monomania to describe political, racial, or religious fanaticism. Nothing is more destructive, he wrote, "than a happy sense of one's own—or one's nation's—infallibility, which lets you destroy others with a quiet conscience because you are doing God's (e.g. the Spanish Inquisition or the Ayatollah or the superior race's (e.g. Hitler) or History's (e.g. Lenin-Stalin) work."[13] Berlin neglected to mention that monomania can also be a private affair. It can be a misanthropic malady that has no desire to conquer the world, but wants to trade its intricacies for something deceivingly simple, something that reduces it to fragments masquerading as totality. Turning the world into a compact personal obsession is unquestionably less dangerous than enforcing devious political doctrines;

13. Isaiah Berlin, "Notes on Prejudice," *New York Review of Books*, October 18, 2001.

nonetheless, it is rooted in a similar belief in authority, a lethal attachment to a discipline that promises to put complexity on hold. Like essentialist ideologies, it too can radiate onto the rest of society, debauching the most unlikely citizen with its promises of ontological harmony.

The nineteenth-century psychiatrist Pierre Janet was the first to establish a cogent connection between this desperate quest for harmony and obsessive behavior. After years of recording his patients' idées fixes, he concluded that the compulsive surrender to one thing or one person helped severely depressed characters endure their destructive tendencies. In order to escape the burden of dissatisfied selfhood, they relished the loss of freedom brought about by psychological hardships. A peaceful marital life, Janet alleged, rather than providing his high-strung patients with equilibrium, often pushed them over the edge. The ostensible gratification of domesticity dragged them down like an insidious albatross. Just as tranquil happiness is seldom the stuff of novels, it also has an adverse effect on these personalities. What usually "rescued" Janet's patients from their depressions was a domineering figure or a set of stringent compulsions that would rebuild their divided selves, substituting "objective" pain for "subjective" woes. A violent relationship or a crippling disease (even a *maladie imaginaire*) had the advantage of being a palpable development, one unfolding in real space, not in the confines of their own solitude. These patients traded one type of harmony (domestic, uneventful) for another—far-reaching and immaterial.

What else lurks behind these solipsistic modes of existence? What explains the common need to hide behind a system or an ideology? In most of the cases I examine, these nervous bouts of activity conceal the profound fear that life's ugly little secret is perhaps that there is not enough worth living for, let alone guarding or preserving. This explains why the figures in this book need to invest in a clear mission that will help counteract that void. This goal is usually abstract; it leads to lasting answers that offer a sense of protection that, in Kandinsky's words, will guard against "the nightmare of materialism."[14] Whatever is being undertaken is acceptable because it will eventually bring to experience something valid, something that exudes authority.

As the analysis of Flaubert's letters will show, there is a deep correlation between this desire for validity, this urge to find authority from above, and artistic production in general. Psychoanalysts have argued

---

14. Wassily Kandinsky, *Concerning the Spiritual in Art* (1912), trans. M. T. H. Sadler (1914; New York: Dover, 1977), 17.

that the moment of creation often occurs when the subject feels attacked by a convergence of disorderly emotions.[15] If this disorder is not converted into some form of coherence, the subject's initial excitement might turn into depression. Because they convey chaos and can only be insufficiently stabilized in everyday life, one writer asserts that these affects "require a move that will give them the sense of direction, a purpose that will restore control."[16] This suggests that the moment of creation is directly triggered by a protective urge. Likewise, the obsessive focus of my characters (a love-object, devotion to learning, to collecting, worrying about one's body) is designed to prevail upon overpowering and disorderly emotions. As soon as these feelings start plaguing the individual, he or she begins a counter-work of restructuring. Instead of giving these thoughts the upper hand, they are reigned in, literally recomposed into something else.

While recent scholarship has been remarkably active in rewriting the nature of mental illness, it would be incomplete without the inclusion of monomania as an everyday pathology, as complex and as creatively charged as hysteria or fetishism. Its manifestations, I argue, are direct responses to the daunting demands of freedom, to the anguishes of a self-hood told it can and should be its own master. This book documents the disorders that have surfaced from the unstructured quality of the everyday. It asks its reader to imagine why dangerous compulsions often arise without identifiable causes. The quieter the moment, the more unbearable the affect. Tranquility, in fact, exacerbates the symptoms of obsessive characters, which might explain why Berlioz experienced his darkest depressions when the world around him bore no trace of crisis or confusion. "Sometimes, I can scarcely endure this mental or physical pain (I can't separate the two), especially on fine summer days when I'm in an open space like the Tuileries Garden, alone."[17] It is not coincidental that Berlioz, with his revolutionary use of the idée fixe, the recurring theme in *La Symphonie fantastique* evoking his passion for Harriet Smithson, was the first artist to

15. Jean Guillaumin, *Le Moi sublimé: Psychanalyse de la créativité* (Paris: Dunod, 1998), 65. Guillaumin notes that "the root of the creative process stems from the urgency with which the artist seeks to restore a stable support system that will offer protection . . . against the onslaught of unruly inner attacks." Unless otherwise noted, all translations in this chapter are mine.

16. Ibid., 9.

17. Hector Berlioz to his father, February 13, 1830; quoted in David Cairns, *The Making of an Artist, 1803–1832,* vol. 1 of *Berlioz* (London: André Deutsch, 1989), 330. The reference came to my attention upon reading Kay Redfield Jamison's *Touched with Fire: Manic-Depressive Illness and the Artistic Temperament* (New York: Free Press, 1993), 122.

make music and monomania coincide.[18] The compulsive repetition of a theme stood assertively for the absent loved one. In the curious configurations of passion, where selfhood surrenders itself zealously to the object of desire, obsession adds a seductive sense of presence. The musical idée fixe embodies the absent lover, itself an aesthetic incarnation of an idealized self. So the returning theme provides not only a double of Berlioz's infatuation, but amply fills the intolerable gap of absence. Obsession, by returning so aggressively to a topic, to an individual, becomes a full-time occupation, a great padding against loss. By projecting all his energies onto the musical equivalent of his idée fixe, Berlioz, like the characters in this book, finds a new center, an unexpected receptacle to absorb his pain while endowing it with aesthetic permanence.

—⚏—

Monomaniacs are keen managers of temporal spacing; whether it is in the realm of art or of love, they possess the sharp ability to split reality into differentiated fragments, each to be endowed with a specific function. Parceling, appropriating, and controlling are some of the tell-tale signs of their condition. Even though our own rather benign fixations are far cries from the nineteenth century's full-fledged monomanias, they nevertheless show signs of hazardous pathologies. Under their alleged ordinariness is concealed a love-hate relationship with permanence, a less than noble need to dominate. While this book pivots around works that have made most manifest the psychological necessity of obsession, I have found it important to take my first sustained example from an idée fixe that is familiar to most of us, jealousy, an emotion that mimics most faithfully the doctrinaire excesses discussed in these pages.[19] It too is rooted in a desperate instinct of preservation, a sickly fear of change. But on close consideration, what it seeks to preserve has much less to do with the other person than with the need for an absolute truth, for a certainty that will ground and direct.[20] Amorous jealousy tells us less about the fear of un-

18. In a letter to Ferrand, Berlioz describes the "history" of his *Symphonie fantastique:* "I conceive an artist, gifted with a lively imagination . . . who . . . sees for the first time a woman who realizes the ideal of beauty . . . that his heart has so long invoked, and falls madly in love with her. By a strange quirk, the image of the loved one never appears before his mind's eye without its corresponding musical idea. . . . This double obsession ["idée fixe"] pursues him unceasingly . . . in every movement of the symphony" (Cairns, 359. [85/514]).

19. This section owes a great deal to Masha Belenky, whose dissertation on jealousy kept me up in suspense many a night! Masha Belenky, "The Poetics of Jealousy in Nineteenth-Century French Texts," Ph.D. diss., Columbia University, 2002.

20. In his book *L'État amoureux* (Paris: Payot, 2002), Christian David claims that *the state*

faithfulness than about our need for unblemished validation. The self will only be convinced of its own worth by the faultless devotion of another. Jealous monomaniacs hold themselves and their victims to impossibly high standards. The severity with which the *jaloux* berates the alleged infidel explodes with the violence of a religious inquisition. Aggressive jealousy can be a great cover up for the self's actual loss of control. While a majority of forsaken individuals bear their fate stoically, monomaniacal lovers devise rigid strategies to trump their relationship's breakdown and make it look like somebody else's failure or weakness. These strategies, themselves powerful idées fixes, are terrific diversions against the intolerable act of waiting, of not knowing. A full-time operation, they involve setting up multiple tricks and traps to contain or confront the fugitive, great focal points that will end up deflecting energy from the self onto the other. Born out of anxiety, the acts of stalking or trailing, eavesdropping or spying, end up alleviating restlessness and grant a sense of mission and purpose. So this detective work gives birth to an alternative world, an ordered universe that is structured and nourished by the very doubts that had undermined it. The dread of not knowing makes way for the desire to know something *for sure*. Catching the beloved in an act of betrayal affords a different (satisfying in its own right) type of mastery. The incessant queries and accusations of infidelity anoint the doubter with the status of a self-righteous judge. The inquisitor is no longer the abused; the defensive position is now held by the suspect. The endless drilling, in fact, punctuates the intolerable suspense with a welcome rhythm, with a pattern that restores a semblance of order.

Nobody has demonstrated better than Stanley Cavell the controlling impulse that legislates jealousy.[21] Othello's murderous passion, he argues, has very little to do with Desdemona's alleged inconstancy, revealing rather the Moor's desire for supreme power. Buried under Othello's wrath is the disappointment that he is no longer God's equal, having lost his prized certainty. To Cavell, Othello's crisis began when he placed "a finite woman in the place of God. . . ." [22] In this book, crisis manifests itself when an absolute is put in the place of the human, making the everyday doubly difficult to endure. There is nothing inherently unusual about

---

of being in love does not merely awaken in us feelings for an ideal amorous interlocutor, but for our own ideal self. Through the object of desire, our ordinary self is absorbed, reemerging as one that has congealed into a unified and perfected individual.

21. Stanley Cavell, *Disowning Knowledge in Six Shakespeare Plays* (Cambridge: Cambridge University Press, 1987), 126.

22. Ibid.

investing a person or a project with divine attributes (such mistakes happen every day), but to turn this deification into a way of life, an end in itself, makes the obsession not a means but an end. So under the pretense of reclaiming the object of desire, the *jaloux* is reclaiming something quite different, namely, his or her immovable place in the universe.

Does this imply that the direct cause of pathological jealousy (Desdemona's handkerchief) is less noteworthy than the preexisting image of one's self and aspirations? At all costs, the victim of jealousy believes, love must be preserved the way it has begun. So it is love, the construct, not love, the interaction, upon which the monomaniac seizes. Therefore, it would be far less traumatic to impute the dwindling of love to a rival than to its inevitable erosion or, still worse, to one's own inability to keep it alive. The rival, then, rescues love from its own self-destructing mechanism. The jealousy that he or she inspires conveniently deflects doubt from the self onto the other; furthermore, by investing the love-object with such importance, the self experiences reflected glory. As Freud puts it: "It is only when they are able to be jealous that their passion reaches its height and the woman acquires her full value, and they never fail to seize on an occasion that allows them to experience these most powerful emotions."[23] Freud makes it perfectly clear that jealousy is a compensatory activity. It works toward preserving something that would have weakened in a matter of time. It is a crafty system of postponement, whereby the subject keeps desiring that which is out of reach, just to allow the illusion to last longer. It is far less daunting to pick an inaccessible object, one who will never grant satisfaction, than to realize that once the desire has diminished, then the love-object will drag us back into normalcy. Doomed to descend into habit, desire is the all-too-human *trompe-l'œil* that barely conceals its own shallowness. Some have seen in this drama the mad attempt to run away from the abysmal emptiness of desire; is it not better, ultimately, to keep alive an imaginary rival than to stare inevitable absence in the face?[24] Beyond this powerful urge to nurse a rival's existence

23. Sigmund Freud, "A Special Type of Choice of Object Made by Men," in the *Standard Edition of the Complete Psychological Works of Sigmund Freud,* trans. under the general editorship of James Strachey and Alan Tyson, 24 vols. (London: Hogarth Press, 1953–74), 11:167. Hereafter SE.

24. Mikkel Borch-Jacobsen puts it this way: "much better to . . . resurrect tirelessly the image of the rival than to be confronted with the abyss of desire; far better to identify guiltily with those who forbid the completion of our desire than to face the void of its absence." *Lacan: Le Maître absolu* (Paris: Flammarion, 1995), 119. My translation. The book is available in English as *Lacan: The Absolute Master,* trans. Douglas Brick (Stanford: Stanford University Press, 1990).

is the even more complex and muddled desire to recover sovereignty in order to dispel once and for all the suspicion that nothing lasts, that everything is merely mortal. The jealous rage, therefore, targets the imperfect self; it is hate directed against its own impotence.

Another reason jealousy plays such a crucial framing role for this book is its relationship to stasis, to the dream of an immobile, unchangeable self. We are primarily great preservers, haters of change. As Freud points out, we always try to get back to an earlier rendition of ourselves, a complete, unbroken version of what time has soiled and split apart. Even though we love to court goal-oriented activities, what we really strive for is "the inertia inherent in organic life."

It seems, then, that an instinct is an urge inherent in organic life to restore an earlier state of things which the living entity has been obliged to abandon under the pressure of external disturbing forces. . . . Those instincts are therefore bound to give a deceptive appearance of being forces tending towards change and progress, whilst in fact they are merely seeking to reach an ancient goal by paths alike old and new. . . . If we are to take it as a truth that knows no exception, that everything dies for *internal* reasons—becomes inorganic once again—then we shall be compelled to say that *"the aim of all life is death"* and, looking backwards, that *"inanimate things existed before living ones."*[25]

The crushing statement—"the aim of life is death"—is not only central to the monomania of jealousy, but to the obsessive temperament in general. Visions of immobility and dreams of converging identities fulfill this stubborn desire for the unchangeable. Cavell alerts us to their hazards, stressing the precariousness of any identity that relies so completely on another being's allegiance:

That the integrity of my (human, finite) existence may depend on the fact and on the idea of another being's existence, and on the possibility of *proving* that existence, an existence conceived from my very dependence and incompleteness, hence conceived as perfect and conceived as producing me 'in some sense, in [its] own image'—these are thoughts that take me to a study of *Othello*.[26]

The dream of absolute possession, Cavell stresses, is really just the pitiful urge to be legitimized by the lover's adoring gaze. But what are the chances that this gaze will remain so constant?

25. Sigmund Freud, "Beyond the Pleasure Principle," SE 18:36, 38. Italics are Freud's.
26. Cavell, *Disowning Knowledge,* 127–28.

The tension between motion and stasis, losing and keeping, is central to all forms of obsession. The jealous mind, like that of the collector or the hypochondriac, is plagued by a love-hate relationship with the status quo, hating it while desperately trying to maintain it. What does this frantic search for motion conceal? Why is stasis so terrifying and yet, in the end, so sought after? Because by definition, the idyllic moment is always doomed to turn into something less intoxicating, while the bliss of passion produces a strange amnesia capable of dissipating the anxiety of being oneself.[27] As soon as this anxiety reemerges, the obsessive lover is moved to generate a new type of panic, one that will parrot the initial excitement, only with a negative twist. From a clue (a chance encounter in an unexpected place, a prolonged absence, a contradiction), a new narrative will be set in motion, investing the love object with hidden motives that will serve the cunning purpose of reproducing the mystery and excitement of the initial encounter. Jealousy has the unique ability to exist at the fringes of the known and the unknown; it is born out of the desire for absolute knowledge, but will perish, taking love with it, if it ever gets that knowledge.

The obsessive lover wants to craft a marvelously sterile world, a museum of feelings, where portraits inevitably become still lifes. Knowing everything about the other is a form of framing, of freezing. It is an attempt to defy the serpentine nature of experience, a desperate insurance policy that will guarantee that some things will never change if prudently kept under glass. It is this autonomy, with its symptomatic urge to turn the mutable into a world of its own, that I explore throughout the book. In this scheme, doubt functions either as love's agent, keeping the lover's investment going by postponing a mediocre reality, or as the immediate cause of obsessive behavior. Doubt is the ultimate destabilizing factor, the curse that keeps us stuck in an in-between realm, where one can be sure of nothing—neither meaning nor its unalloyed absence.

27. In his study on depression, *La fatigue d'être soi: Dépression et société* (Paris: Odile Jacob, 1998), Alain Ehrenberg asks whether post-Nietzschean individualism has not proven just too arduous to carry out. Our capacity to endure the pressures of the quotidian has been weakened, even worn out, by the ongoing onslaught of choices we need to make ourselves. Having learned to distrust authority, we end up shouldering a daunting number of decisions and responsibilities. There is no magic formula, no transcendent end in sight. Having relinquished the temptation of being cared for, we have transferred back to ourselves the decisions that used to be made by others, leaving only ourselves as guides. Ehrenberg argues that to be master of one's own fate takes a drastic toll, possibly ushering back a subliminal craving for authority. Depressed individuals are caught between the desire to surrender to this providential "master" and the powerful urge to keep control over their lives.

—ᵐ—

Of the nine chapters that make up this book, the first two (presented out of chronological order) introduce real-life manifestations of obsessive disorders. While Pierre Janet's case studies provide a foundation for the more speculative chapters, Flaubert's letters demonstrate how the making of art, or what he liked to call art's revenge over life, can overcome the fears and phobias hidden at the heart of obsession. The seven remaining chapters are by no means comprehensive analyses of the works at hand, but attempts to read in forgotten moments of unforgettable texts the pathological workings of obsession.

—ᵐ—

Pierre Janet's two-volume study *Obsessions et la psychasthénie,* with its assemblage of over sixty different types of obsessions, is an important point of departure for this book. It sets the stage for the fictional and real characters who will appear in these pages—individuals whose stories reveal the double-edged nature of obsession and who have been either destroyed or rescued by their compulsions. As Janet demonstrates, and this also explains my choice of examples, these are disorders that might strike any of us, disorders that often stem from discrete afflictions such as *tedium vitae* or mild depression. As I explain in these introductory pages, my chapters (perhaps with the exception of Baudelaire and Nodier) draw on cases that begin with mild psychological disturbances and then blossom with unexpected force into veritable pathologies, distressing conditions that embrace obsession as the only viable remedy. Janet struck gold when he made the connection between his mostly female patients' monomaniacal tendencies and their inability to balance the two opposing sides of domesticity—the freedom to rule over one's domain and the crippling consequences of confinement in that same domain. New symptoms come with new sets of obligation, and to gain mastery over one's domestic world did not necessarily summon up feelings of liberation. The stationary quality of *la vie d'intérieur* had a catastrophic impact on certain individuals. Janet noted that as a result of being emotionally and intellectually enclosed, many of his female patients resorted to pathological forms of domestic diversions. Their compulsion to clean their house over and over again, to oversee to an extreme degree their children's routines, disrupted, while correcting, the amorphous rhythm of their lives.[28] Do-

28. On the relationship between domestic stillness and the frantic rhythms of the mar-

mesticity, by combining personal and impersonal time, freedom and constraint, structure and lack of structure, thus becomes a metaphor for the ambiguities of modern experience.

—·—

Flaubert certainly falls into Janet's category of obsessive characters. Like them, he resists desperately what Jean-François Lyotard identifies in *The Inhuman* as "free floating attention," the "free association," and "working through" that enables the individual to "go with the flow," and take stock of life's rhythms.[29] Life is so hideous, Flaubert writes to one of his confidantes, that the only way to endure it is to turn it into art.[30] Survival is a matter of finding the perfect sentence, the *mot juste*. Flaubert proceeds with the fastidiousness of an architect, far more concerned with the quality of his materials, the precision of his perspectives, than with a grand design that might provide a large scale explanation of the world. What he harvests from this rigor is "a divine form, something as timeless as a principle."[31] By retreating into the precise world of grammar, he comes to exemplify a more general desire to do away with the intricacies of life-as-exchange. Monologue, we will discover, is far easier to master than dialogue. No wonder, then, that fastidious art-making can become such an idée fixe, reigning alone in its ability to trade the battles of life for those solved and dissolved with ink. Understanding the dynamics of this barter—artifice over lived experience—will set the course for the more extreme forms of obsessions to be encountered in this book. Like the monomaniac whose time is perfectly managed by obsessive rituals, Flaubert's painstaking writing routine enabled him to compartmentalize his life so efficiently that it straightened out, at least for the time of his writing, life's unruly and rumpled surfaces.

—·—

Where Flaubert could not tolerate the free-floating nature of the everyday, finding his order in dogged writing habits, Charles Nodier, one of

---

ketplace, see the enlightening article by Gillian Brown, "The Empire of Agoraphobia," *Representations* 20 (1987): 134–57.

29. Jean-François Lyotard, "Rewriting Modernity," in *The Inhuman*, trans. Geoffrey Bennington and Rachel Bowlby (Stanford: Stanford University Press, 1991), 30–31; quoted in Marder, *Dead Time*, 11–12.

30. Flaubert to Mademoiselle Leroyer de Chantepie, May 18, 1857; Gustave Flaubert, *Œuvres complètes*, vol. 2, ed. Jean Bruneau (Paris: Pléiade, 1980), 717. Unless otherwise indicated, I quote the Pléiade edition of Flaubert's letters; translations are mine.

31. Flaubert to George Sand, April 3, 1876. Gustave Flaubert, *Préface à la vie d'écrivain*, ed. Geneviève Bollème (Paris: Seuil, 1963), 271.

the pivotal figures of French Romanticism, was actually the first writer to propose monomania as an antidote to the increasingly alienating rhythms of modernity. By highjacking Esquirol's term and injecting it with a mystical aura, Nodier extracted from "reflective" monomania the promise of a new secular religion, one that would restore control to madmen and eccentrics by bestowing upon them a sense of divine control.[32] Their obsessive escapism, their fanatical resistance to life's inevitable impoverishment, was suddenly interpreted as a cure against the flatness of everyday life.

—⁂—

A similar idea had already been aired by Kant, as impressed by the madman's ability to embrace a systematized form of "non-sense," as he was by the "rational" rigidity that such a system bestowed on the mad person's life. Kant marveled that such compulsive displays of unreason functioned at least as effectively as their "reasonable" counterparts; they provided a key to life, a rationale that was maintained thanks to the paradoxical cogency of a fixed idea. Unwittingly conjoining Nodier's wishful escapism and Kant's curative *vesania*, Baudelaire brought this idea to life in "Mademoiselle Bistouri" (Miss Scalpel), one of his most penetrating prose poems. Hers is also a world where obsession provides astonishing emotional coherence, one where the idée fixe becomes an aesthetics in its own right, a tool as redemptive and as dangerous as the scalpel itself.

—⁂—

To George Eliot's Dorothea Brooke, the real tragedy of life, at least at the onset of the *Middlemarch* narrative, is the oppressive insignificance of the everyday. An admixture of platitude and possibility, it offers no weighty answers, always hovering between meaning and emptiness. With its amorphous stretches of empty time, the everyday, to use Blanchot's words, threatens her both as the "tragedy of nullity" and as "the site of all possible signification."[33] What this chapter examines is how her escapism ties in, helps us grasp, the clashing principles developed in Wor-

32. Charles Nodier, "Rêveries psychologiques de la monomanie réflective," in *L'Amateur de livres*, ed. J. L. Steinmetz (Paris: Castor Astral, 1993), 50.

33. Maurice Blanchot, "Everyday Speech," *Yale French Studies* 73 (1987): 14. "Whatever its other aspects, the everyday has this essential trait: it allows no hold. It escapes. It belongs to insignificance, and the insignificant is without truth, without reality, without secrets, but perhaps also the site of all possible signification. The everyday escapes." Translation of "La parole quotidienne," in *L'Entretien infini* (Paris: Gallimard, 1969), 357.

ringer's groundbreaking essay *Abstraction and Empathy* (1908). Abstraction, he argues, is an urge rooted in our desire to escape from the threateningly familiar, the oppressively mundane. *Middlemarch* pits abstraction against empathy, the dreadful Casaubon against Ladislav, revealing how certain natures (impressionable, fanatically prone to compulsive reading) feel tyrannized by their empathetic nature, perceiving it as a threat, a dangerous harbinger of personality fragmentation. *Middlemarch* documents the unsettling voyage from abstraction to empathy, from ideal constructs to "incalculably diffusive" acts.

—⟶—

If Eliot uncovered the dangerous temptations of abstraction, Thomas Mann's *The Magic Mountain* unravels another psychological riddle. How can illness, something potentially lethal, behave like a solution to life's inconclusive nature? Like the surrender to abstract knowledge, intense preoccupation with their ailments helps certain individuals simplify the complex world by reducing it to the confines of their own bodies. Anorexics, for instance, make their lives revolve around self-imposed trials, turning the absence of food into the plenitude of being in full control of their hunger.[34] The hypochondriac's busy schedule, likewise, is regulated by a rigid routine that will mercilessly strike back at the *horror vacui*. Like the sanatorium's elite clientele, Hans Castorp in *The Magic Mountain* begins to accumulate ailments as feverishly as the bibliophile hoards books. Disease begins to function like an aesthetic principle, a type of collecting that restores form to a messy universe. Left alone in their rooms or their hospital beds, hypochondriacs turn their surroundings into a sanctuary, not dissimilar to the monk's cell. There, they can peacefully devote themselves to their affliction, like studious and concentrated scholars with a rare manuscript—recording and footnoting every anomaly. It is its messianic misanthropy, its circularity, that will allow us insight into the mechanism of obsession.

—⟶—

Elias Canetti's works are filled with monomaniacs, creatures haunted by an idée fixe. Their dedication to a single guiding principle entranced and repelled Canetti from the outset of his writing life. *Auto-da-Fé* is the

---

34. A description of this reversal is found in Éric Bidaud's *Anorexie mentale, ascèse, mystique: Une approche psychanalytique* (Paris: Denoël, 1997): "Anorexics make the void compact . . . turning it into the paradoxical figure of plenitude. They fetishize it" (145).

chilling demonstration of scholarship as a method of dissociation from the world. Kien uses his books, his conference papers, to cut himself off from everything except his own sense of hegemony. Canetti's case-study of a Sinologist gone mad helps us grasp our own uncanny ability to float in and out of hidden power structures. Like his author, who was known for his ability to surrender his entire soul to a book, to a friendship, he gives himself over to the immutability of his subjects. Like Canetti, Kien wants clarity in a darkened world. And like Kien, his greatest creation, Canetti explores what it means to be hostage to an obsession that can only save you by making you blind.[35]

—m—

If scholarship can be the attempt to recreate a perfectly unified and self-contained universe, then it shares a great deal with the mourner's attachment to the lost object. There is a striking link between the attachment to a perfect artifact and melancholy. In Freud's theory of melancholy, the tyrannical "demon of noontide" springs from the placing of one's existence against a perfect, albeit lost, moment of being. Of course, no such perfection ever occurred, but the psyche could not endure without such myths. Melancholy, like some of the previously analyzed symptoms, can also play itself out as an obsession. It is a startling replica of other mono-maniacal tendencies, also turning an affliction into a perverse system of survival. The melancholic can hang onto his or her loss with stunning perseverance, dwelling on the pain with uncanny single-mindedness.

I analyze this will to pain in Nina Bouraoui's *La Voyeuse interdite*, a book that demonstrates stunningly how melancholy can be the weapon as well as the cure, an auxiliary that sustains the subject, causing it to reenact a past trauma over and over again, making the initial scenario so familiar that it takes on a reassuring fascination. The pain, now tamed and appropriated, has turned into a self-contained world, where the original victim has gone from being the passive actor to the stage-manager of intolerable suffering.

35. See Slavoj Žižek, "Selfhood as Such Is Spirit: F. W. J. Schelling on the Origins of Evil," in *Radical Evil*, ed. Joan Copjec (London: Verso, 1996) in which he quotes Schelling's paradoxical view. Either the individual "persists in himself, in his purity . . . and thereby loses himself in empty expansion; or he gets out of himself, externalizes himself, by way of 'contracting' or 'putting on' a signifying feature, and thereby alienates himself, that is, he ceases to be what he is." Kien, not as a scholar, but as an individual, is precisely caught in this no-win situation. When he does manage to live in his own head, he is without a world, useless outside the bounds of his scholarly production; when he is in the world, he loses his mind.

———ﬗ———

What is monomania to us, today? In no way does it pale next to Ahab's murderous single-mindedness, but in the realm of aesthetics, it has shifted from private passions (i.e., Balzac's monomaniacs are moved by greed, gold, or girls) to a faceless, perhaps even defaced, relationship to things public. A recent model of monomania has surfaced in art and literature. Whether the sex-by-numbers portrayed in Catherine Millet's *La Vie sexuelle de Catherine M.* or Sophie Calle's artistic fixations, we are confronted with a new form of obsessive-compulsive *mal du siècle*. Calle, rather than sticking to a rigid pattern, is constantly reinvented by her monomanias (and it is significant that she has more than one); they are the reflection of life's transitory condition. By no means a way to unify the self, they give rise, instead, to new possibilities of self-making. Rather than "fixing" reality by anointing it with Platonic permanence, Calle intervenes in the fabric of the everyday by imposing an intensely codified grid on situations that have spun out of control. It is chance (the bête noire of nineteenth-century monomaniacs) that feeds her idées fixes, but it is a chance she has made her own. And because the stakes of her rituals are so low—deciding upon the color of food, determining which letter of the alphabet will guide her daily routine—this monomania has no chance of becoming doctrinaire. In fact, it has shed the very attachment to authority that so characterized her obsessive predecessors. What it does instead is to challenge the public's own secret craving for an art form that duplicates the seemingly transparent structure of authority.

1
Pierre Janet

The Phobia of Everyday Life

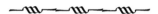

The early twentieth-century physician, philosopher, and psychiatrist Pierre Janet (1859–1947) could be renamed the great poet of obsessive disorders. Traveling on the margins of sensationalism, his case-studies remain remarkable for their ability to connect debilitating obsessions to the morbid and destructive need for domination and control. A lecturer in psychology at the Sorbonne (1898) and a professor at the prestigious Collège de France (1902–1936), Janet is one of the great forerunners of our contemporary fascination with the poetics of the everyday; he would have been the first to agree with Henri Lefebvre who urged his readers to seek "a philosophical inventory and analysis of everyday life that will expose its ambiguities—its baseness and exuberance, its poverty and fruitfulness—and by these unorthodox means release the creative energies that are an integral part of it."[1]

Positioned between two centuries that would split his thought into two contrasting directions, Janet spent his career learning about the mixed blessings of the everyday. More lucidly than many of his peers, he connected his patients' narratives of domestic despair with the contradictory status of the quotidian—its baseness and its promise. Janet pulls out of his patients' stories a bizarre brand of suffering, one caused by this mysterious alliance of opposites; he explores a possible therapy that would cure, or at least explain, why obsessive behavior so often erupts onto a perfectly anodyne domestic stage. Thanks to his work, a great complement to some of the nineteenth century's most wrenching narratives of personal suffering, we are apprised of the insidious perils that lurk behind a seemingly successful family life. Had he been Emma Bovary's doctor, he would have shown great interest in her compulsive shopping

---

1. Henri Lefebvre, *Everyday Life in the Modern World* (New Brunswick, N.J.: Transaction Books, 1984), 13.

sprees. Janet, indeed, was invariably struck by the number of patients who responded to the assault of the everyday by succumbing to a variety of obsessions and manias, the list of which is both daunting and comical: "Obsessive shame for one's facial features; obsessive shame of speaking; obsession about being a child; obsessive guilt toward the cat's escape; obsession about religious crimes; obsessive thoughts about forming a pact with the devil; obsession about intestinal worms. Mania for metaphysical research; mania for the perfect love; mania for predictions and oaths; mania to summon up perfectly a visual recollection."[2] These mercurial desires hide a host of guilty longings that Janet taps into with great success. At times his accounts display such empathy that they would not be out of place in one of Chekhov's tales. Some of his most convincing cases read in fact like short stories waiting to be turned into novels. This chapter will chronicle some of his boldest hypotheses about obsessive natures and will serve as a frame for the book's exploration of the two antagonistic sides of obsession—the productive and the destructive.

In addition to those listed above, Janet's two-volume *Obsessions et la psychasthénie* records over sixty different types of obsessions. Both alternatives point to an unbearable restlessness, a deep anxiety bred by the slow, inevitable, course of everyday life. Habit is so deadening to some of these patients that they create bizarre counter-poisons, often in the form of alternate habits, less oppressive because rebellious and self-willed, but no less perilous. The aim of these obsessive patterns, Janet observes, is to escape from an intolerable sense of porousness, a Beckett-like anticipation of a dreamy future that never materializes. As these patients confide their desires and frustrations to their doctor, they often take on the rhetoric of mystics or martyrs. Janet notes, not without commenting on his own role as a mentor, that as soon as they find a guide, albeit tyrannical, their controlling impulses fizzle out and metamorphose into a devotional absolutism. Janet makes it clear that these are the two interchangeable sides of the same obsessive trait. In order not to experience the emptiness within, the debilitating *horror vacui*, these patients fall into either of these patterns in order never to have to confront their brittle selves.

There is no doubt that Janet's writings have inspired many breakthroughs in the understanding of obsessive-compulsive disorders. Janet

2. Pierre Janet and Fulgence Raymond, *Les obsessions et la psychasthénie*, vol. 2 (1903; repr., New York: Arno Press, 1976). All subsequent references to this work come from this edition, followed in the text by *Obsessions* and page numbers only. All translations are mine.

was perhaps the first to see that the obsessive is unable to negotiate the complexity of interpersonal relationships. Whenever an intimate encounter is about to take place, whenever a conversation hits a socially uncomfortable point, it is likely that obsessive characters will fall apart. What is intolerable to them is that crucial moment of hesitation whereupon their identity is about to be decided, about to emerge from the unpredictable relationship with the other. What occurs effortlessly for most people takes on a daunting quality because it is an unresolved interaction, where the outcome is still to be decided. The obsessive character views the world through a Manichean lens: one needs to dominate or be dominated, in control or controlled. Without these clear-cut roles, the patient experiences a terrible sense of panic and needs to retreat to a preexisting rigid role.[3]

Janet is also the shrewd painter of the commonplace. He reports with graphic detail the case of a patient's obsession with intestinal worms to prove that the parasite represents the invisible malaise that gnaws at his patient's peace of mind. This particular woman is afflicted with the mysterious need to concentrate all her energy on this *ver araignée* (spider worm) that allegedly courses up and down her intestine, spreading its hairy paws across her stomach. Janet suggests that, despite her phobia for the animal, she must be obtaining some form of comfort from this fatal beast. What it provides, amidst the horror and disgust, is the certainty of a constant, ever-returning presence. Her pathological need to spend the good part of her day tormented by the worm's imaginary peregrinations—"the poor woman . . . spends days double-guessing herself on the worm's existence" (*Obsessions,* 334–35)—leads Janet to a double speculation. On the physiological front, this obsession is surely rooted in an invasive gynecological procedure; the surgery had not only triggered a deep depression, but it had left her with an excruciating sense of openness. Literally, the intervention had made the woman's body vulnerable to all kinds of real and imaginary invasions. On the psychological front,

3. See, for instance, Leonard Salzman's "Therapy of the Obsessive Personality," in *Essential Papers on Obsessive-Compulsive Disorder,* ed. Dan J. Stein and Michael H. Stone (New York: New York University Press, 1997), 152. "The obsessional is particularly incompetent in the area of interpersonal relationship. Relationship involves participation, which, in turn, implies some need of dependency as well as commitment and exchange that grow out of some trust in the relationship. The demand for self-sufficiency obviates and aggravates as he grows older." Salzman is commenting on the zone of indeterminacy, the uneasy moment when the participants let their identities be molded by this new encounter. Janet showed with superb foresight how his obsessive patients were terrified by a halfway metamorphosis. The patient either took the lead, or surrendered to the other.

Janet mentions a neglected childhood and poor nutrition, both also unmistakable sources of emptiness.

Even though such analyses can appear as rather superficial bits of speculative medicine, failing to reach much analytic complexity, they nonetheless demonstrate how Janet, as the good novelist *manqué* that he is, had a brilliant way of turning the interpretation over to his readers, forcing them to flesh out the sketchy and compressed nature of his own finding. What Janet is best at discovering is the link between his patients' obsessive phobias and their radically impoverished self-perception. The worm, even though the patient experiences it with the uttermost disgust, becomes the bridge between the inner and outer world. Its peregrinations compel the patient to use the doctor as mediator of her secret life.

Janet's classification of manias is equally riveting, running from the search for perfect love to the all-consuming desire to remember *perfectly* a past memory. My focus is on those patients who are desperate to turn their excruciating sense of loneliness into something that will save them from themselves. I will follow Janet's belief that the need and failure to be controlled or overly directed is one of the great triggers of monomania. This book argues that obsessive characters are urgently drawn to the disciplined life, seeking guidance in a powerful leader. Rules, even if cruelly administered, provide a linear quality, a sheltering framework. This explains why when left to their own devices, asked to function autonomously, these characters immediately duplicate these rules, inventing dour and thankless tasks for themselves, creating an opprobrious inner tyrant. The tyrant's mission, and this is one of Janet's great insights, is to wipe out their unusually sharp *horror vacui*. Being governed by somebody or something rescues one from the emptiness of the everyday. Better that one succumb to obsessive rituals than to the flatness of depression. The *brouillard*, the mist that overwhelmed Emma Bovary after her marriage to Charles, is infinitely more oppressive, infinitely more difficult to live with, than the perilous, but electrifying charge contained in obsession. Obsession, even though it ends up consuming one's life, is a poisonous delight.

Janet grasps with remarkable lucidity the escapist potential of obsession. Even though she might be in excruciating pain, a woman who has focused all her energies and passion onto a lost lover has actually gained access to a private and elevating religion of suffering. This condition provides by its very abstraction an antidote to the vapidity of life. Many of Janet's patients are women who mirror the quiet heroines of nineteenth-century French literature. As Maupassant achieved through Jeanne, the depressive protagonist from *Une Vie* (*A Woman's Life*), Janet's cases are profound commentaries on the plight of women whose identities are primarily shaped by great biological turning points—puberty, sex, marriage, and aging. Janet focuses a great deal on the lonely women who, once deprived of their *raison d'être*, often abandoned by their lover, husband, or child, experience a crushing existential void, an abysmal degree of sorrow. But Janet does not stop there. He demonstrates how these women fend off their demons of loneliness by producing certain repetition compulsions. Such women are waiting for some kind of tyrannical trap to fall into, substituting their self-imprisonment to an often dangerous authority that is sure to engulf them. All Janet's cases are not so dire, but a typical pattern might be the story of the "poor" forty-one year old he names CK....[4] Recently widowed, and plagued by dozens of hypochondriac obsessions, her entire body is a great mass of suffering. She is attacked by migraines, fatigue, and kidney pains, and her bodily ailments have started eating at her personality, causing her to feel that her "moi," the core of her being, is dissolving: "It is a frenzy that throws all the psychological symptoms into contagious confusion. What are the causes of such disorder?"[5] CK's story reveals the following: all this disorder, all these confusing sensations, suddenly evaporate when she runs into one of her old boarding school teachers. Coincidentally, this woman (some ten years older than she) also suffers from compulsive disorders (cleaning mania) that paradoxically result in terrible slovenliness. CK takes her old teacher under her wing and makes it her mission to "clean her up." She reprimands her, coaxes her, and forces her to pull herself together. The teacher, in like manner, forces CK to confront her phobias and finally manages to calm her anxieties. Janet paints an idyllic picture of these two obsessive personalities, reunited and channeling their troubles into a joyful common plight. "Here they are, thrilled with one another: they direct and support each other, like the blind and the paralyzed, and thanks to this mutual bolstering, they remain perfectly reasonable for five years" (*Obsessions*, 402). Note that Janet uses the verb to direct ("diriger"). He has made these two women's illness and recovery revolve around the lack (and subsequently the restoration) of direction. Neither is capable of orchestrating the cacophonous voices within herself; she will only be

4. I will first quote Janet's patients the way he does, with an ellipsis at the end of the abridged name, and then provide a simplified initial.

5. Obsessions, 401. This description occurs in the section "Illness of Isolation—Amorous Obsession, Cessation of Direction" ("Maladie de l'isolement—Obsession amoureuse, Cessation de direction").

"saved" by taking control of the other's disorder. The two women become each other's vocation. By turning his patients' complex complaints into a rather commonplace narrative of private life, Janet humanizes the causes of their illness. He also follows a process that metastasizes from vulgar hypochondriac tics and complaints to the productive handling of an idée fixe. Instead of depicting his patient as a pariah, he offers a very simple explanation. Without purpose, without a master plan, CK's life turns back onto itself; her lack of love and purpose becomes the wide empty stage upon which a narrative of anguish and repetition is allowed to develop. Janet conflates her serious medical predicament and a very clear sense of loneliness. Unfortunately, and here the story really does end like a second-rate nineteenth-century sentimental novel, his patient is accused of having an illicit affair with the teacher. The two women are so shocked by the allegation that they decide to go their separate ways and never meet again.

Without the companionship of her former mentor, CK is possessed once again with a compulsion to repeat, and the nagging inner voices preside anew over her day. It seems, however, that their cruel way of disrupting her life is less onerous than the silence of solitude. The rekindled obsession, at least, provides a dialogue, an interlude to a life where the only other intrusion would be white noise. Janet demonstrates throughout his study that one of the predominant feelings of obsessive personalities is a floating sensation. Patients are assaulted by indescribable symptoms that eat away at the solid core of their being. Janet distinguishes between the inner obsession—inchoate, often rooted in an "inability to focus," typified by a self divided against itself and assailed by a "pitiful struggle by a divided soul in quest of itself" (*Obsessions*, 406)— and outer obsession. The latter is inflicted upon the patient from an outside force. It literally casts out the first obsession, exorcising it by coercion.

In another case-study, Janet describes Mademoiselle Byl..., a young woman who will move heaven and earth to marry her parents' gardener (*Obsessions*, 395). Since her seventeenth year, she has betrayed bizarre behavioral symptoms, all related to what Janet calls "the overwhelming shame of self." This shame has caused the young woman to lock herself in the house, refusing ever to venture into the streets. Janet draws this explanation out of her: "I am not like other young girls, I am ugly, I look like a cat; don't you see how shameful it is for a girl like me to go out . . . I am a monster" (*Obsessions*, 396–97). She goes on to explain that being such a nonentity, such a blotch on God's creation ("I even offend God"), she could not possibly ever dream of a marriage with somebody of her own

rank. Is this why the romance with the gardener coincides with her becoming much more settled? Janet puts the pieces together: the young
man's arrival on the scene, his becoming the object of her entire attention,
saves her from her own self-inflicted shame; she has finally met somebody who could put her "nothingness" to good use. Indeed, by becoming the servant to a servant, her inferiority would actually become
productive. The anguish of self-loathing would give way to the intoxicating desire to serve. "She would start cooking, she would pass herself
for a servant, since that's all she was good for" (*Obsessions*, 397). Her fixation on the gardening assistant leads her to debasing rituals: she stops
washing her hands to be "more like him" (*Obsessions*, 397), undoubtedly
sending her parents into hygienic fits. Janet, although he shows some
skepticism toward the parents' intrusion, also reads the situation as a
disturbing social breach. He never gives much reality to the suitor, concentrating entirely on the patient's "off-color" behavior. But after commenting briefly on the impropriety of the *liaison*, he goes back to the
nagging question—what lies at the roots of obsession? Why will patients
attach themselves so frantically to an "unsuitable" person? He stresses
that the young girl's behavior is a direct consequence of her lack of self.
"There is no more doubt about this," Janet writes, "[such] love is nothing
but the expression of the profoundest obsession of shame" (*Obsessions*,
297); her blatant lack of self leads to the type of asocial behavior that
should never be confused with legitimate love. Janet's utter confidence in
what makes for real versus erroneous love is more than suspect, but it
should not obscure the real validity of his theory of existential despair. He
states that the object fixated upon is usually incidental, and what matters
is not the flesh-and-blood recipient, but the ontological need to invest
oneself completely in one thing. Anybody who needs such a degree of en-
gagement suffers from a pathological sense of hollowness. Janet guarantees that Mademoiselle Byl's passionate attachment to the gardener has
nothing to do with the man himself. He simply embodies the figure who
will both duplicate and eradicate her worthlessness. By loving somebody
her family despises, she will defy any sense of expectation and devote
herself wholeheartedly to duplicating the nothingness she claims to embody. At least this is Janet's interpretation.

   If there is an undeniable paternalistic tone to this case-study, Janet does
show small signs of uncertainty about his method. He admits that taking
a patient in simply on account of her "wrong" sentimental choice is problematic. She is being "locked up" ("*internée*") just because she has fallen
in love with the wrong man. This, after all, is a seemingly innocuous

"folie" and it does seem remarkable that parents would drag their children to the doctor every time they are about to make the wrong sentimental choice. But parents, to Janet, are just as noteworthy as the children they bring in. Janet, as a good reader of nineteenth-century family histories, stresses that his patient's symptoms are duplicated, sometimes even exaggerated, by those of her mother and father.[6] He reviews the family's medical history and concludes that her problem is inherited. This does not stop him from taking the situation in hand. Janet commits Mademoiselle Byl to the hospital with the idea that she will find in the doctors' care and attention a substitute to the gardener fixation. And indeed, the effects are impressive. Stunned by the doctors' kindness, she gradually lets go of her obsession: "She was extremely surprised to be treated, not exactly as mad, but as sick by relatively reasonable people. The change, the astonishment of meeting kind people shook her up, and in a few days, she lost her fundamental feelings of incompletion . . . and renounced her ill-fated marriage" (*Obsessions*, 309). A modern reader has every right to view this as doctor playing God. But Janet's self-assuredness in the matter is mitigated by a certain skepticism toward his own profession. In fact, he only takes partial credit for having saved the young woman from her "grosse sottise," her great goof (note how he uses an infantile idiom, parroting the parents' language). When she suffers a relapse, he turns to what he believes to be a more effective cure for her obsessive traits. He places her on a strict regimen, a demanding series of physical exertions that would channel her excess of energy into mental improvement: "We resumed treatment by handling her more firmly; putting her on a real schedule, we forced her to focus on her concentration, her will, and her memory . . . the improvements were slower to come, but more secure. She has shed her hesitation, her shyness, her shame, and, more to the point, she has forgotten the infatuation that caused all this" (*Obsessions*, 399). Janet's conclusion is too abrupt to satisfy our interest in the workings of obsession. Five lines hardly do justice to any case. However, his insight about redirecting his patient's thoughts, forcing her to change her focus from the morbid to the constructive, is important. As in the previous case-study, Janet has grasped the simple, but essential, fact that obsession is a condition that can only be expunged if it is allowed to metamorphose into something else. Janet's "practical" treatment also points to a very simple

---

6. "The father is a pathologically indecisive *aboulique*, the sister a *psychasthénique*, riddled with stomachaches, headaches, attention deficit, maniacal attention to detail, and phobias," *Obsessions*, 396.

fact: physical activity returns the patient to the everyday that she has traded for a symbolic realm. Janet treats this otherworldly realm as a dangerous illusion, a seductive prison that traps the subject. His analysis resembles Ludwig Wittgenstein's attack on metaphysical language. As the critic Toril Moi explains, the language of metaphysics "holds out a promise of meaning, but when we try to grasp it, it escapes. . . . Wittgenstein thought that such language trips us up." Wittgenstein proposes not a physical counter-training like Janet's, but "a kind of philosophical therapy, which aims to free us from the mental straitjacket that makes us believe that we *must* think of a certain question. . . . His task, he wrote, 'is to bring words back from their metaphysical to their everyday use.'"[7] Wittgenstein's attack on metaphysical language is singularly relevant to the alternate worlds dreamed up by Janet's women. Any language that so blatantly rejects the everyday, making its practitioners prey to concepts that promise full disclosure, "gives the impression of being profound and meaningful [when . . .] in fact [it] means nothing."[8] The temptation is to embrace a realm that will never deliver anything but abstractions. Such attachment to what is not present, to what will plunge the subject deeper into unreality, points to the dangerous desire *not to understand* what is directly around us, favoring instead an ideational region. To Janet, fantasies, delusions, and any kind of abstract doctrine are signs of ontological weakness: "Abstract intelligence is the lowest degree of thought, remaining when all the superior functions that constitute the real—will, attentiveness, connection with the present—have disappeared" (*Obsessions*, 461).

Janet situates this abstract realm at the intersection of helplessness and authority. He is convinced that the roots and cure of obsession hover around issues of power. As I indicated earlier, the typical compulsive character resorts to obsession as an unconscious corrective to loneliness and lack of direction. Metaphysical language provides a different kind of loneliness, no less alienating, but tantalizing and glamorous. Janet's patient Simone is a case in point.[9] Her life alternates between authoritative behavior, helplessness, and "the sense of hollowness" (*le sentiment du vide*); the various ways in which she combines these elements makes her either prey to a life of petty obsession or to grand mystical aspirations. In

7. Toril Moi, "'It Was as if He Meant Something Different from What He Said—All the Time': Language, Metaphysics, and the Everyday in *The Wild Duck*," *New Literary History* 33 (2002): 659.

8. Wittgenstein; quoted in Toril Moi, "It Was as if He Meant Something Different," 659.

9. Janet refers to her as Sim..., but for ease of reading I will call her Simone.

a remarkable confessional moment, she describes the failed dynamics of her married life. Because of her husband's lack of vision, his failure to offer her a novelistic dream-life, she is forced to provide the missing elements herself; but nothing, it turns out, is more arduous than to play both sides of the conjugal dialogue: having a dull interlocutor turns her right back onto herself, cast in the position of having to write all the lines. Wedded to his flatness and to her own impossible aspirations, she is sucked into terrible ennui. "Alone, I am bored, my husband does not make my head work hard enough, he knows nothing and teaches me nothing, he does not astonish me. . . . I know myself, I have exhausted my own circle of thoughts, I need to be given new ideas, new impressions. . . . My husband has good common sense, but that bores me to death. . . . A husband should always be superior to his wife. . . . He does not know how to make me suffer a little. You cannot love somebody who is unable to make you suffer" (*Obsessions,* 406). Simone's self-diagnosis is remarkable for a number of reasons. She is formulating the frustrations voiced by the great adulteresses of nineteenth-century European fiction. Like Emma Bovary, she abhors the *tedium vitae* that has substituted itself for marriage. Like her, she might claim that "the most important thing in love is not love, but emotion and above all novelty" (*Obsessions,* 407). She pines for a husband who would feed her a vision that she could never procure herself. Rather than reflecting her thoughts, he would spawn his own, intoxicating her with his fantasy and intelligence. These thoughts, almost cribbed from Flaubert's Emma, are tied to the subject's hollow self-perception. By not making her "head work hard enough," her husband leaves her to stew in her own obsessive thoughts, leading her to interpret his common sense as mere commonplace. Janet is perplexed by these subjects begging to be enticed out of themselves, saved from their own limitations, wrenched from their familiar tics and ruminations. Each of them has a firm definition of what the other ought to be: he or she should effortlessly and with full control provide a space of escape, not of repetition.

Janet grasps exactly how Simone's boredom generates an almost interchangeable craving for knowledge and suffering. Both elements are powerful enough to obliterate the present. And the present is precisely the problem. Knowledge—that is, the expertise of something exotic and impenetrable—will blissfully overwhelm her, taking her far from her stagnant, everyday self. Suffering, likewise, will intensify the present moment. Everything will feel more urgent, more complicated; everything will be a diversion from the straightforward, the painfully prosaic. Simone's masochism is not so much a desire for pain as a need for greater mental rewards. The daunting void that plagued her melancholic fictional sisters has to be filled: Janet shows that it will either be replaced by the compulsively minute or the quest for unattainable transcendence.

Like Emma, Simone turns to a lover. But unlike her fictional predecessors, she receives a curious type of sentimental gratification from her transgression. In one of her letters, she describes him in these chillingly eulogistic terms: "He is an astonishing man. He has never shown a second's worth of distress, emotion, pity, kindness, relaxation (*laisser-aller*); always master of himself . . . and cold to the point of making you die of sadness . . . he had the gift of stopping your slightest effusion, forcing you to take back the smallest sentimental sentence to the point that however horribly he would humiliate me, I never once could shed a tear in his presence" (*Obsessions*, 404). It is not surprising that Janet uses Simone's case as one of his central case histories. As in the story of CK, he is drawn to the woman's humiliation. Her story touches him: he refers to her as "this little lady" ("cette petite femme" [*Obsessions*, 406]), saddened that her lack of sophistication has blinded her and led her to accept the lover's callous ways. His patient has admitted to him that despite her infatuation, she is not satisfied by her lover—"he had no consideration for her needs and only thought about himself. She was far more satisfied in her marriage" (*Obsessions*, 406). At this point, Janet makes his inquiry pivot around the question: why would you take an abusive lover if you are far more satisfied by your husband? She answers with an impressive degree of lucidity: "There was around that sensation something very different, fear, remorse, an intense emotion that constricted her throat and made the whole thing much more spicy (*pimentée*) than with her husband" (*Obsessions*, 406). Janet portrays the affair as a source of anxiety. But the very fact that she is filled with any trepidation at all, that she feels full rather than empty, is crucial to understanding this destructively positive mechanism. Simone would much prefer the anxiety her lover inflicts upon her, because it invades her from without, not from within. For once, it is not she who has generated this energy, however negative it may be. What a liberation, Janet implies, when one can let go of one's own obsessions and passively endure those of another. Duplicating the passions she had picked up from books, teachers, or religious figures, she revels in an emotion that takes full possession of her being. Her pain, her constricted throat, are by no means hypochondriac inventions. They stem from a painfully real situation, from the genuine contempt and brutality that the lover inflicts upon her. Parroting Emma Bovary's quixotic fantasies, she prefers pain and a certain sexual frustration, because "I did not have that

heavy sensation that I could predict exactly what would happen next."
(*Obsessions*, 407) Recall Emma watching with growing disgust Charles'
eating habits. What repelled her was his inability to turn food into a pure,
Eucharistic experience. Food is only food, when it is Charles who is mas-
ticating. Likewise, words are practical and pedestrian when Charles utters them. Simone's lover, conversely, magically turns words into barely
comprehensible concepts. Far from resenting this, she is mesmerized by
what she does not understand. His power, then, resides in *her* ignorance,
her sense that he is so far superior to her, that whatever he utters must be
important, not just worthy, but nourishing and vital.

Basking in her lover's abstractions fills Simone with mystical elation. It
provides her with the type of "excitation" she needs in order not to be depressed. Without such excitation, these *abouliques* (Janet uses this word
frequently, meaning something similar to *dysphoric*) remain depressed.
This is exactly when they fixate on order; their lives, indeed, are only tolerable when they can be organized into cogent patterns. Sounding again
like Schopenhauer, Janet ties this to boredom:

[These individuals] remain unhappy, because they cannot achieve mentally the
pleasure of the present [*la jouissance du présent*], which is the only remedy against
boredom. They cannot tense [*se tendre*] up, so they seek tension all over the place;
if they find this tension in alcóhol or morphine, they will become alcoholics or
morphine addicts; if they find it in divine love and religious emotion, then they
will experience mystical delirium, but if they find their source of excitation in a
human being, they will fall in love and when this person abandons them, they
will experience the very same disorders as a morphine addict deprived of morphine. It will not be long until *l'obsession amoureuse*, obsessive love, will develop.
(*Obsessions*, 407)

This short excerpt deserves to figure prominently in all histories of melancholia. The French verb "se tendre," which translates as "to tense up," is
a brilliant characterization of what the obsessive character craves. Janet
notes that his patients have somehow been deprived of the mechanism
that triggers this tension. The "healthy" person, he is suggesting, manages to create tension from within, without the help of stimulants or radical allegiances. Such a person might get excited reading a book and, at
the same time, enjoy thinking about work without having to resort to an
extremist position. People such as Simone (and her mother for that matter) are fundamentally incapable of such casualness; whatever situation
is played out must immediately be invested with a life or death outcome.
It is not infrequent for these types to go from one obsession to another;

Janet cites mystical exaltation, passion for literature, for poetry, or even fierce involvement in one's work as some possibilities.

As in the bulk of his cases, Janet frames Simone's symptoms with incidents from her family history. Simone's mother was "absolutely wretched" (*épouvantable*); "a hateful woman whose mania for authority [*manie de l'autorité*] almost reached delirium. She would neither tolerate in her parents, her husband, or any of those who came near her, any gesture, word, or idea that she did not previously dictate. . . . [S]he wanted to organize everything, up to the minutest detail, and would succumb to great violence if she felt the slightest divergence" (*Obsessions*, 404). Her daughter, Janet's patient, desperately tries to fight this same need to control and organize, creating two distinct sides to her persona. First comes the predictably staunch perfectionism, second a weakness of will, accompanied by "the constant propensity to daydream (*rêvasserie perpétuelle*)" (*Obsessions*, 404).

The compulsive perfectionism comes at a high price, since maintaining such order is a painful, often a highly self-conscious *faute de mieux*, a shift from much higher aspirations. Simone, indeed, "maintains order in her life," but at the cost of "torturing herself, having the simultaneous desire to let herself go" (*Obsessions*, 405). Janet is drawn to these Janus-faced conditions, these lives that appear harsh and unbending, when in fact fraught with misery and inner doubts. Behind their inflexible masks, he writes, authoritarian individuals are people whose "beliefs, focus, and willpower depend entirely on a particular moral *milieu*, ruled by great uniformity. Instill contradiction into this equilibrium and their precarious . . . mental synthesis will be shattered" (*Obsessions*, 404). Such patients have lost the ability to adapt to circumstances. Their imagination has been frozen over. When something new tries to break through this frosted ground, the patient panics, unable to fit the new information into his or her preexisting system. The tragic inability to absorb the new explains the other side of such figures. Simone, for one, explains that her compulsions have very little to do with the situation at hand; in fact, they conceal an impossibly high aspiration: "As long as I can remember . . . all the silliness [*sottises*] or the good actions [*bonnes actions*] that I have committed were all rooted in the same cause, a yearning for a perfect and ideal love to which I could surrender my entire being, through which I could entrust myself to another—God, man or woman—who would be by so far my superior that I would neither need to think about my behavior nor take care of my own life" (*Obsessions*, 405). What is striking here is the patient's lucidity. She recognizes that her actions are mere stand-ins for her quest for domination. As her wish-list indicates, she seeks a leader—God, man, or woman—who would rob her of her free will. "To find somebody . . . I could blindly obey . . . certain that he would save me from all lapse and would lead me in a straight line . . . toward perfection. . . . How I envy Mary Magdalene and Jesus' ideal love: to be the ardent disciple of an adored and deserving master; to live and die for one's idol, believing in him without the shadow of a doubt . . . being held in his arms so girdled, so small, so wrapped up in his protection, that I would cease to exist" (*Obsessions*, 405). All the elements that traverse Janet's work on obsession are contained in this passage. She pines after "somebody," a being with no fixed identity, a hidden God whom she would "obey blindly." This notion of blind obedience has powerful Christian connotations. She proves the degree of her faith by blindly surrendering to commands that exist, it would seem, merely to test her devotion. The content of the order is irrelevant since all it really reflects is its recipient's absolute surrender to authority. Being led "in a straight line," being saved from the arabesques of ambiguity, is her dearest dream. Once she finds the ruler of her life, Simone curls up in a womb-like position, "so small" that she will "cease to exist." This willful surrender is a barely concealed death wish. She is unwittingly admitting to Janet that if she ever could play Mary Magdalene to Christ, then she would gladly see her identity eroding to the point of non-existence. What appeared to be a cruel and domineering streak is in fact the pitiful need to be turned back into nothingness. By giving herself over to such a dominant object of desire, she finally endows her life with resolution. All of a sudden, the prosaic quality of her routine has metamorphosed into something that is unfathomable and hypnotic. So Janet makes clear the two options: either you surrender to cult-like behavior or you script the most rigid and matter-of-fact scenarios to live your life by. If we think back to Simone's mother, we note that her own allergy to the unpredictable, her inability to take on a dialogical relationship with the world, was what drove her to adopt the second option, a cruel and codified life.

In a case similar to Simone's, reported in *L'amour et la haine* (a compilation of the classes he delivered at the Collège de France), Janet describes another variation on obsessive escapism. This time it is Léonie, a forty-five-year-old who, from the early years of her marriage, had lost all interest in her husband and two children. Léonie, however, leads a double life. Known to all the hypnotists for her alleged magnetic powers (she is a *somnambule extra-lucide*, a clairvoyant sleepwalker), she becomes the key player in a series of adventures. The most famous is her participation in

Les fouilles du château de Crèvecoeur (*The Excavations of Château de Crève-coeur*), a case published in 1862 as a booklet. Apparently, a treasure, which nobody could find, was buried in the large *caves* under the castle. Only Léonie's clairvoyance promises to uncover it. Prey to the greed of quack-doctors, she is almost buried alive (up to her mouth) under the *château*; from her muddy tomb and from the depths of her trance, she directs the operations. This bizarre situation, according to Janet, far from being de-grading or disappointing (her success or failure in the excavation is not mentioned), becomes her personal triumph. All she needed, Janet pro-nounces, was a mission of her own, a cause, something that would pro-vide her with an identity: "Is this nothing in the life of a woman? . . . such events change a life, fill it, invigorate it. Our Léonie would become a char-acter (*un personnage*). Being a character is an enormously important hu-man attribute. We all want to be a character, to be Mister Somebody (*monsieur quelqu'un*) rather than Mister Nobody (*Monsieur Personne*). How many neurotic people (*névropathes*) don't even know how to be wives or mothers and believe themselves to be poets, mathematicians, anything, just as long as they can play a part in life."[10] Again, Janet is as-sessing the role of boredom and loneliness in the construction of obses-sive behavior. He is drawn to the type of woman who requires an above-average amount of intellectual stimulation or else she will be un-able to "metabolize" her *tedium vitae*.[11] Obsessive behavior no longer looks like a genetic curse, but like the result of a legitimate human need. No woman should have to limit her life to the four walls of her home and expect to be ecstatic about it. What interests Janet, beyond this stifling lonesomeness, is the urge to be dragged into extreme and dangerous sit-uations. He is surprised to find that suffering is a relief, not a burden. It brings a sense of drama and welcome crisis to a life without surprises.

Pépita is another of these housebound women who lead a double life. A bored housewife, she engages in the most dangerous of habits: she at-taches herself passionately to an "abject individual, an alcoholic, ether-addict who used to beat her and rob her of her possessions" (*Amour*, 253). But rather than suffering from this abuse, Pépita thrives. Her delicate health suddenly flourishes, her mood improves, and she is no longer the ailing woman she used to be. Like Simone, she abhors normal life, which

10. Pierre Janet, *L'amour et la haine: Notes de cours recueillies par M. Miron Epstein* (Paris: Editions Médicales Norbert Maloine, 1932), 273–74. All subsequent references to this work are followed in the text by *Amour* and page numbers only.

11. For more on this matter, see Elissa Marder, *Dead Time: Temporal Disorders in the Wake of Modernity* (Stanford: Stanford University Press, 2001).

she finds painful and vulgar (*pénible et vulgaire*). She blossoms when indulging in extravagant adventures with dire consequences: "All these troubles, problems, trials, give me such pleasure that I can't go back to the *vie de tricot* (humdrum life) with papa and maman. . . . On my own, I'm bored; my husband doesn't make my head spin enough. I need different ideas, different emotions. What I need is a husband vastly superior to me and who would change all the time" (*Amour*, 253). Janet focuses on the need for intellectual stimulation. Without voicing it clearly, he implies that a great deal of his case-studies are superior women, who are not allowed to cultivate their minds and are going insane.

A more unsettling side of Janet's research is his tendency to call these obsessive patients weak-willed; they *allow* themselves to be overwhelmed by an idea, something that crawls into their psyche like a living entity, like the famous *ver araignée*, the spider worm, that had invaded his patient's intestine. This spider is a good metaphor for Janet's research. It brings up once more his belief in the two types of obsessions: those generated from within and those from without. None of Janet's patients is able to contend with those operating invisibly, weaving invisible webs inside the body or soul. Conversely, when the obsession is focused on a lover, especially the disciplinarian type many of Janet's patients gravitate around, then the patient finds temporary solace and release.

What this suggests is that nothing is more destabilizing than the nagging and invisible melancholy that distorts and infiltrates the patient's whole universe. In contrast to this invisible predator, the order and discipline that the cruel lover inflicts provides the obsessive type with a welcome focal point. The implacable imprecations, at least, come from an identifiable source; the patient does not feel as though she is going mad, giving into something she cannot grasp. She is simply doing what she is told. The inexorable inner voices, on the other hand, pound in all directions, filling the patient with boundless dread. Part of Janet's therapy for these cases is to deflect this sense of boundlessness; he works on his patients' need to question everything by forcing them into a disciplined train of thought. The discipline of medicine itself seems to replace the discipline of love.

So what we have is one syndrome and two manifestations. For what it is worth, the second type of obsession is less painful than the litany of unanswered, ever-repeated questions and doubts. As Janet shows in his chapter on vocational scruples (*scrupules de la vocation*), the types who succumb to the inchoate feel the urge to turn every sentence, every thought into a question. This questioning disease (an offspring of *la folie du doute*) is the condition that bespeaks the individual's loss of certainty. He describes his patient We..., a twenty-four-year-old woman, consumed by the mental mania of asking questions about everything in the following way: "She racks her brains to find out whether or not she has seen crosses or saintly figures in the sky. She tries to remember whether she *really* did see them; sometimes she thinks she did, other times, she does not. . . . She also asks whether the saints spoke to her" (*Obsessions*, 379). While a doctor today would diagnose this doubting disease as a straightforward symptom of obsession-compulsion, Janet interprets this mania as the expression of mental weakness, as the inability to reach a positive or negative solution. This is not much of a diagnosis, but it takes us back to Janet's staunch belief that most of his patients are ill because they cannot manage themselves without a set of directives. He decides to treat We. with the following treatment: "We managed in five months to alter considerably this patient's state. With incomplete hypnoses, focusing exercises, and a whole education of the will, she has become infinitely more sure of herself, but it is obvious that she is still not cured" (*Obsessions*, 38). Forcing precise points of focus on his patients, educating their will (it is not clear from most of the case-studies how Janet does this), would prevent the mental unraveling that also strikes the thirty-seven-year-old patient: Xyb. who is the case-study in his chapter on "Criminal obsession as guilt" (*obsession criminelle sous forme de remords*). This woman has lost the ability to finish anything she has begun. Having fired her *blanchisseuse*, her linen-maid, she begins wondering obsessively about her violent outburst against the innocent woman. Either the guilt of having fired her, or the guilt of having shown indecision by taking her back, fills Xyb.'s entire days. All her thoughts attach themselves to the figure of the *blanchisseuse*. She sinks into the most debilitating inertia, complaining that she sees everything through a thick fog. Like Penelope, she embroiders, but each time she is about to complete her task, she unravels it, *just so it remains unfinished.* "It seemed to her that she had no right to finish anything. She also keeps herself from getting to the bottom of things, or carrying any feeling to its end. She has lost interest in her children, and remains quite indifferent to what people tell her" (*Obsessions*, 449).

This sense of incompleteness drives Xyb. to debilitating inertia. She is surrounded with disorder, as though her inability to organize her thoughts, to decide between right and wrong, is transferred to the chaos of objects. Janet has grasped how dangerous this floating sensation can become. Leading some of his patients to suicide, others to a permanent state of frozen horror, it operates against one's linear sense of time. One of the consequences of Xyb.'s inability to complete a task is her troubled relationship with temporality (*le trouble du sens du temps*): "She always used to be lax with time, but now her indifference to it goes beyond everything; she lets whole days go by without noticing: 'The day went by like a minute,' she said, 'I was waiting for it to be nine and suddenly, it is already night time, and I don't know why; I'm like an animal (*une bête*) who has lost its sense of time" (*Obsessions*, 449). She has produced a monster in her own head, a spider-worm that will not let go of her. The linen-maid has come to metonymize all the loose ends in her life; with her unambiguous cleanliness, she serves as the blank slate upon which Xyb. casts all her inner demons. Only an idée fixe will be able to fend off the vaporous guilt that is destroying her life. Born out of despair and indecisiveness, it will bestow a focal point on a soul that has all but lost its center. This explains why Janet establishes the connection between guilt and the idée fixe. In essence amorphous and mercurial, the opposite of certainty, guilt never stands for one simple thing. It becomes the passepartout emotion, the unsettling pest that needs to turn into something else, something certain. Whether Othello's jealousy or Ahab's white whale, the idée fixe has that virtue of turning the uncertain into a dead certainty.

Tyrannically ruling a household, hampering children from any autonomous conduct, and, above all, wanting to be everybody's stage manager, puts an enormous burden on one's willpower, turning it into the measure of all things. There is no escape from such self-inflicted coercion except perhaps through the radical excision of selfhood. Rigid schedules and immaculate floorboards only provide a temporary satisfaction and the perfection might not last longer than the next obsessive thought. In the end, however, tired of being leaders and authority figures, such characters pray, not for a Prince Charming, but for a figure who will allow them to switch from omnipresent taskmaster to invisible servant. This dialectic suggests that the flip side of compulsive behavior is an overpowering desire to serve. Simone's quest for ideal love, notably, is far removed from any sense of reciprocity; purely immaterial, it can never be satisfied—hence its strength and mystical appeal. The projected ecstasy rests in a reveling in the void, in a melancholic knowledge that the coveted object will always be out of reach. Perfectionism is always radically intolerant of the real, unless the real embodies absolute mastery.

In his recent history of authority, Gérard Mendel notes how individuals and groups are drawn to absolute power (*le pouvoir absolu*), no matter how informed or educated they are. "Even when warned by experience, it is surprising how easily a fantasy, an abstraction, a doctrine, or the words of a writer can elicit the leap from immanence to transcendence, becoming a legitimating principle."[12] Janet's work helps us grasp just how obsession plays into this need to be overpowered. Being held hostage by an idée fixe (whatever its nature) makes one vulnerable to the particular idea, but immune to one's own personal torments. Absolute power claims for itself both sides of every argument, leaving but one choice to the irresolute—surrender. Janet's obsessive patients, even when they are at their most domineering, are simply yearning to surrender to a force greater than themselves, one that will rescue them from their crippling sense of irresolution. Their fanatical choices—religion, unconditional love, relentless routine, even immaculate domesticity—stands for the clarity and determination they cannot reach on their own.

What continues to impress in Janet's cases is his will to reinsert his patients' obsessions into a re-enchanted quotidian. The patient's boredom, for instance, becomes the pretext for a rich meditation on emptiness (*le sentiment du vide*), one that will slowly allow for a new history of the patient. Like Nietzsche who advocated for new academic disciplines, Janet suggested some startling changes in the ways of analyzing illness: "A major study is still to be done on the relationship between objects and feelings. For instance, one would realize that happiness and sadness are usually tied to some form of ownership. The study of objects, then, should be linked to the study of emotions" (*Amour*, 10). Nietzsche had also proposed an unconventional way of understanding the intimate, of linking the forgotten elements of the everyday to a personal history of mankind. "So far, all that has given color to existence still lacks a history. Where could you find a history of love, of avarice, of envy, of conscience, of pious respect for tradition, of cruelty? . . . Has anyone made a study of different ways of dividing up the day or of the consequences of a regular schedule of work, festivals, and rest? . . . Has anyone collected men's experiences of living together—in monasteries, for example?"[13]

Rather than beholding our prosaic world as the enemy of meaning, as the foe of profundity, why not become the cunning observer, the active interpreter, of the seemingly trivial? Why not be the re-creator, instead of the victim, of small things? The characters of this book are all loathe to rethink their relationship to the everyday, and Blanchot's idea of applying

12. Gérard Mendel, *Une histoire de l'autorité: Permanences et variations* (Paris: La Découverte & Syros, 2002), 110.

13. Friedrich Nietzsche, *The Gay Science*, trans. Walter Kaufmann (New York: Vintage, 1974), 81–82.

"a glimmer of consciousness to a mechanical gesture, or practice phenomenology while polishing a piece of old furniture" would terrify them. The triumph and the curse of the idée fixe is that it protects from possibility—both its threat and its promise. It shields from the possible epiphanies wrought by "new impressions [that] come into being beneath this familiar domestic duty." But stuck in their fear of change, what these obsessive natures end up learning from Janet's investigative empathy is that "consciousness rejuvenates everything, giving a quality of beginning to the most everyday actions."[14]

14. Gaston Bachelard, *The Poetics of Space*, trans. Maria Jolas (Boston: Beacon Press, 1964, 1994), 67; quoted in Nancy Ries, "Anthropology and the Everyday, from Comfort to Terror," *New Literary History* 33 (2002): 725.

2

Flaubert

The Revenge of Art on Life

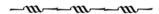

That's not to say that great authors, great artists are all ill,
however sublimely, or that one's looking for a sign of
neurosis or psychosis like a secret in their work, the hidden
code of their work. They're not ill; on the contrary, they're
a rather special kind of doctor. Why has Masoch given his
name to a perversion as old as the world? Not because he
"suffered" from it, but because he transformed the
symptoms, he set a novel picture of it by making the
contract its primary sign and also by linking masochistic
practices to the place of ethnic minorities in society and the
role of women in those minorities: masochism becomes an
act of resistance.

Gilles Deleuze, *Negotiations*

Nietzsche, himself no stranger to disease or depression, once re-
marked that people long to be organized out of fear of their own frailties.
Their hatred of "the laisser aller, of any all-too-great freedom . . . implants
the need for limited horizons and the nearest tasks—teaching the narrowing of our perspective."[1] This narrowing of perspective, this active
self-limitation, helps bring back a sense of order and agency. Order is the

Most of the letters in this chapter are taken from Jean Bruneau's four-volume edition of
the *Correspondance* (Paris: Gallimard, 1973–1998); henceforth *Correspondance*. Some of the letters are taken from the very useful compilation of Flaubert's letters edited by Geneviève Bollème in *Préface à la vie d'écrivain: Extraits de la correspondance* (Paris: Seuil, 1963); henceforth
Préface. Others are taken from Gustave Flaubert, *Œuvres complètes*, 4 vols., ed. Jean Bruneau
(Paris: Pléiade, 1980); henceforth *Œuvres*. All translations are mine.

1. Friedrich Nietzsche, *Beyond Good and Evil*, trans. R. J. Hollingdale (London: Penguin,
2003), chap. 5, no. 188.

opium of the depressed, the counter-poison to fragmentation and inner tumult. It suffices to read even a fraction of Flaubert's letters to be convinced that the only way he could fend off periodical despair was by building his life around the merciless and iron-clad discipline of writing. To a friend, curious to learn how he suddenly seemed cured of his *crises*, he writes: "You ask me how I cured myself of the nervous hallucinations that used to plague me? In two ways: 1. by studying them scientifically, that is, by trying to be aware of them, and, 2. by the strength of my will." What horrified Flaubert most about his hallucinations was that they made him tumble into a formless world, where his "brain was shot through with a whirlwind of ideas and images" and his ego "ripped apart like a vessel in the storm."[2] These cataclysmic images, where the body loses its unity, are decisive for grasping not just Flaubert's obsessive relationship to language and to the rituals of writing, but for understanding the motor that drives artists to produce in the first place. Before scrutinizing the ways in which a compulsive relationship to style boosted Flaubert's psychological immune system, I will review some of the findings of three psychoanalysts (Didier Anzieu, André Green, and Jean Guillaumin), who have recently produced superb studies on the connection between creativity, disease, and healing. What all three have observed is that the moment of creation often occurs when the subject is feeling attacked by a convergence of disorderly emotions.[3] If this disorder is not converted into some form of coherence, the subject's initial excitement might turn into depression. These affects, Guillaumin writes, "require a move that will give them a sense of direction, a purpose that will restore control."[4]

It is this intense sense of purpose that helps melancholics resist succumbing to the whirlwind of images described above. Having a firm aim helps the mind mobilize, while triggering at the same time a significant number of protective mechanisms. Conversely, if the momentary crisis is

2. Flaubert to Mademoiselle Leroyer de Chantepie, May 18, 1857, *Œuvres*, 2:716. Flaubert was particularly fond of this old Mademoiselle, a highly intelligent and troubled spinster wracked by anxiety and religious doubt.

3. In his excellent study *Le moi sublimé: Psychanalyse de la créativité* (Paris: Dunod, 1998), Jean Guillaumin notes that "the impetus that leads to creative activities comes from the urgent need, felt and cultivated by the artist, for the restoration of a stable external support . . . , which would help protect against overexcitement [*pare-excitation*] produced by the onslaught of unruly internal attacks" (65). He portrays the artist as the constant target of inner battles that can be resolved only by the "restoring" stability of the creative act. The act of creation functions as scaffolding that prevents the fragile inner edifice from collapsing.

4. Ibid., 9.

not rerouted into something productive, then it will fracture rather than restructure the subject's ego. This is why overwrought emotions imperatively need to be mediated by a constructive framework. Art has the strange capacity of providing this framework. Because it brings together the formed and the formless, its production grants, in the words of Didier Anzieu, a second skin, a protective agency that keeps these frightening emotions at bay, while in fact letting them soak into our being. Anzieu analyzes this osmosis in terms of the mother-child relationship. While the mother "engenders" her double, gives birth to something she has herself produced, she is also recreated by it, forever altered by its conception.[5] The autonomy of pregnancy, the tranquil self-enclosure of gestation, dramatically ceases after birth. Creating a work, likewise, is as much about fusion and sameness as it is about mutation and estrangement. But the moment of creation itself, the pure mental energy that goes into writing, into making up one's own surroundings, channels overwhelming emotions into feelings of ordered tranquility. While this intense act of emotional reorganization is at work, the artist is taking part in a remarkable performance, juggling two separate realities, playing the role of the producer and the produced. The new reality, born from the need to reconfigure a collapsing worldview, displaces the old with a freshly constructed one. The act of creating has enabled a passively-experienced emotion to turn active and resolute.[6]

The artist looks with awe at this new product, outgrowth of his or her mind, created in part to regain control. It is both the need for and the loss of control that gives the work of art its multiple status. It is at the same time a therapeutic response to the onslaught of uncontainable emotions and a remarkably self-contained environment where these emotions are miraculously turned into their own air-tight universes. Once the work is concluded, the artist is projected outside of him or herself, reinvented as the audience of his or her own production. This process is then duplicated in the reader / spectator who will now judge the success or failure of this conversion. If the transition from chaos into form has operated properly, then *the public* will enjoy its own version of unreal-reality.[7] This dual

5. Didier Anzieu, "Le Moi-peau: Vers une métapsychologie de la création," in *Psychanalyse du génie créateur* (Paris: Dunod, 1974). Again, I am indebted to Guillaumin for pointing out these sources. The English translation of *Le Moi-peau* is *The Skin Ego* (New Haven: Yale University Press, 1989).

6. It is clear that Flaubert deflected his unease toward the world into a rigid respect for the work itself. He restored balance by putting into writing the energy he often denied to life.

7. Guillaumin puts it well: "[The spectator,] bound to the work through its violence . . .

process allows us to perceive the art work as simultaneously creative and destructive. Destructive because (and in Flaubert's case) the artist uses art to sever fundamental ties with the world, being often far more content to suffer with his self-inflicted sentence (écrire pour ne pas vivre) than to speak in his own voice. The pathology of this omniscient and yet absent voice bespeaks the desire to erase personhood by creating a by-product of the self.[8] Such doubling frees the author to view his or her production as other. This owning / disowning allows a fantastic sense of freedom and irresponsibility at the same time that it increases the profound fear of fragmentation.[9] Losing oneself in one's own creation might be solacing, but cannot be sustained over a long period of time without becoming something pathological. Transmigration is never without dangers. As will be shown later in this book, Canetti's breakdown upon finishing Auto-da-fé reveals how lethal the identification between work and author can be.

Monomania sets in when writing becomes a replacement activity for life itself. Work, friends, and the normal activities that structure the everyday are all staved off and replaced by the all-encompassing, all-excluding act of creating an alternate universe. This territory is not as solitary as one might think. Despite the consistent analogies between such space and dark retreats (Flaubert talks about hibernating, Tournier refers to his "terrier," his mole-hole,[10] his den, and Le Clezio invokes his "étouffoir," his

---

its systematic organizing of the negative into the positive . . . is now able to project himself freely, to be overtaken by, and even to 'luxuriate' (s'éclater) in the work, while nonetheless feeling miraculously protected by it," Le Moi sublimé, 13. Guillaumin adds these remarkable words on the absent / present nature of this interaction: "I suppose that . . . it is probably this odd presence-absence . . . that provides the work with . . . its capacity to reenact . . . through the negative hallucinations born from its white pages . . . the virtual fantasies of the author and of the public," ibid., 18. The work constitutes a photographic negative of its author's fantasy; Guillaumin compares the relationship between work and author to that of turning a glove inside out; ibid., 22. These fantasies, however, will turn against the writer unless he can eventually detach them from himself, read the words he has written as though they were authored by a stranger. This separation speaks directly to the monomaniacal principle. The idée fixe has a brutally disembodied quality; its "enabler" starts beholding it as an independent entity. In the case of hypochondria, for example, the idée fixe is the body's deterioration. The malade imaginaire starts viewing his own body as a separate entity, something he can scrutinize the way a detached spectator might.

8. "To destroy oneself through the act of creating, rather than to run the risk of being severed later from one's creation and to exist as oneself," ibid., 15.

9. Guillaumin explains this in terms of the fantasy of self-genesis (autogenèse). "To be the sole creator of one's identity could be one of the deepest motivations for creating art: that is to say, to have been fertilized . . . by none other than oneself," ibid., 26.

10. See the interviews by J. L. de Rambures in Comment travaillent les écrivains (Paris: Flammarion, 1978). Again, I am indebted to Guillaumin, who uses this volume extensively.

smotherer), what is clear is that these creative spaces are first and fore-most theatrical stages upon which many scenarios are unraveling, not least the quiet melodrama epitomized by the writer who has opted for art over life. In these intensely private chambers, rituals are anticipated and carried out with an astonishing level of formality. The "writing-room" smacks of the sanatorium (the author is both doctor and patient) with a touch of the boudoir, where the wooing of inspiration is about to take place. Most remarkable about this courtship is the uncertainty of its out-come. The author is redirected by the words he or she has just produced, but the outcome of the course is not known, as mysterious to its unwit-ting author as it is to its future reader. When the author becomes specta-tor, he or she is actually reading as though for the first time. From this results a gap that will separate the producing self (trance-like, sleep-walker of sorts) and the non-producing self. The "stuff" being created will be viewed as foreign material (the work of a daimonic intruder, a mysterious alter ego who "unscrambles" the message for the outside world), astonishing for its own creator at the moment of rereading. Rereading words produced in this altered state triggers a combination of recognition and estrangement.[11]

The feeling of control that accompanies the act of locking oneself up to write, the pride in having unsuspected resources, reinforces the notion that creating has set one in a world apart. It is strengthening, both despite and because of its ability to isolate. When Mondrian or Flaubert discusses the relationship of their straight line or perfect phrase to a sense of onto-logical security, they are splitting the world between the rigid (with its connotations of self-discipline, rigor, and control) and the arabesque, the overly lyrical *I*—all things that might well lead them out of their invul-nerable worlds.[12] To these artists, but also to those individuals whose bouts with obsession will traverse this book, there is a real terror involved

11. Guillaumin discusses the awe felt by the author, on the brink of finding out what se-cret his or her work is about to reveal. These discoveries occur through what he calls "sud-den apparitions"—the rapid condensations that lead to creative discoveries. Explaining how little these revelations have to do with their recipient's conscious life, he notes that the secret hidden in the work ends up being the author's own secret. "The secret they deliver . . . is in an odd way, for the writer himself, his own astonishing secret," *Le Moi sublimé*, 26.

12. See the derision that Flaubert aims at Colet when she gives in to syrupy excess. Janet Beizer speaks admirably about Colet's destabilizing effect on Flaubert. Because Colet writes in a style that he has finally overcome (the early Flaubert, as he himself is more than happy to admit, is dripping with sentimentality), she summons up all his stylistic wrath. See Janet Beizer, *Ventriloquized Bodies: Narratives of Hysteria in Nineteenth-Century France* (Ithaca: Cor-nell University Press, 1994).

in the unrestricted, the potentially mutable. What turned out to be most appealing in their dogged devotion to the idée fixe is its way of eluding dialogue. Living "naturally," conversely, is synonymous with giving oneself up to potentially uncontrollable powers.[13]

The monomaniac has no desire to change his or her mind, and this suppressive constancy provides a gratifying sense of power. The same power emerges in Baudelaire's contempt for any aesthetics (or indeed any individual) that picks the natural over the artificial. Art-making is not about surrender to the real, to circumstances; it is about overcoming its constraints. To Baudelaire, the woman who willfully ignores biological imperatives and creates for herself a supremely artificial persona has elevated herself into an art form. Her victory is entirely personal and absolutely empowering. It is a solitary success she is celebrating, one that excludes the possibility of a real interaction. This "unreality" principle enables her to create an impregnable realm where she reigns with unchallenged mastery. Her artifice has constituted itself as a therapy against the rules of necessity. Making art is about remaking the world according to a private image of perfection.

The act of creation provides a therapeutic space (of comfort, retreat, freedom from society's judgment) while revealing to the self a hidden world that could only come to the fore in this mysteriously private way. So one of the paradoxes of creation is that it forces the known and the unknown to collide, producing a third reality. It is not quite the reality that Plato feared from the sensual sounds of music or the tear-inducing emotions of sentimental tales, but the curious initiation into a dormant self. It is the combination of this opening and closing that constitutes the profound originality of monomania. The unleashing of open spaces breeds dangerous imaginings, while the comfort of a sealed-up world comes with a measure of risk. We are speaking of a script where both parts are played by the same person, who basks consequently in a sense of absolute power. During his or her residence in this privileged context, the creator-conductor lives spiritually rent-free, magically exonerated from any con-

---

13. Recall Mondrian's eulogy for plastic art in "Down with Traditional Harmony!" (1924). "The truly plastic has always been expressed through the *equilibrated relationships of planes.* But modeling, perspective, the softening of lines and colors—in short, the whole superficial *trompe-l'œil* technique of traditional art—have veiled the truly plastic. The new art protests against such debasements, which originate in individualism, the lower intellect, and natural instinct. By individualism we mean the state of the individual who is limited and dominated by his own 'ego.'" *The New Art—The New Life: The Collected Writings of Piet Mondrian,* ed. Harry Holtzman and Martin S. James (New York: Da Capo Press, 1993), 190.

tractual obligation to society. Such a space provides respite from any interaction with the world. It freezes time, endowing the present with a sovereignty where all thoughts and discoveries are only mediated by the self. The author has produced his or her own reality, fulfilling the dual fantasy of the all-mighty creator and the blissfully passive convert. This fantasy of autonomy occurs in like fashion in our monomaniacs. Their obsessions too have granted them a disturbing sense of invincibility over and immunity from the ordinary course of affairs. But while their extremist behavior allows them to surrender to forces greater than themselves, it also binds them to an ideational tyrant, the reflection of their own unattainable ideal self. Once this ideal image has taken hold, it will prove impossible to live up to or to live without.[14]

—⁂—

In the letter that opens this chapter, Flaubert describes his torments as all-invasive: they manifest themselves as a "whirlwind of ideas and images," (*tourbillon d'idées et d'images*), they enter his body like a gust of wind, a shattering onslaught of visual and cerebral hallucinations. Nothing is more uprooting than to wake up to a world that has splintered into thousands of particles. The son of a doctor, raised in a household full of scientific stringency, Flaubert is enraged by the manipulative aspect of a condition that he ought to be able to cure, or at least identify. Writing, unlike his temperamental physical fits, seems to be a controllable entity. On a good day, it might even assume a therapeutic status; it turns him from patient, helplessly maimed by a disease that somebody else must take charge of, to the active healer of his own condition. From sufferer, he becomes master of his malady, victorious over the beast within him. In order not to succumb to his mood, Flaubert trains his pen to convert his anxieties into formal exercises, still lifes that can no longer plague him

14. André Green puts it this way: "To think that the ideal becomes the standard against which the self judges its actions and thoughts, to think that it can become the most unforgiving tyrant, keeping us forever in its debt, while casting in an inhumane light those living without it. All this makes us aware of the tremendous hardship that comes with idealization. To this sense of ideal, of merciless imperative . . . the analyst can only oppose another ideal—that of measure." André Green, "Obsessions et psychonévroses obsessionnelles," in *Encyclopédie médico-chirurgicale: Psychiatrie* (Paris: Editions techniques, 1965), 3:37370. But measure is precisely what destabilizes the types we are discussing. So Green is all too aware that his patients will never be able to substitute "boring" reason to the irresistible desire to idealize. As he adds later, the very pull of the ideal is that it requires absolute adhesion to a unique and inalterable principle. It is the need to be guided and mistreated by this ruthless model that explains its draw.

since they have become models of literary perfection. Form is the antithesis of hallucination, for it is the enchanter that tames the disorderly
into ultimate order. Flaubert's search for control, his praise of insensibility, is a curious version of William James's own melancholic afflictions.
The latter writes to his daughter from Bad Nauheim, describing his fits of
"dissatisfaction with one's self, and irritation with others, and anger at
circumstances" as resulting in "stoney insensibility." James equates this
stoniness to his depressions, whereas Flaubert ultimately welcomes it as
redeeming.[15]

Do not show your passion, but sublimate it into style. We are reminded
of Hobbes's proclamation: madness is a matter of "too much appearing
passion." It is not the actual emotion itself that is unsettling to Flaubert,
but the temptation to be dragged down by it and the sickly need to ex-
hibit it to others. The heart must never speak and the artist must assume
a god-like self-sufficiency; it is the only way he will be protected from the
danger of others. The same detachment that Flaubert requires of his narrators, he mercilessly exacts from himself. He is willing to renounce all
human contact for the price of peace of mind. "I will renounce everything,
as long as I can have peace, that is, my freedom of mind."[16] This peace
corresponds to a strange communion with the self, but a self from which
all excess has been scooped out. Critics who have examined the pathology of self-sufficiency have equated it with "a revulsion for all that is
physical and spontaneous, existing beyond the shaping and distancing
powers of the mind."[17] Whatever matter or event cannot be reshaped

15. Quoted in J. H. Rubin, *Religious Melancholy and Protestant Experience in America* (New
York: Oxford University Press, 1994), 20.

16. Flaubert to his niece Caroline, March 14, 1879, *Préface*, 286. As William Paulson
pointed out when he read this manuscript, one must also take into account Flaubert's circumstances at the time he wrote these words: "The context of this remark is Flaubert's poor
financial situation and the need to reduce his expenditures, accept a government pension,
and pay back some debts . . . [This] does put 'I renounce everything' in a somewhat less absolute light than the reader might infer from the quotation's presentation here." Paulson is
right to note a certain one-sidedness in this presentation, but as with the book in general,
my intent is to analyze those particular moments in Flaubert's letters when the monomania
appears. There is no question that Flaubert was capable as well of great empathy and
expansiveness.

17. This is Louis Sass's assessment of Baudelaire's aversion to sex. What he understands
as a fear of giving into the lawlessness of the senses I equate with Flaubert's distrust of emotions. Louis Sass, *Madness and Modernism: Insanity in the Light of Modern Art, Literature, and
Thought* (Cambridge, Mass: Harvard University Press, 1994), 87. Even though Sass's book
concentrates primarily on the relationship between art and schizophrenia, it greatly helped
me conceptualize some of the notions surrounding melancholy and monomania.

mentally has to be dismissed as "infected." It was Walter Ong's *The Presence of the Word* that viewed the solitary mechanics of silent reading as an offshoot of this condition. Writing and reading both require a willful separation from the world. They can only develop in an in-between space where dialogue is banished. As another critic points out, writing not only "tends to require and to encourage silent reflection," but also has the ability to "freeze thought, by organizing it in a visual space; it thereby offers a new image of an independent mental universe."[18]

What we take for granted when we read—the silence, the access to a private mental universe—becomes a disproportionate drive for Flaubert. This contemplative mode of reading, a strictly personal space of meditation, a locus that can be fully controlled and then nurtured by the individual, becomes a way to live with almost no need for a flesh-and-blood interlocutor. Reading and writing, unlike conversation, provide a steadying mental organization. When we read, we translate information into our own private language; it is about our ways of conceptualizing, not the ways of others. Curling up with a good novel suggests that we have made ourselves feel at home in the world. In Flaubert's case, as the self-sufficient bliss sets in, as the withdrawal intensifies, reading and writing simply increase the level of intolerance toward the world: "One must get used to seeing in those around us mere books. The sensible man studies them, compares them, and does all he can to turn them into a profitable synthesis. The world is nothing but a harpsichord for the real artist. It is up to him to pry out of it sounds that either delight or chill you to the bone."[19] To view people like books has the advantage of turning them back into still and unchanging matter. They will start to count less than the powers of observation that have framed them. Framing is as important to Flaubert as it is to a painter who needs to adapt reality to the canvas size, perspective, and color. It is the act of framing, indeed, that tames chaos, that turns the formless into the harmonious. Witness this curiously Platonic letter to George Sand, in which Flaubert wonders whether a book can produce the same effect as the naked wall of the Acropolis: "I wonder whether a book, independently from what it says, could not produce a similar effect. In the precision of the assembly, the rarity of the elements, the polish of the surface, the harmony of the whole, is there not an intrinsic virtue, a sort of divine form, something as eternal as a principle?

18. This quotation from Louis Sass is part of his larger analysis of Ong's theory of silent reading, ibid., 93.

19. Flaubert to Ernest Chevalier, February 24, 1842, *Œuvres*, 1:96.

(I speak as a Platonist) . . . so the law of numbers governs feelings and images, and what seems on the outside might just be in there."[20] The book, like the temple's wall, is geometrical. It has to respect the contours of its subject, forcing the artist to labor precisely until "the harmony of assemblage" is achieved. Through this perspectival fastidiousness, Flaubert hopes to find a guiding principle. Such an act of restoration can only occur with the help of a merciless and steadfast gaze, a perfectly reliable lens, ever ready to make intelligible the inchoate. It is not a matter of looking at exceptions, but rather making the unexceptional, the everyday, into a principle, something recognizable in spite of its being askew.

Flaubert's radical imprecation—treat people like science experiments, make a synthesis out of the human muddle—is the idée fixe that holds up his aesthetic revolution. To all his friends, especially those who practiced writing (Louise Colet, George Sand, and Louis Bouilhet), he urged a drastic dodging of the inter-subjective experience, a zealous attempt to shun dialogue and make all communication monological: "Life is such a hideous thing that the only way to bear it is to avoid it. And one can avoid it by living in Art, in the incessant quest for the True revealed in the Beautiful. Read the great masters, attempt to grasp their procedures, and get closer to their soul, then, you will conclude your study with intoxicating dizziness. You will be like Moses descending from Mount Sinai. His face was encircled with rays of light for having contemplated God."[21] Such avoidance of the world is best understood in terms of a conversion experience: to eschew this "hideous" life, one must convert it into something that only exists in art. This is no simple Bovarysm: Flaubert is not preaching the Quixotic, he is not telling his correspondents to imitate literary models and indulge in a derivative type of existence. What he proselytizes, rather, is a retreat into a world of craft, a life of sentences and of commas, where the only value judgments will be about grammar and style, rather than about sweeping ethical truths. Paradoxically, writing becomes the site of divestment, rather than investment; stripped to the sum of its syntactical parts, it gains a simplicity that makes it more akin to carpentry than to psychology. Along with this belief in precision, Flaubert gives Mademoiselle de Chantepie tips about how to meditate. Contemplation detaches you from worldly disappointment, but it needs to be

20. Flaubert to George Sand, April 3, 1876, *Préface*, 271.

21. Flaubert to Mademoiselle Leroyer de Chantepie, May 18, 1857, *Œuvres*, 2:717. This letter was quoted briefly in the introduction. Although it certainly does not summarize Flaubert's philosophy (there is, after all, a *bon vivant* in Flaubert, both aesthetically and socially), it sheds light on the monastic possibilities of art making.

complemented by an almost ritualistic daily set of activities. The domestic compulsions we found in Janet's housewives are converted by Flaubert into scholarly compunctions. One must exhaust oneself through activities, mental and physical. "There is a sentiment, or rather a habit, that you seem to be forgetting, and that is the *love of contemplation*. Take life, its passions, even yourself, as the *subject* of intellectual exercises. . . . Take on a study plan, make it rigorous. . . . *Force yourself to find regular and tiring work*. . . . Try to stop living in yourself."[22] This letter, a great example of Flaubert's empathetic relationship to his interlocutors (despite his self-professed curmudgeonly nature), offers a simple solution to life's existential travails—escape from your unanswerable metaphysical quandaries by exhausting yourself through an impersonal relationship to the world. Flaubert was the first to admit betraying regularly this principle. He grants to Louise Colet that his greatest sin was not only to put himself so shamelessly into his writing, but to have turned love into his great compulsion."[23] As to love, it has been the great question that has occupied my whole life. What I did not give to pure art, to the vocation itself, went there; and the heart I was studying was my own."[24] But love is the type of idée fixe that always eludes fixedness. Like the great truths that we pitifully run after, hoping to hang them in our mental frames, they will always baffle us. This is why our quest must be infinitely more sober and technical. So Flaubert's therapeutic, rather than helplessly passionate idée fixe, lies in his urge to fix the disorderly world, not by pontificating and offering solutions to grand problems, but to make style a form of match-making; it is a fitting-room where signifiers will finally be matched to the perfect signified. Witness Flaubert's analysis of Renaissance art. "How ought one to get anything out of all that [Renaissance discoveries] *in the name of beauty?* . . . By studying which shape, which color, corresponds to such or such a person, in particular circumstances. What you have is the relationship between tonalities and lines. The great coquettes understand that, and just as real dandies, they do not dress according to fashion magazines. . . . So what does that *proper effect* depend on? On the exact relationship, one that eludes you, between feature, facial expression, and dress."[25] It is the incessant return to a *rapport exact*, the recur-

22. Flaubert to Mademoiselle Leroyer de Chantepie, *Œuvres*, 2:716–17; italics in original.

23. "The less *one feels a thing*, the better one will express it as it is (the way it *always* is, in and of itself, in its generality, abstracted from all its ephemeral contingencies)," Flaubert to Louise Colet, July 5, 1852, *Œuvres*, 2:127; italics in original.

24. Flaubert to Louise Colet, July 5, 1852, *Œuvres*, 2:124.

25. Flaubert to Louise Colet, January 29, 1854, *Œuvres*, 2:519; italics in original.

ring desire to find the right color and then to match it with the rest of the universe that is a tell-tale sign of Flaubert's aesthetic monomania. If Flaubert cannot fathom the "hideous" quality of life, it is because nothing seems ever to fit right, nothing is simply a matter of geometry or color coding. Flaubert's idea of writing is fundamentally static. When the proper sentence, with its properly harmonized lines, sounds, and grammar, has been written, then the world is at peace. The modern vice is to make believe that the world is rational, a geometric utopia that comes with directions. The only geometry we can hope for is on the page. So what is hideous is not so much that life is not geometric, but that people treat it as a vulgar problem to be solved.

Art escapes such trivial totalizing; it seeks the padding of a spiritual convalescent home, the magic mountain that records the tiny movements of life, leaving out the great unruly passions. Art is a therapeutic mode of stagnation: "Being that my great fear is passion and movement, I believe that if happiness is somewhere, then it is in stagnation."[26] Flaubert advises his friends to hibernate—"do what I do: break with the outside world, live like a bear—a polar bear—send everything to hell."[27] He admits living in absolute seclusion: "I live absolutely like an oyster. My novel is the rock that ties me down and I have no idea what is happening in the world."[28] Art creates the sound-proof environment, the coffin-like anti-world that temporarily cures his agitation. Plagued by the inadequate correspondence between the real and the "idée," he resorts to writing as a mental gymnastics that calms down "the irritation of the idea until we find in it an exact, precise, and adequate equivalent."[29] The recovery, however, is a curious one. It is a self-generated affair. Its dynamics (the shift between torment and recovery through the peace of art) never leaves the confines of his own head. Its mechanism is not unlike smoking or sleeping, two eminently "useless" but restorative enterprises: "I write for myself alone, the way I smoke and sleep. It is something so personal and intimate that it is almost animalistic. . . . [I]t seems to me that my work would lose almost everything from being published. There are animals that live underground and plants that cannot be plucked and are therefore overlooked. There are perhaps spirits created for adverse corners. What is their use? None! Couldn't I be from that breed?"[30]

26. Flaubert to Ernest Chevalier, August 13, 1845, Œuvres, 1: 249.
27. Flaubert to Alfred Le Poittevin, September 16, 1845, Œuvres, 1:251.
28. Flaubert to George Sand, September 9, 1868, Œuvres, 3:797.
29. Flaubert to Louise Colet, December 13, 1846, Œuvres, 1:417.
30. Flaubert to Louise Colet, August 16, 1847, Œuvres, 1:467.

Writing performs the same evanescent therapy as blowing smoke into thin air. As Richard Klein notes, "the cigarette accomplishes a small revolution in time, by seeming to install . . . a time outside itself."[31] Flaubert not only looks for a time that can develop outside of the movements of his own psyche, but acknowledges that his mania for writing resembles that of inhaling, or exhaling; writing is a tic, a nervous habit that takes on a life of its own. Tics endow life with a rigid form of temporality, punctuating time in such a predictable manner that they soon become ends in themselves. Literally, the commas and the semi-colons take over, themselves enormous dilemmas that manage to outshine the conflicts of the outside world. Commas can be playfully moved around without the risks involved in manipulating people, their sentiments, and reactions.

It is this passion for structure and perfectly paced narrative that signals the monomaniacal temperament. Free-association and even a certain degree of incoherence are taboo. It is a matter of principle to keep so-called spontaneity at bay, to eradicate any expressions that could be construed as personal. Sentimentality is a literary disgrace that must be tamed and turned into something impersonal, painstakingly constructed, and as far as possible an absolute denial of one's own life. The rejection of the personal zone leads to Flaubert's relentless mocking of a meandering style, an earnestly self-absorbed prose. It explains why his recurrent references to punctuation are about composing and structuring with a vengeance. Flaubert keeps the repressed as inhibited as possible. He admits to George Sand, "I feel an indomitable repulsion at writing anything from the heart. . . . Has God ever given his opinion? That explains all those things that choke me, that I would like to spit out, but that I swallow back down."[32] There is no concealing the pathological nature of his writing-habits. Even though the idea of revealing parts of himself repulsed Flaubert, he admits being overcome with the need to "spit out" whatever is tormenting him. But he resists, and it is this resistance that turns the narrative away from the temptations of the sentimental and gives it a pure life of form.[33] Art is not created for its own end and therefore is not a Kantian disinterested activity, but a cure for its practitioner.

---

31. Richard Klein, *Cigarettes Are Sublime* (Durham, N.C.: Duke University Press, 1993), 8. Smoking, as Flaubert jokes with his friend Chevalier, is like everything great—glory, love, dreams, friendship—it goes up in smoke. Rather than invalidating it, this is a reminder that nothing great can keep from evaporating. September 2, 1843, *Œuvres*, 1:188.

32. Flaubert to George Sand, December 5, 1866,*Œuvres*, 3:575.

33. This is reminiscent of Foucault, who comments on art's ability to send the individual back onto himself, creating a high degree of isolation. Art "encloses itself within a radical in-

Flaubert's strict observance of structure betrays a phobic relationship to a world that cannot so easily punctuate the "real story." Writing, then, is about covering up. The adamancy with which Flaubert covers up the real story—his or that of his friends, the stories he suggests he is repressing—reveals an ideology of restraint. Unlike the patient of psychoanalysis, who is considered on the way to recovery as soon as he or she relinquishes coherence and forsakes all narrative ordering principle, Flaubert balks at incoherence in life or in art. How reassuring to think that reality can be relived from within, in the scene it composes. Style is the mastermind behind the stage, and this disembodied crystallization of the self is what does all the worrying and all the organizing, standing as Flaubert's proxy. Thanks to such neutrality, Flaubert's writings can never be reduced to parts of his life; style has a life of its own. It is predictable, reliable, and above all, not contingent upon anything else except its own internal laws.

Flaubert's monomania, then, lies in the attempt to bottle up experience so it can be relived in isolation. It is the stubborn pursuit of a quest that makes no sense to the outside world, but enables one's own universe to hold together. Many years ago a cartoon from *The New Yorker* portrayed Monet shooing away a frog from one of his water-lilies, because it interfered with his vision of what the perfect water-lily-representation should be. The cartoon's joke came from the literal-minded notion that Monet could not abstract the frog from the scene and then go ahead and paint what he had to. Flaubert shares a great deal with the mock-Monet; it is not hard imagining him after countless interferences giving up on a reality that can be so easily disrupted, and turning instead to the unbendable world of grammar and syntax. Because he de-dramatizes the content of writing, reducing it to its formal or factual components and organizing it into armies of metaphors and metonymies, Flaubert manages to be both outside and inside of his creation. He is the general who oversees the grand plan and remains aloof from the splattering and casualties.

Flaubert once referred to himself as an eye that could record information without being affected by it. "Better simply be an eye."[34] How can one be an eye that is separate from an evolving psyche? How can an eye become an autonomous organ, unattached, all-seeing, and never seen? Part of Flaubert's obsession with anonymity is epitomized by this god-

transitivity . . . curv[ing] back in a perpetual return upon itself, as if its discourse could have no other content than the expression of its own form." Michel Foucault, *The Order of Things*, trans. Alan Sheridan (New York: Vintage Books, 1970), 300.

34. Flaubert to Louis Bouilhet, March 13, 1850, *Œuvres*, 1:602.

like gaze that encompasses everything without ever being part of the picture. This aloofness betrays the desire to avoid the world's commotion, while creating a smaller, perfectly docile movement. The eye scans reality, zooms in on a particular feature, character, or event, and then envelops it.

These eyes can only see when they are placed outside the body, expelled from their own frame. Once anonymous they become faithful cameras, unflinchingly recording the world without ever needing to take their cue from a presiding consciousness. It is as though Flaubert's own *histoire de l'œil* relates the adventures of an absolutely disaffected consciousness. Whether or not they belong to Gustave is irrelevant; they are Flaubert's, the craftsman. On a textual level, there is nothing intersubjective about these eyes, since they never make contact with those they observe. However, they focus on the unexpected, behaving as erratically as a Tolstoyan narrator, who in the guise of a horse or an illiterate serf, manages to convey a more real, because oddly decentered, vision. Flaubert writes to Mademoiselle Leroyer de Chantepie that his literary heroes were never trying to make a point or trying to conclude. They were simply putting facts in front of us. Like God, they abstained from commentary, turning the material over to their readers to battle with, making discomfort and alienation an integral part of the reading process.[35]

Flaubert's medical eye is not Cain-like. It has no conscience, nor does it fill the beholder with fear and awe. Rather, it is a private eye, greedily collecting data that will not necessarily be of any use. There is a gratuitous amount of looking and recording going on behind the scenes; but even though this inter-galactic eye has infinite depth of vision, it nonetheless will never let itself be incorporated into somebody else's subjectivity. It can see, but cannot be seen; like a tape-recorder, it quietly monitors the world, taking in events and sounds. Like this invisible eye, the monomaniac turns out to be a voyeur, turning the disparate into the separate, the shapeless into the peculiar, singling out that which, under the guise of incongruity, is central to the unity of his being. Flaubert discusses endlessly the issue of perspective: around the end of his life, he still insists that "there is no Truth, just ways of seeing,"[36] reiterating what he had written almost thirty years earlier, namely, that the secret of art lies in the *rapport exact*, the perfect correspondence between the formal and

35. "They were simply putting facts in front of us. Homer, Shakespeare, Goethe, all God's first-borns (as Michelet had it), were careful not to do anything but *represent*." October 23, 1863, *Œuvres*, 3:353.
36. Flaubert to M. Léon Hennique, February 2–3, 1880, *Préface*, 290.

the intelligible. Born out of solitude, the fixed gaze, the eye that never blinks, has the rigidity of a statue. The world can finally be turned into a closed book.

The will to make things narrow, to take them out of their broader context, is one of the most fundamental prerequisites of Flaubert's survival. He applauds the strength it takes to stay away from sweeping truths. For the passerby, though, eavesdropping outside Flaubert's study, the narrowing of vision comes across as an extreme form of anti-social behavior, a dangerous retreat from the world. In an early letter to Louise Colet, Flaubert compares the writer's den to a mole-hole. One must close oneself in and continue, head bent, to work like a mole.[37]

The mole is blind, and yet it works with extraordinary alacrity. What it achieves is considerable, all the more remarkable in that it had to stay buried to accomplish it. The mole analogy puts Nietzsche's remark in a different light. What is so reassuring about enclosure and self-protection that it directs vision altogether inwards? Does such a dispassionate form of creation exonerate the artist from taking responsibility for the content of his work? Could it explain in part Flaubert's astonishment at *Madame Bovary*'s trial, at the accusations and infatuations leveled against his "immoral heroine," at the investment in a work created in a vacuum? The point was, he had thought, to concentrate on the sentences, the metaphors, and the research; this was not a treatise on human nature. When he writes that "man is nothing, the work is everything," he means that the private life of the artist is as irrelevant as are the possible ways readers might identify with the characters. A work is above all craft.

Man is nothing, the work is everything! I seek above all beauty. This discipline that can be rooted in a false point of view is not easy to follow, and to me at least, it is a kind of perpetual sacrifice I offer to Good Taste. It would be awfully pleasant to speak my mind, and to relieve Mister Gustave Flaubert with sentences. But what is so important about that Mister . . . I search for beauty above all. Goncourt is very pleased when he picks up in the street a word that he can stick in a book, and I am very satisfied when I have written a page without assonance or repetitions. . . . It is indeed writing itself that is my goal, I can't deny it.[38]

Flaubert *would like* to pour his heart out in writing, but he sacrifices himself instead to a set of aesthetic imperatives. This choice—restraint over intimacy—speaks volumes about the reasons behind the narrowing of

37. Flaubert to Louise Colet, September 22, 1853, *Œuvres*, 2:437.
38. Flaubert to George Sand, December 1875, *Œuvres*, 4:1000.

perspectives discussed above. As in all the cases examined in this book, even if the self-inflicted limits placed on the individual entail harsh sacrifices, they also usher in a blissfully disconnected state. This separation, surprisingly, allows for a different kind of intimacy, one where the rejection of the world strengthens the self's sense of integrity. The pain and loneliness of writing disciplines and heals the unruly self. So even if art is taking a tremendous toll on Flaubert's life, it graces him with a particular ecstasy, an approximation of the unifying *idea* he keeps coming back to. "I lead a jagged life, devoid of all external joys, and where all I have as sustenance is a sort of perpetual rage. . . . I love my work with the same frantic and perverted love the ascetic feels for the hair-shirt that scratches his belly."[39] Paper and ink are infinitely more compliant than flesh and blood. So if to write well is Flaubert's aim, then it has nothing to do with a particular topic. It is about the pleasure inherent in perfecting something for its own sake, of completing a task, and thereby dispelling confusion through symmetry. It is essential to refer to the much-quoted letter to Colet about writing a book about nothing. Nothingness, here, stands for the plenitude of style, the absolute satisfaction of a form that can never be accomplished outside the page. Predicting that abstraction is the way of the future, Flaubert trumpets the antithetical relationship of art and mimesis. Considering that nobody advanced with more conviction the cause of the realist novel, it is indeed remarkable that he could simultaneously perfect it, while craving a work of pure abstraction.

What seems beautiful to me, what I would like to write, is a book about nothing, a book without external links, that could hold itself up by the mere internal strength of its style, just as the world stands in the air without any support. . . . The most beautiful works are those with the least amount of matter. . . . I believe the future of art is in that direction. . . . That is why there are no ugly or beautiful subjects; from the perspective of pure Art, one could almost establish axiomatically that there is no subject at all, style being itself an absolute way of seeing things.[40]

How to reconcile Flaubert's consuming passion for documents and encyclopedias with such an extraordinary eulogy of abstraction? How can a writer, who devoted years of his life researching details so minute that they might go unnoticed by the most observant of readers, pine so desperately for the immaterial? One could argue that Flaubert's will to ex-

---

39. Flaubert to Louise Colet, April 24, 1852, *Œuvres*, 2:75.
40. Flaubert to Louise Colet, January 16, 1852, *Œuvres*, 2:31.

haust all information is part of his love-hate relationship with openness. Even more striking is that the very world he contains and stifles through his writing is the one he refuses to harness in "real life" conversation. Flaubert shows no propensity to theorize about life, to cut it into neat frameworks; his metaphysical tidying-up only occurs through writing, through a vigorous compartmentalization that dispels part of his *horror vacui*. But while this factual ballast shields him from some of his existential turmoil, letting the facts swell up the pages of his novels, it still leaves room for a different kind of yearning. Wanting to write a book about nothing attests to the enticing side of the void. The "nothingness" he pines after is a rich inner space, an emptiness that has lost its anguish. The simultaneous cowering from and craving for the void, for a time of stagnation, is a constant in the monomaniacal imagination. Many of the characters in this book are attracted and repelled by free time, drawn to and squelched by obsessive activity. Movement, while it fends off the demons of introspection and provides temporary relief from anxiety, does not satisfy the soul's craving for a higher order; it is a mere temporary solution. Idleness, however, richer in existential possibilities, can breed an intolerable sense of dread. Flaubert the researcher is always in conflict with Flaubert the idler. His goal-oriented temperament is engaged in a subliminal fight with his platonic urges; facts fill the void while perversely exacerbating the desire for the ethereal and the harmonious, for a space that should house an ecstatic sense of presence.

Flaubert's ideal work of art has no external ties; like a tight-rope walker, it would bypass subject matter at any moment and still stand erect in mid-air. If Flaubert's idée fixe is indeed the will to expunge as much matter as possible from his books, then he is prey to an unbending ideal, an impossible vision that can only hope to offset the fluidity of life. These two conflicting desires, the one carried out in writing, the other in dream, are addressed head-on in Flaubert's letters. He was well-aware that his retreat into an obsessively controlled space had caused him to give up a great deal of life's promise. Living a reduced life of momentary perfection, however, seemed infinitely preferable to the alternative.

Flaubert's deep antipathy for flux came from his equating passion and loss of control. He refers to passion as a disease that ultimately drives the subject outside of itself, away from the all-restorative idea. Flaubert's misogyny, his claim that he understood women less and less, is a strangely adequate index of his artistic creed, with its increasing closing-off from the world. When he feels the pressures of Colet's passion, he responds with a conveniently high-minded Platonism—instead of loving me, he groans, try to love art "exclusively, ardently, devotedly. It will not let you down. Only the Idea is eternal and necessary."[41] This so-called idea is not only a great protection from Colet's possessiveness—you cannot own me since I belong to my work—but it becomes a great opportunistic excuse for getting out of amorous attachments. Art, throughout the *Correspondence*, is a double escapism, using its masculine status to critique the uncontainable, unfathomable quality of women. Witness how this translates into an attack on ardent women, "les femmes ardentes": "Women, those whose heart is too ardent, whose spirit is too exclusive, do not understand the religion of beauty, unless feeling is involved."[42] To Flaubert, who in this respect is Baudelaire's soul-brother, women are the antithesis of abstraction; they are congenitally unable to cultivate form for its own sake, always confusing beauty and egotistical sentimentality. With women, content will always override form, spilling dangerously over that terrain that was to remain untouched. Form is Flaubert's chastity belt, his great excuse for remaining aloof. "What I love above all is form, as long as it is beautiful, I care for nothing beyond that. . . . For me the only things that matter in the world are beautiful lines, well-turned sentences, harmonious, singing. . . . Beyond that, nothing."[43] Even though Flaubert is provoking Colet (he writes to Sand some twenty-five years later that his claim that he preferred sentences to people was preposterous),[44] he still uses art as a defense, almost a physical deterrent.

Flaubert's aesthetics exist in a neutral zone, a no-man's land, where the battles fought can all be solved with ink. Only a sustained relationship with commas and dashes can produce serenity. "I get drunk on ink the way others do on wine. But writing can be so difficult that at times, I am crushed with exhaustion."[45] Writing is a monkish exercise; its reward is to be left in perfect solitude, far from the needy crowd. The only way to find peace, he writes to Louise Colet, reminding her that she is certainly not the one who will give it to him, "is to fix oneself on any old pyramid, as long as it is high-up and solidly based."[46] But unlike Mondrian, who

41. Flaubert to Louise Colet, August 8–9, 1846, *Œuvres*, 1:283.
42. Flaubert to Louise Colet, August 6–7, 1846, *Œuvres*, 1:278.
43. Flaubert to Louise Colet, August 8, 1846, *Œuvres*, 1:278.
44. "No! Literature is not what I love above all else. I did not explain myself properly. . . . I spoke of entertainment. . . . I am not such a boor that I prefer sentences to human beings." Flaubert to George Sand, March 3, 1872, *Œuvres*, 4:491.
45. Flaubert to Mademoiselle Leroyer de Chantepie, December 18, 1859, *Œuvres*, 3:65.
46. Flaubert to Louise Colet, May 30, 1852, *Œuvres*, 2:100.

turns his back on nature, Flaubert takes it head on. He knows the soil as intimately as the farmer, the body as precisely as the surgeon. The difference is that he braves it from above or from within; he uses it, but is ever vigilant that he should never become one with it. The world can only be somebody else's dwelling place.

Flaubert's advice to his fellow-humans? Lock yourself inside of art, treat people like books, keep your heads down like moles, avoid life and know that you are as doomed to loneliness as a polar bear; and realize, man is nothing, art is everything! "This is why I love art. There, at least, in the world of fiction, everything is free—There's where you quench everything, that you do everything, you are king, you are the people, active and passive, victim and priest. No limits. . . . Art has often given me a revenge over life."[47] The world, unless it is transformed by art, is a desolate place. Its fragmented quality, its anarchical play of uncontrollable circumstances will drive you to madness. Flaubert often wonders what would have happened had this not been the case and had his life been "external rather than internal."[48] As Sartre puts it, Flaubert had to forsake the self in order to give birth to his art. Writing is the result of a profound *malaise,* and Flaubert chose literature, Sartre writes, "because the latter, in its abstract autonomy . . . was transmuted into an inhuman end and symbolized Alienation as an absolute commitment."[49] Art is the ticket to *not* belonging, to acquiring a marginal space that could not be converted into anything practical. Sartre also calls this *l'Art-Névrose* and *l'Art-Rupture,* since the artist commits himself to fail (even in his artistic creation) "so he no longer coincides with his self."[50] This explanation takes us back to the escapist side of monomania, its inability to append playfully the different parts of life.

The desire to box in reality and to follow a scripted line of action may well stem from the fear that reality might just stop holding together, suddenly exploding into tiny dissociated fragments, with nothing to hold onto anymore. Such feelings of panic explain the self's desperate clinging to one type of belief or model: the idée fixe is the wonderfully secure agent that reorganizes everything into a single meaning; it is a powerful magnetic force that turns the heterogeneous into the homogeneous, the plural into the single, the open into the closed. Open societies are feared,

47. Flaubert to Louise Colet, May 23, 1852, *Œuvres,* 2:91.

48. Flaubert to Louise Colet, April 24, 1852, *Œuvres,* 2:82.

49. Jean-Paul Sartre, *L'Idiot de la famille: Gustave Flaubert de 1821 à 1857* (1972; repr., Paris: Gallimard, 1988), 3:330.

50. Ibid.

and the monomaniac would much prefer a secure habitat where the world can be treated as a book—picked up, put down, opened, and finally closed. Paradoxically, Flaubert's ideal book is like a window that lets the light out, not in. As long as reality can be kept out, as long as the individual can wall himself in, then art can begin.

3 The Cult of the Unreal

Nodier and Romantic Monomania

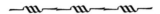

Some call'd it madness—such indeed it was . . .
If prophesy be madness; if things viewed
By poets of old time, and higher up
By the first men, earth's first inhabitants,
May in these tutored days no more be seen
With undisorder'd sight.

Wordsworth, *The Prelude*

This is why I would rather consider this abnormal condition
as a veritable blessing, like a magical mirror through which
man is summoned to see himself as beautiful, that is, as he
should or could be, a kind of angelic excitation.

Baudelaire, "Le Poème du haschisch"

Not well-known in the English-speaking world, overshadowed by
Nerval, Gautier, and Baudelaire, Charles Nodier (1780–1844) was an elusive, but pivotal figure of French Romanticism.[1] Often cast off as a "brilliant, lovable, and sporadic genius,"[2] he is the eternal precursor, setting the
stage for those literary revolutions that end up forgetting their architects.
Like many of my other examples of artistic monomania, his work is yet another illustration of Flaubert's famous pronouncement that "I write in order not to live." Most comfortable within the *genre fantastique*, Nodier used

1. A version of this chapter was published in French as "Charles Nodier: Pour une dé-
matérialisation de la lecture," in *L'Œuvre d'identité: Territoires de l'art*, ed. Catherine Nesci and
Didier Maleuvre, special issue, *Paragraphes* (October 1996): 61–75. I would like to thank
Catherine Nesci for being so encouraging and enlightening at the time of its writing.
2. Ch.-A. Sainte-Beuve, "Charles Nodier," *Revue des Deux-Mondes* 22 (1840): 379.

his writing as a refuge against the unsettling plight of Modernity: what besides literature could restore to the world a sense of the divine? Like his German predecessors (chiefly Friedrich Schlegel and Novalis), Nodier strove to counteract what Marx would perceive as the bourgeoisie's dogged attempt to drown "the pious exaltations of the past . . . in the freezing water of selfish calculations."[3] Literature, then, would be a direct counterpoison to life's disappointments.[4] Unlike Baudelaire whose work constituted the prime example of an idealist who could not even believe in his own ideals, Nodier's work is built around the conviction that ideals, dreams, and essentially any type of "unreality" are imperative to fend off the meaninglessness of modern life.[5] His would be merely a regressive conservatism if it were not converted into this notion of the idée fixe. Nodier was one of the first writers to translate a medical notion into a literary mode:

Monomania comes naturally in two forms—explicit and harmless (the doctor's realm) and militant, occasionally even homicidal (the jury's). . . . I will be entertaining you for a moment with a type of monomania that transcends both categories because its manifestations are intimate, individual, grave, and poignant for the poor soul it has attached itself to. I have taken the great liberty of naming it *reflective monomania (monomanie réflective)*, a tag yet unused by philosophers. It frequently surfaces in societies where civilization has been worn down by an incessant desire for progress. It is this kind of monomania that ends usually in suicide.[6]

3. This excerpt from *The Communist Manifesto* is quoted by Michael Löwy and Robert Sayre in *Révolte et mélancolie: Le romantisme à contre-courant de la modernité* (Paris: Payot, 1992). These critics have inspired me to see Nodier in the light of a particularly partisan antimodernism. They read certain strands of European romanticism as "chivalric enthusiasm," a way of re-enchanting the world. One of the most conspicuous characteristics of this reaction is a return of religious traditions; these traditions, according to Max Weber, drive "human beings to banish the supreme and most sublime values of public life" and find refuge either "in the transcendent kingdom of mystical life or in the direct and reciprocal fraternity of isolated individuals." Max Weber, *Le Savant et le politique* (Paris: UGE, 1963), 93; quoted in Löwy and Sayre, *Révolte et mélancolie*, 46.

4. Paul Bénichou describes the atmosphere around Nodier as full of that peculiar "fervor in mourning of its objects, animated by an otherworldly temptation that is nothing but the embodiment of despair." If art is sovereign, he adds, it is because "it is not the object of doctrine, but of regret. It is a manifestation of a lost paradise, of the Impossible. The desolate Primitivism of the 1800s prefigures the bitter divorce between the ideal and the real." Paul Bénichou, *Le Sacre de l'écrivain* (Paris: Corti, 1973), 219; my translation.

5. Note Elissa Marder's statement: "Neurotics are often very reliable prophets. This is hardly surprising since they base their sense of the future upon their internal, unconscious convictions about the truth of the past." Elissa Marder, *Dead Time: Temporal Disorders in the Wake of Modernity (Baudelaire, Flaubert)* (Stanford: Stanford University Press, 2001), 88.

6. Charles Nodier, "Rêverie psychologique de la monomanie réflective," in *L'Amateur de*

Even though Nodier's definition of monomania hardly made a mark, it is indeed the first to connect obsession with the profound need to re-create one's world from within. Not only did he understand that the idée fixe was a commitment, a monastic vow of sorts, but he grasped well before its time that certain obsessions do not easily fit the confines of medical or juristic thinking. He concentrates on compulsions so discreetly carried out that they often go unnoticed, silently suffered and yet no less grave than those highlighted by the glamour of scandal. Nodier is mesmerized by a monomania that generates a strange bliss, a cultivated state of disjunction that stretches a screen between the real and the ideal. His "reflective" monomaniacs have indeed trained themselves to achieve "an intimate state of mind that isolates gleefully all the realities of life; [monomania] can dispossess itself . . . of the past, the present, the future, and even of hope in order to shape the world according to its own choice, a world upon which [the monomaniac] possesses all the attributes of God's power."[7] By converting life's complexities into one insuperable idée fixe, these anguished characters manage to regain focus and control over a world that has been slipping away. Their idea is so pervasive that it blocks out whatever does not fit its composition; it has the weight of divinity (the attributes of God's power) and is abstract enough to outstrip temporality itself. Thanks to its intensity, it enables its recipient to shape, rather than to be shaped by, the world. Only an ardently focused mind can achieve such detachment. But in order to accomplish this fusion, he or she has to demonstrate an ardor, an intensity of belief that the outside world could only interpret as insanity. This intensity, however, is not to be confused with the fanaticism of those who are ready to perish for their beliefs.[8]

---

livres, ed. Jean-Luc Steinmetz (Paris: Castor Astral, 1993), 48–49. My translation. Another illustration of monomania occurs in Nodier's delightful story "Le bibliomane" in which he pokes fun at the liberality with which the term *monomania* was used to explain *away* a wealth of situations. Theodor is a monomaniac *par excellence,* who only lives to collect books. When he realizes that his copy of Virgil is not the definitive 1676 edition (which is a third of a line taller), he collapses and dies from the shock. Before dying, he compulsively repeats to anybody who will hear him the fateful phrase: *a third of a line, a third of a line.* The doctor writes up the case in the *Journal des Sciences médicales,* labeling Theodor's condition *maroquin monomania* or *bibliomaniacal typhus.* The jargon is out: even the priest, repeating blindly the findings of the *Journal,* concludes that Theodor's condition *is* unmistakably *typhus de bibliomanes.* The story has a wonderful way of being both a textbook study of monomania and the playful derider of a term doomed to flatten the complexity of human experience.

7. Ibid., 50.

8. "This sacred monomania is fanaticism, a fanaticism so intimately connected to our blindest weaknesses that it will always elude the vulgar superficiality of our judgments. Nobody who is alive is allowed to judge fanaticism," ibid., 60.

"The reflective monomaniac . . . is neither a fanatic, nor a hero: he is the faulty logician of the real world who derives a bitter voluptuousness from his substituting the immortal for the mortal, the decaying present for an eternal future; he is . . . a sort of spiritualist . . . countering nothingness with his unshakable convictions."[9] All our monomaniacs are afflicted with this heavy sense of nothingness; they all find a way of resisting it by forging passionate relationships with the immutable. But what distinguishes Nodier's types is that they pad this void by trumping it with a different kind of lack: they have taught themselves radical modes of self-abnegation, tapping into the "passionate predisposition to suffering" that will enable them to reach a higher plateau of being.

Nodier was taking up some of the very same themes that shot through the works of E. T. A. Hoffmann, whose celebrated *The Golden Pot* illustrated the artist's losing battle against the growing power of the philistine. Whereas Hoffmann also introduced the Fantastic genre to bring the reader back into the illogical and autonomous realm of art, Nodier expected this same reader to undergo a conversion. He not only pressured his audience into questioning its faculty of judgment, but concentrated on the languages of madness, in particular, the manifestations of idées fixes and monomania. Today's psychiatrists might want to read Nodier's essay on reflective monomania to rethink the effect of obsession on everyday types of behavior. The two tales I evoke here are *La Fée aux miettes* (*The Crumb Fairy*) and one of the great gems of French nineteenth-century literature, "Jean-François les bas-bleus" ("Jean-François Blue Stockings"). These two works are striking in that they reveal the narrow relationship between the sacredness of art and Nodier's conception of *monomanie réflective.*

Nodier's peculiar brand of monomania offers an escape from a disintegrating spirituality by hastening worldly dispossession and providing an obsessive and single-minded substitute for prosaic entanglements. Rooted in the ability to create an alternative inner world, it facilitates the collapse of present, past, and future into one unified picture. Most interesting to this book is how this form of artistic monomania manages to be illness and cure simultaneously. If writing is indeed the consequence of an essential malaise, then how can it also be the first step toward its remedy? Once his readers have determined why Nodier's characters need to construct a "self-willed world" ("un monde à leur choix") and unequivocal shelters, it will be their turn to enter a closed, but restorative uni-

9. Ibid., 54.

verse. These goals will have been carried out if the character's idée fixe has transmitted itself to the reader, who will be swayed in turn by that exquisite "spiritual ecstasy" (*extase de l'esprit*) described above. Only the most candid mode of reading will achieve this, inducing a trance-like state barely distinguishable from that of the believer being preached the divine word. Nodier expresses this idiosyncratic approach to reading in his preface of "Jean-François les bas-bleus." "Believe me, I would never write a Fantastic story unless I believed in it as sincerely . . . as in the daily facts of my life; and in that respect, I don't think I am any less intelligent or reasonable than those strong intellects who deny the Fantastic absolutely. . . . In fact, what separates me from them is my way of seeing, feeling, and hearing."[10] The Fantastic can only bear its fruit if both author and reader willfully suspend their disbelief and abandon themselves entirely to the new reality. This makes for a curious eucharistic transaction where absorption and meditation are at the core of the process. Nodier's brand of Romanticism acts as a challenge to the reader's rationality. But since writing is a way of healing the world, the prescription ordered by this doctor-writer is for the reader to change expectations: one needs to estrange oneself from the world before being able to see it as it is. This estrangement (*méconnaissance*) is not merely a Platonic legacy, although there is no doubt that Nodier's poetics are reminiscent of Plato's theory of Ideas. It is intimately connected to the anti-mimetic program of abstract art—a useful connection as it explains the "separatist" psychology of Nodier (in Latin *abstractio* means separation) and his desire to reject the real for a radical spirituality. It is not simply a matter of defeating life with literature, but of understanding every literary act as a choice, an ongoing negotiation with two conflicting desires: belonging to the world or resisting its deceptive fascination. It is on the latter act of resistance that Nodier will build "an economy of the Fantastic."[11]

Nodier wanted to turn every act of reading into a metaphysical Bildungsroman, which explains his devotion to an aesthetics of the Unreal: "everything positivistic in life is bad; everything good is imagined."[12] What he means by positivistic is whatever pertains to the concrete world

10. From Nodier's introduction to "Jean-François les bas-bleus," in *Smarra, Trilby, et autres contes*, ed. Jean-Luc Steinmetz (Paris: Garnier Flammarion, 1980), 415.

11. "Une économie de l'extraordinaire." See Roger Bozzetto's "Nodier et la théorie du fantastique," in "Nodier," special issue, *Europe* 58 (Spring 1980): 70–78.

12. Nodier, *La Fée aux miettes*, in *Smarra, Trilby, et autres contes*, ed. Steinmetz. All references to *La Fée aux miettes* and "Jean-François les bas-bleus" come from this edition, followed by story title and page number only; translations mine.

of the everyday. It is not that Nodier attempts to revive an idealized golden past; rather, he believes that whatever has been lost must now be resurrected from within. The "elsewhere" (*l'ailleurs*) that Nodier summons up is altogether internal; it sets in motion our ability to lose ourselves in the playful realm of art.[13] "In order to make the Fantastic tale interesting," he writes in the preface to *La Fée aux miettes*, "you have to be convincing, and . . . one can only be convincing if one is convinced."[14] There will have to be a fusion between writer and subject for the content of the book to spill into life. Nodier's artistic production (he was active between 1799 and 1844) relies on an intermingling that would force the audience to rethink the aims of literature. His work, indeed, is propelled by a messianic impulse that builds on a rhetoric of religiosity both to solace human narcissism and to counteract the anxiety of death by the *montage* of fiction. If all art can be conceived as a *montage,* a piecing together of fact and fiction, then this particular montage is born of two major impulses: the desire to withdraw from the world and the desire to re-enchant it.

Why include Nodier's diminutive story "Jean-François les bas-bleus" among classics like *Middlemarch* or *The Magic Mountain*? The powerful tale about a lunatic-genius, even though it has fallen through the cracks of the anthology books, deserves its place next to Hoffmann's *The Sandman* or Schlegel's *Lucinde.* As Baudelaire does in his prose poem "Mademoiselle Bistouri," Nodier dissects the exemplary quality of mental illness. He makes evident its infectious nature, stressing its formative role for the "ordinary" individual. Both Baudelaire's and Nodier's narrators see in their mad companions ways of escaping their own mediocre lot. Pining for a modicum of transcendence that they are unable to generate themselves, they find, deep in the disturbing tics of their interlocutors, a source of inspiration, the recognition of a power that might help them live better lives.

Nodier's tale, one of the most striking stories of early Romanticism, pon-

---

13. Whatever had trickled down from Kant and Schiller certainly manifested itself in this notion of the ludic. It is never clear, nor is it important, to confirm any facts in Fantastic literature. Todorov identifies this level of indeterminacy as modalization, something we find in Gogol's *The Nose,* in Chamisso's *Peter Schlemihl,* and in Kafka. The narrator never commits himself to historical truth, leaving the reader to wonder whether the story was not all a dream. The character's *malaise,* then, communicates itself to the reader, who ends up inheriting the condition of uncertainty.

14. Nodier, *La Fée aux miettes,* 224. See Bozzetto, "Nodier et la théorie du fantastique." Bozzetto shows how Nodier dreams of converting every act of reading into a metaphysical Bildungsroman.

ders in less than thirteen pages the productive role of obsession, the therapeutic need for the idée fixe. Nodier tells the story of a young man, greatly gifted intellectually, who is assigned to tutor a young nobleman. He falls desperately in love with the latter's sister but, realizing that the union is impossible, devotes himself heart and soul to his studies. He goes mad, but this madness surfaces only when he is forced out of his monomanias—science, his studies of the occult. The tale's pertinence to this study, and to the analysis of the idée fixe in general, is that his madness only manifests itself in the face of triviality. Like an allergic reaction, it strikes only when it rubs against the flatness of the quotidian. Nodier investigates what it is that lies beneath Jean-François's inability to invest ordinariness with meaning, while his fellow-humans greedily speculate on meteorology or on the fickle undercurrents of conversation. Jean-François, and there lies his strength, is rendered catatonic by anything except concepts of a higher order. Like the addict who takes drugs to intensify the present moment or to dispel the emptiness of living, Jean-François "uses" the likes of mathematics to extricate himself from a similar sense of hollowness. He can only participate in social transactions once they have been purged of their all-too-human ingredient, and his mind, having expelled all prosaic matters, has constructed a natural barrier against ordinary language.

One of the most remarkable characteristics of this young man's madness was that it only manifested itself in trivial conversations, when he was dealing with familiar things. If asked about sunshine or rain, a performance, the newspaper, gossip, county news, he listened attentively and answered politely; but the words that flowed from his lips poured out so tumultuously that they got muddled before the end of the sentence, in such confusion that it was impossible to decipher his thoughts. He would go on, though, more and more unintelligibly, substituting with increasing intensity his natural and logical speech to the baby-talk of a child who does not understand his own words or the senile sentences of an old man who has forgotten their meaning.[15]

Jean-François panics when asked to engage in the art of sociability. The alleged pleasures of everyday life—the latest entertainment, harmless prattle, or even the vagaries of the weather—plunge him into confusion. Unless it fits within the confines of his idée fixe, he cannot enter in a dialogue with his fellow-humans. He manages to utter polite sounds, he parrots civility, but these false conversations end up producing a crisis that arrests all communication.

15. Nodier, "Jean-François les bas-bleus," 418.

Nodier's work often dwells on individuals who are curiously addicted to thought for its own sake, to modes of thinking that can bypass human contact altogether. Anything that does not inflame such intellects makes them dysfunctional. Even though in today's medical framework, Jean-François might be labeled with a number of chemical disorders, in Nodier's context, he is the symbol of a disjunction that could, in more moderate ways, strike any of us. Worldliness causes pain because it is situated in an inescapable present; we must react to it, respond to its demands, and fit it within our mortality. Otherworldliness, however, enables us to escape from this condition, matching us with something greater than ourselves, something that retains its future promise, enticing by its sheer sense of possibility. This mystical yearning is what affords Nodier's characters their dual sense of intoxication and despair.

Nodier's *idiot savant* only regains his composure, his brilliance, when asked about quasi-unanswerable questions such as the planets, the nature of the universe, or complex ethical matters. Intellectually stimulated, asked to transcend the prosaic, he is not only persuasive, but masterful. His admirer, the story's young narrator, understands that the only way to engage with him is to egg him on with such intricate questions. He quizzes Jean-François about space, the planets, astronomy, the nature of matter, merely to hold his attention, desperate to bask in this privileged mode of transaction. "Science's most arduous questions . . . were child's play for him, and their solutions sprung so fast from his mind to his mouth that one might have mistaken the result of reflection and calculation for a merely mechanical operation."[16] It is certainly in tune with the pathology of monomania to prefer the mechanical, the formulaic, to questions involving plural answers. Nodier's holy fool captures the essence of a phenomenon without ever having to run it through the ordinary channels of communication. Bypassing the human makes him both an object of scorn (to the villagers, he is the local idiot) and of awe (to the educated, he is something of a seer). But to Nodier, there is a dramatic lesson to be gleaned from such a personality: seen through the eyes of the young narrator (the story is loosely based on Nodier's own experience), Jean-François is a great example of the ravages operated by the quotidian. He goes mad because the world does not offer the right kind of fodder for his

16. Ibid., 419. See also how his madness recedes when the conversation gravitates around "a moral or scientific question of some weight. Then the diverging and scattered beams of his sick intelligence compressed themselves in a concentrated beam . . . endowing such brilliance to his discourse that it became difficult to doubt that Jean-François would have been any more erudite were he in full possession of his reason."

mind; madness, at least, allows him to remain in a realm that is altogether abstract, promising to delay the inevitable boredom and insipidity of the habitual. There is nothing trite about the story. The clichés about early Romanticism as the site of metaphysical escapism do not apply here. Nodier's narrative is the excruciatingly moving account of those individuals who cannot adapt to the concrete. Shocked into madness by disappointed love, Jean-François instinctively turns away from the world, only able to focus on ideas. His is also the ability to sense the future—he "feels" the *mise-à-mort* of Marie-Antoinette and dies shortly after the death of his unattainable beloved.

Unlike some of Janet's more domestically oriented patients, obsession here is exclusively turned to the *idea* part of the idée fixe. Bliss overcomes the otherwise simpleton when his brain is asked to perform complex tasks. While all other demands function literally as depressants, pushing down his mood until he becomes dysfunctional, the practice of pure thought, the raw electric charge of brain power, lifts him to an altered state. Nodier's exploration of insanity (today we might identify such symptoms as a variation on Asperger's syndrome, where the afflicted individual performs brilliant scientific feats, but is physically incapable of engaging in any forms of intimacy)[17] serves to reinforce his belief that a fearful schism is growing between the increasingly material *Zeitgeist* of an epoch that has overlooked the art of contemplation and individuals who simply cannot find a home within these pragmatic demands. The narrator wonders whether "Jean-François had two souls, one that belonged to the crude world where we live, and the other that purified itself in the subtle space he believed he could break through with his mind."[18]

Nodier felt that his contemporaries had chosen the world by default. Its emptiness, indeed, was increasingly looking like a "wasteland of thought where a fallen world skids toward nothingness," a gap that resembled "a terrible uncertainty between false and real."[19] How paradoxical that Nodier prescribed the Fantastic, the most uncertain of genres, to treat this condition of uncertainty. It is not just that he turned to themes and characters utterly divorced from a recognizable reality, but he picked

17. Nodier's story "Une Heure ou la vision" is also tangentially about mental illness; its protagonist is afflicted with a form of schizophrenia. This interest in mental illness (in the type of phenomena that seduced the Surrealists—sleepwalking, dreaming, speaking in one's sleep) testifies to Nodier's desire to explore paranormal phenomena.

18. Nodier, "Jean-François les bas-bleus," 422.

19. Preface to *La Fée aux miettes*.

a style that would exaggerate the rejection of the world. One of Nodier's most brilliant interpreters, Jean-Luc Steinmetz, has noted that one could read Nodier's entire work as an attempt to cure this sense of doubt by setting up a *thérapie de l'extraordinaire*, a therapy based on the construction of a fantastic alternative to life.[20] Not exactly a talking-cure, this literary therapy would provide a state of suspension where writer, narrator, and reader could immerse themselves in a new form of reality. The extraordinary is a variation on the restorative art of sleep; it reclaims the powers of the imagination while providing a metaphysical supplement to a world that has lost the ability to dream. Nodier envisions this rather abstract mode of being as an "intermediary state;" his brand of the Fantastic could simultaneously be viewed as a form of protest and a utopian reconciliation. Redemption and reconciliation are two key words in Nodier's vocabulary and help us grasp the hopes he placed in a literature that would establish, against all odds, a perfectly autonomous realm, a symbolic architecture upon which to transfigure the world.

This desire of re-enchantment pushed Nodier's work in the direction of abstraction. His writings are grounded, on the one hand, in the dissolution of form and, on the other hand, in the rejection of a prose based on external events and experiences. This expulsion of the real has as much to do with the non-figurative as it does with the dissolution of content into form, coupled with the radical rejection of any experience evocative of ordinary life. In fact, Nodier's prose cannot be co-opted; it shares with abstract art the inexorability of an unquestioned belief. Shielding itself from history, it plays out a curious dialogue where the anxiety of the void, the *horror vacui*, can only be filled by another kind of void, a pregnant void, that will counteract the damaging effects of relativity.

While Nodier's abstraction addresses the absence of belief, it resists miming a blissful "elsewhere." Here is how the narrator of "Jean-François les bas-bleus" translates this elsewhere: "What pure peace surfaces in this cloudless region that is never unsettled, never deprived of sunshine, and that laughs, as peaceful and luminous, whether above our hurricanes or above our sorrows."[21] This peaceful deserted space smacks of the "desolated primitivism" that Sarah Kofman recognizes as the world before the Fall.[22] In such a world, there is no beginning or end, no tumult or con-

---

20. Steinmetz develops this notion of therapy in his remarkable "Le veilleur de nuit," chosen as the introduction to *Smarra, Trilby, et autres contes*, 27.

21. Nodier, "Jean-François les bas-bleus," 423.

22. Sarah Kofman, *L'Enfance de l'art: Une interprétation de l'esthétique freudienne* (Paris: Galilée, 1985), 197.

spiracies; it is a world that can even do without literature, since it is un-remittingly uneventful. In such a world, art would be thoroughly devoid of external references; it would not feed on anything outside of itself and therefore be both the world and its representation.

Nodier's plot structures function according to autonomous norms. Like music, they produce, to quote Novalis, an indirect effect.[23] It is this indirect quality that will allow both narrator and reader to be revealed. The themes, then, are not important as such, but as "revealing prisms,"[24] witnesses of a melancholic malaise that will end up being formidably fertile. The profoundly abstract intuitions of La Fée aux miettes and "Jean-François" are results of a fluctuating world where the self is more and more divorced from others, and where the "I" mourns the cloudless region evoked earlier. The narrator of La Fée aux miettes explains his need for osmosis, his craving a return to an unbroken universe, as the quest for an enveloping soulmate who would enable him to leave behind his frag-mented existence. "What I needed was an entire soul, a soul . . . to wrap myself around, that would entangle and absorb me in its will; a soul I could turn into, losing myself and becoming it, a soul that would make me into something that was a million times more me than what I am, and yet be still me. Oh, it cannot be described."[25] Nodier's spokesman reveals un-wittingly the dangerous passivity within monomania: he wants some-body or something to absolve him of decision-making. By divesting himself of his own will to act, relying instead on a higher force, he unwit-tingly points to the perilous side of such escapism. By seeking somebody to take charge, Nodier's character surrenders his ability to control his own actions. Such a desire to give oneself over to an all-encompassing alter-ego is reminiscent of melancholia's predicament; the melancholic, indeed, tries to settle in a closed universe that predates language and that obliterates the self. Returning to Nodier's essay on monomania, the idée fixe is the padding that protects against an unwanted condition. No wonder, then,

---

23. One might also evoke the concept of pleasure for its own sake. Reevaluated in Todorov's extraordinary dissection of the symbol, we now can trace this concept of au-tonomous art back to K. Moritz, who equates it with a divine form of uselessness. Ethics and aesthetics must be kept apart; beauty is inherently useless. "The concept of uselessness, inas-much as the latter has no goal in sight, links itself . . . to the concept of the beautiful, inas-much as beauty has no need for a goal, no need to exist outside of itself, and in fact is valuable and meaningful in and of itself." K. Moritz, Schriften zur Ästhetik und Poetik, Kritische Aus-gabe (Tübingen: Max Niemeyer, 1962); quoted in Tzvetan Todorov, Théorie du symbole (Paris: Seuil, 1977), 187.

24. Jean-Luc Steinmetz, "Aventures du regard," Europe 58 (1980): 23.

25. Nodier, La Fée aux miettes, 335.

that Michel, the protagonist of *La Fée aux miettes,* can only find this protective solace in the form of an inanimate portrait. Only art, indeed, seems
to rescue him from his fallen condition, painting a new picture of a promising world. Utopia, then, can only be produced via an imaginary world that
will counteract the careful calculations of reason. One of the great models
of this otherworldly drive is E. T. A. Hoffmann's *Princess Brambilla.* Much
admired by Baudelaire, this text describes characters who turn dispossession into art. Hoffmann's description of the dispossessed human condition is a remarkable harbinger of modern theories of melancholy.

The soul of King Ophioc must still have quivered with the memories of those
blissful first days of creation when man lived harmoniously with the outside
world. This must have given him that immediate intuition of truth; often, he felt
that the forest, the shrubs, the springs were talking to him, that golden arms out-
stretched themselves from under the clouds, making his breast swell with burning desire. But then, everything collapsed again, and the dark and terrible
demon that had taken his mother brushed against him with its frozen wings
and, irrevocably, he saw himself abandoned by Her.[26]

This astonishing excerpt contains not only the roots of a theory of melancholy, but one that is remarkably akin to Nodier's notion of the idée fixe.
Can art, transformed into an ardent ritual, replace the feeling of loss and
abandonment with a firm sense of belonging? What Nodier describes as
monomania is the ability to build something up that will obscure all the
dissatisfying aspects of reality. Art emerges, it is clear, when the gap between "immediate truth" and the "concept of anxiety" is closed and then
spoken. It is this created space that will yield to a visionary and redemptive form of existence. However, just as it is the case with Hoffmann's
King Ophioc, the elation of a dream-world is also liable to collapse back
into habit. To Nodier, the only way in which the illusion will remain is
through a sustained madness or suicide. "The habit of these visions will
dull their effect; the eventual return of disillusionment will extinguish
them altogether; ecstasy will disappear like a schoolchild's soap bubble.
. . . Since it has become clear that the ideal was nothing but a lie, the ecstatic state seizes upon the rigidities of rational life with cruel sorrow; manipulating these sorrows . . . reveling in them, sure that at least reality will
not turn into something else."[27] Life will always fluctuate between bliss

26. E. T. A. Hoffmann, "La Princesse Brambilla," in *Romantiques allemands* (Paris: Pléiade,
1963), 2:1016. My translation.
27. Nodier, "Rêverie psychologique," 51.

and despair; the dream cannot be sustained for very long. Sorrow is the logical alternative to ecstasy—the only emotion to carry similar intensity.

The tension voiced by Nodier's characters—Michel in *La Fée aux miettes* or Jean-François—can only be alleviated by experiences that enable modes of absorption and osmosis. If this yearning for unity is so unrelenting, it is because fragmentation is sensed everywhere. Here we return to the problem that has been addressed elsewhere in this book, namely, that these melancholy-prone characters cannot sustain a world without fusion. Without a cohesive worldview, these uprooted souls commit the most extreme of actions. Only when they are allowed their idée fixe, their *monomanie réflective*, can they turn disarray into metaphysical order. A total fusion between individuals and their idée fixe is the only way to fill the anxiety of emptiness and displacement. To be able to be one with another (animate or inanimate), and still remain oneself, would make life not only endurable but philosophical.

These idealistic notions only make sense in the context of Nodier's belief in an ascetic mode of being. Asceticism, indeed, goes infinitely farther than a mere substitute to life. It is an integral part of the *thérapie de l'extraordinaire* in which life will be experienced again both as uncanny and as harmonious. The world will neither be explained, nor flattened by sweeping explanations, but animated by a joyous melancholy. This joy, initially missing from his life, is finally provided by the portrait of Belkiss the fairy. It is through the artistic representation of the ideal that "an immense, burdensome, indefinable joy, usually absent, and that probably eludes most mortals, radiated through Belkiss's portrait."[28] It is clear that the joy inherent to the work of art (the portrait) is not one that cancels out the present; in fact, it is "a burdensome joy," produced by both lack and its fulfillment. For the individual who knows how to look, to read, and to believe in the impossible, this joy is the sum of all human emotions. Michel is the *insensé*, the senseless creature, who has been deprived of his reason (he is akin to Novalis's *sinnberaubt* and to Baudelaire's Mademoiselle Bistouri); he represents the meeting of subject and object, soul and world, happiness and grief.[29] Witness these claims from Novalis:

28. Nodier, *La Fée aux miettes*, 335.

29. Jean-Marie Schaeffer, *L'Art de l'âge moderne: L'esthétique et la philosophie de l'art du XVIIIème siècle à nos jours* (Paris: Gallimard, 1992), 108. This indispensable book has been translated by Steven Rendall as *Art of the Modern Age: Philosophy of Art from Kant to Heidegger* (Princeton: Princeton University Press, 2000).

The predisposition for poetry has a great deal in common with the predisposition toward mysticism. It is a predisposition for what is particular, personal, unknown, mysterious, still to be revealed, and for the necessary-contingent. It presents the unrepresentable, it sees the invisible, it feels the non-material. . . . The poet is the senseless being in the real sense of the word. . . . He represents profoundly the subject-object—the soul and the world. . . . Poetry has a great deal in common with the prophetic and religious predisposition, with the visionary sense. The poet orders, fuses, chooses, invents—without understanding himself why he acts this way rather than an other.[30]

Like the protagonists of E. T. A. Hoffmann, the first task of this *insensé*, indeed, is to destroy the fake-real (to distinguish the artist from the philistine, in order to reconstruct a universe that will be able to provide the proper setting for a life in art).

If Nodier is one of the most fundamental authors of French Romanticism, it is because he understood the task of literary creation as one of reconstruction. To grasp the urgency of this reconstruction, he needed to exaggerate it, dissecting the metaphysical sense of absence, and turning it into an obsession, a metaphysical idée fixe. Absence, then, is crucial in Nodier's work, because it underlines the passage from the destruction of reality to the reconstruction of another reality. Nodier's narrators, characters, and readers are all called upon to perform a colossal amount of self-alienating activity; they practice exhaustively their roles as enlightened marginals, perfecting with a Loyolan tenacity their retirement from the world.

Everything seems to point to the fact that Nodier was writing for the already converted. Like Rousseau's demanding contract in the *Rêveries* (where he claims suggestively that there will be no reader capable of understanding him), Nodier's contract seems also to imply that few readers could match the rigor of his interior vision. "If I were to write another Fantastic tale, I would do it differently. I would only do it for those who have the unrivaled happiness of belief, those honest peasants from my village, the sweet and good children who have not benefited from communal education, and the soulful poets with heart who do not belong to the academy!"[31] These remarks are slights to the established academics and poets. Nodier's point is to rid himself of those highly educated readers by lim-

30. Novalis, *Schriften*, ed. P. Kluckhohn and R. Samuel (Stuttgart: Kohlhammer, 1960), 3:685–686; quoted in Schaeffer, *L'Age de l'art moderne*, 108. My translation is from the French.
31. Nodier, *La Fée aux miettes*, 225.

iting the access to his tales to the simple of heart and of mind.[32] Only those who do not ask sophisticated questions will have understood the answer. Nodier forces the reader into an anti-hermeneutic circle where narrative has been almost completely deprived of the traditional elements of storytelling—mimesis, descriptions, and psychological portraits.[33] The dynamic between reader and story reveals the peculiarities of a text based on a quasi-theological system of appeal. How can one read, indeed, if the narrative offers only two possibilities: to believe or not to believe? What becomes of those who refuse to treat reading, and art in general, as a closed system that will allegedly resolve the worldly contradictions? Will they have no chance of grasping the meaning of the work? How does one deal with a type of reading that not only disregards the reader's hunger for meaning, but rejects plot for an internal teleology that resembles more than anything else a negative theology?

There will be no blatant conclusion in many of Nodier's stories, for it is not closure that is at stake, but the slow path toward an essence. After the long narrative of Michel's journey in *La Fée aux miettes*, just as the narrator is about to relate the outcome of his life story, the manuscript is stolen, and as one of the characters remarks, it will never be read. Reading, therefore, rests upon the unsaid and the reader learns by virtue of what has been withheld. We might never know how the story ends, but this is not important. Not surprising is that Nodier is impossible to paraphrase, and indeed his texts deal in the ineffable; their resistance to retelling is a sign that any retelling could only lose the profound sense of the work that operates through communion, rather than linguistic communication. Michel describes the process: "I told you that between the portrait and myself developed a marvelous understanding that replaced speech; it was more animated, faster . . . as though the slightest impressions of my thought would be reflected, by a mysterious power, in these inanimate lines [*linéaments*], in these colors fixed by the paintbrush."[34] This marvelous understanding, similar to Baudelaire's *reine des*

32. This brings to mind George Sand's preface to *François le champi*. She has one of the narrators argue for a literature written in the language of and for the consumption of the peasants. Sand's aim, though, is part of Realism's democratic goal, whereas Nodier's is far more ambiguous. He practices an anti-elitism meant to bring to the fore those who perpetrate a different type of communication.

33. See the excellent article by Catherine Nesci, "Lettre mimologique / Lettres parasites: Imitation et fiction chez Nodier," in *Les Genres de l'hénaurme siècle: Papers from the Fourteenth Annual Colloquium in Nineteenth-Century French Studies*, ed. William Paulson (Ann Arbor: University of Michigan, Department of Romance Languages, 1989), 97–117.

34. Nodier, *La Fée aux miettes*, 295.

facultés [queen of perceptions], is devised as a fantastic syntax in direct contradistinction to a cathartic approach to the story. Such a reading discourages raw curiosity and inhibits a voyeuristic contact with the text. Nodier trades common escapism for a disinterested state of grace (*état de grâce*). Such a state, bypassing the linear, grows out of the suspension of our thinking selves; it results from an osmosis where I and Other, subject and object, can do away with description and still experience a believable representation of the world. Literature, then, has nothing to do with the new; it is essentially contemplative, receiving its gratification from within. Nodier takes the reader from the poetics of Aristotelian catharsis to a form of Augustinian restraint. Michel equates curiosity with ruin: "Baneful instinct that opened the doors of death onto Eve, onto Pandora's box where the miseries of humanity would still be asleep. . . . [S]ince those days, I stopped asking questions. I took my life as it was."[35] This acquiescence contradicts, it would seem, the initial cause of monomania—the nausea emanating from the quotidian. Nodier twists the definition of the everyday and separates triviality from reflectivity. We get our cheap thrills from a sense of fulfillment based on the compulsion to know, not the urge to understand. Nodier's reader, by extension, is asked to nurture a different kind of reading, one where silence and immobility replace dramatic apotheoses. In this type of art, reading does not quench our curiosity, our hunger for information, but rather offers itself as a devotional object. In *La Fée aux miettes,* the genuine object of devotion is the medallion that the old beggar-woman gives Michel to thank him for his generosity. This emblem is predicated on the way Michel interacts with it. He is no longer a spectator, admiring the medallion, but an integral part of its makeup.[36] There is therefore an analogy between Michel's transformation by the devotional object, and the reader's metamorphosis by the text. Both alterations are based on a suspension of disbelief: the only reality that matters is that of faith—not an institutional faith, but one that disregards the assumptions of reason. Nodier and Descartes, in their diametrically opposed ways, work in oddly similar fashions. Both overthrow everything, provoking a *tabula rasa* where the thinking subject puts everything in doubt in order to rebuild the world's foundations. Both worlds, however, end up opposite from one another: if Descartes determines to overthrow everything that

35. Ibid., 349.
36. As Steinmetz notes, he enters "into the sign, he manages to cover the esthetic distance . . . and becomes an essential part of the reflective space." Steinmetz, "Aventures du regard," 20.

cannot be secured by reason, Nodier endorses a reality that is precisely considered mad.

The portrait mediates these two points of view. A fundamental theme in Romantic topology, central to the works of Gogol, Poe, Villiers, and Hoffmann, and particularly important to Nodier, is one in which the mediation of art and life crystallizes with particular strength the ultimatum posed to the reader. Michel, after all, is caught kneeling in front of Belkiss's portrait, undergoing voluntary training in the art of extracting from the portrait its "marvelous understanding." His description is that of a silent prayer that gradually evolves into a purely esthetic moment. This trance, however, is by no means passive; rather than blinding or seducing, it forces the reader into an active position. As Luigi Pareyson has demonstrated, real contemplation is active; it produces a dialectic between object and subject. "During the process of contemplation, the eye is not immobile: having discovered and revealed the work in its formal nature, it follows its features . . . it considers it as the mutual agreement of part and whole, within the economy that preserves it from what is superfluous and lacking, in the coherent legislation that confines it in its indivisible totality and in its perfect structure . . . rather than the cessation of movement, [contemplation] is its sublimation."[37] To Nodier, contemplation is synonymous with a "clairvoyant vision."[38] It is an active state, a clash between the inanimate, the finished brushstrokes on the painting, and the eye capable of harmonizing the part and the whole. It is not because the work of art, to quote Proust, exists before we are conscious of it that we must not pry into its workings. However, this discovery is a private movement, one that can only be brought to life by a vision, or rather, an individual revision.

Earlier in this book, I mentioned that monomania should not always be confused with the drive to conquer and control the world. The destructive misanthropy that so often flings our monomaniacs into universes of their own making does not only stem from the will to correct the world's imperfections, it also derives from a menacing sense of personal decay and disrepair. Flaubert's fear of the sloppy phrase, of the unstructured paragraph, originated in a profoundly uncomfortable dialogue with his surroundings; it was rooted in a *malaise* that drove him to search for order in a writing routine as strict as a set of military exercises. At the first

---

37. Luigi Pareyson, *Conversations sur l'Esthétique,* trans. Gilles Tiberghien (Paris: Gallimard, 1992), 29. My translation.
    38. Ibid., 30.

sign of sentimentality, he could berate his faulty sentence, dismiss with contempt his own mawkishness, and declare victory over the wily advances of emotion. Style became his defense against the threats of a liquefying self. Louise Colet's "uncontrolled" sentimentalism, conversely, became the choice target of his contempt, because it was the mirror image of his fragility and so reminiscent of his own inner turmoil.[39]

As we discussed earlier, life's liquid lack of contours manifested itself in Pierre Janet's patients as a phobic fear of vagueness, surfacing most violently in the intermediary, undefined features of domestic life. Janet's surprising discovery was that his patients often cultivated these disturbing forms by becoming mystically obsessed or fanatically devoted to a person or a cause. Surrendering to devotional bliss, for instance, would circumvent anxiety, reshaping it into a structured way of life. What is remarkable with Nodier is that far from pursuing a cure for the idée fixe, he actually prescribes monomania as a mystical cushioning, a padding that will ease the discomfort that follows intense, but short-lived enjoyment, potent, but half-hearted convictions. He anticipates Aby Warburg's insight that the world became schizophrenic as soon as its relationship to knowledge was split between "inspired-ecstatic and rational-conscious poles, neither ever succeeding in wholly reducing the other."[40] Nodier's protagonists are constitutionally unable to build their lives within these dichotomies, and need the blessed idée fixe to break out of this debilitating split. Such an urge surfaces as soon as this existential schizophrenia manifests itself. It is the result of the following conclusion: what is intolerable is not that we inhabit a fallen world, but that we are always caught between the possibility of bliss and the knowledge that it will soon be blighted. Monomania (*monomanie réflective*) protects Nodier's characters from this doomed choice; but unlike trite forms of escapism (the facile literary consumption Hoffman scoffed at), it is willful and programmatic. It is an appeal to build a counter-world in which one can lose oneself by increasing (not blunting) receptivity to internal sensations; it promises to

39. See Janet Beizer's enlightening analysis of this tension in *Ventriloquized Bodies: Narratives of Hysteria in Nineteenth-Century France* (Ithaca: Cornell University Press, 1994).

40. Quoted in Giorgio Agamben, *Stanzas: Word and Phantasm in Western Culture* (Minneapolis: University of Minnesota Press, 1993), xvii. Agamben goes on to note that "criticism is born when the scission reaches its extreme point . . . situated where, in Western culture, the word comes unglued from itself." The disorienting sensation of becoming separated from one's initial foundation causes the subject to crave a secure world that cannot dissolve. The fact that Nodier's characters attach themselves to the immutable, the invisible, and even the incommunicable suggests that they gravitate toward that which cannot be dismantled since it was never complete in the first place.

dispel emptiness, cast away doubts, while teaching how to abstract one-self from that which is merely transient. A response to the debilitating void within, this monomaniacal break from worldliness actually pro-vides a second skin, similar to that described by Anzieu when he dis-cusses the various protective agents that we summon up to keep uncomfortable emotions at bay.[41] Nodier's brand of spiritual flight pro-vides fusion and distancing at the same time. The retreat into contem-plation becomes a new form of intimacy-building, an encounter that reunites self with body, while protecting it at the same time from a falsely satisfying sense of oneness.

Nodier's appeal to monomania is a cognizant effort to rise above the disappointments of the everyday. It is reminiscent of the techniques used by some of Jaspers's most desperate patients—those who knew that if they should ever "let go" and loosen the tight hold they had on their ill-ness, they would instantly be swallowed up by the vortex of their de-pression. Analyzing this predicament, Blanchot concluded that such patients needed to maintain themselves in an almost unbearable state of tension in order to provide their bodies with the artificial energy of crisis. This energy acted as a positive force in a world that was dragging them down, leading them to a free fall into nothingness. Such a heightened state of crisis provided the psychological excitement they needed to es-cape from their debilitating physical reality. They would do everything to keep their bodies in a near state of frenzy, arguing that "I feel I will go mad if I let go even for a second."[42]

For Nodier, contemplation becomes a stand-in for that tension; the spir-itual exercises practiced by his characters are another ploy to circumvent psychological *effondrement*, a nervous breakdown generated by the com-monplace. So rather than seeking tension from without, Nodier nurtures the exceptional from within. He is Plotinus's natural disciple, under-standing that the soul, "withdrawing to the inmost, seeing nothing, must have its vision, not of some other light . . . but of the light within itself, unmingled, pure, suddenly gleaming before it."[43] The withdrawal is not a flight into the stylized, as we will see in other types of monomania, but into the formless, the untranslatable. By finding a realm so resistant to re-

---

41. See the discussion about Didier Anzieu's *Le Moi-peau* in chapter 2.

42. Maurice Blanchot, "La Folie par excellence," introduction to *Strindberg et Van Gogh* by Karl Jaspers (Paris: Minuit, 1953), 17. Originally published in *Critique* 43 (1951):99–118.

43. Plotinus, *Enneads*, 2nd ed., trans. Stephen Mackenna (London: Faber and Faber, 1964), 112. Mark Cheetham's *The Rhetoric of Purity: Essentialist Theory and the Advent of Abstract Painting* (Cambridge: Cambridge University Press, 1991) alerted me to this quote.

cuperation, Nodier can defeat the sterility of the everyday while simultaneously becoming utterly absorbed in its projected transformation. His contemporaries, he made it clear, were prisoners of a world that was all-consuming and yet gave them nothing substantial in return. He looked to art to perform this reciprocity: it could transform the coarse into the congenial and the commonplace into the therapeutic. Unlike the intellectual abstractions that George Eliot paints in *Middlemarch* and unlike the indomitable structures that Kien craves in *Auto-da-Fé*, Nodier's answer to the insufficiencies of the quotidian is to bask in a formlessness that helps uncover the infinite possibilities of abstraction. What appeared so wretched to Pierre Janet's bored housewives is oddly cultivated as such in Nodier's prose. The everyday, rather than being the evidence of one's ordinariness, is turned into the tabula rasa that will be inscribed with a set of inaugural and unclassifiable inner truths. Precisely because it starts out as the site of insignificance, it will have no trouble welcoming all possible signification. As Blanchot puts it, "whatever its other aspects, the everyday has this essential trait: it allows no hold. It escapes. It belongs to insignificance, and the insignificant is without truth, without reality, without secrets, but perhaps also the site of all possible signification. The everyday escapes. This makes its strangeness."[44]

44. Maurice Blanchot, "Everyday Speech," *Yale French Studies* 73 (1987): 14. Originally published as "La parole quotidienne," in *L'Entretien infini* (Paris: Gallimard, 1959), 357.

4 Between Kant and Hegel

Baudelaire's Dialogue with Obsession

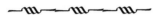

Visited Peckam Asylum (a private madhouse) on Saturday
last. . . . What a lesson! How small the interval—a hair's
breadth—between reason and madness.

Shaftesbury, *Diaries* (November 18, 1844)

In case you don't know it . . . we call monomania . . . what
our ancestors innocently used to call the idée fixe.

Charles Nodier, "Rêverie psychologique
de la monomanie réflective"

Less than a century before Baudelaire wrote "Mademoiselle Bistouri" [1865] (in English, "Miss Scalpel")—a prose poem that presented in full force the therapeutic powers of obsession—Immanuel Kant was taking a vivid interest in *vesania,* an obscure type of madness that drove individuals to organize their lives around a series of obsessively carried out patterns and rules.[1] These rules were not only self-legislated (imposed solely from within), but they provided a sense of order and purpose, allowing their practitioners to function perfectly within the narrow confines of their idiosyncratic and self-ruling universe.[2] In his forays into

1. A version of this chapter appeared in French in *Études françaises* 40, no. 2 (Spring 2004): 115–130 as "Monomanie à deux: Baudelaire et le dialogue avec l'insensé." I would like to acknowledge the works of J. A. Hiddleston, *Baudelaire and the Art of Memory* (Oxford: Clarendon Press, 1999), and Edward Kaplan, *Baudelaire's Prose Poems: The Esthetic, the Ethical, and the Religious in the Parisian Prowler* (Athens: University of Georgia Press, 1990). Special thanks to Julia Przybos for her suggestions. I owe a special debt of inspiration to Daniel Berthold at Bard College. The poem is transcribed in the appendix, pp. 214–216.

2. It was the chapter "De Kant à Hegel" in Gladys Swain's *Dialogue avec l'insensé: Essais*

madness, Kant seemed to have found the proof that the human mind, even at its most diseased, is still drawn to structures and systems. Delirium itself (*insania*), unquestionably one of the most disruptive of disorders, has a way of mimicking reason, of duping the mind by setting up a counterworld that passes itself off as reality. The perturbed intellect translates the "similar" into the "dissimilar," embarking with great confidence on a path that looks uncannily normal. Kant marvels at the diseased brain's ability to process unreality according to its own laws of understanding. There is a disturbing method behind the chaos of delirium.

Lunacy (*vesania*) is the sickness of a disordered reason. The patient disregards all the facts of experience and aspires to principles which can be entirely exempted from the test of experience. Such a patient fancies that he comprehends the incomprehensible, and that such things as the invention of a method for squaring the circle, perpetual motion, the unveiling of the transcendental forces of Nature, and the comprehension of the mystery of the Trinity are all within his power. He is the quietest of all hospital patients; and, because of his self-contained speculation, he is the farthest removed from a state of frenzy. With complete self-sufficiency, he closes his eyes to all the difficulties of investigation. This . . . type of derangement could be labeled systematic.[3]

Like the confined narrator of Perkins's *Yellow Wallpaper*, who, hypnotized by the arabesque designs on her walls, creates an alternative world, one she much prefers to her stultifying quotidian, the mind is naturally attracted to the systematic, to the recurring—whether it is a self-inflicted idée fixe or an attachment to order for its own sake. Listening to the chaotic ranting of the insane, Kant was puzzled to find a sense of "complete self-sufficiency," even an inner peace, which could only elude their sane counterparts. The sane, and this is a proof of their gloriously fallen condition, puzzle their way through the world. Difficulty and lack of resolution are at the core of their existence. Selfhood (of the moral kind) springs from ongoing battles between duty and freedom, between the moral order and self-interest. Not so for Kant's insane: spared from such dichotomies, their relationship to fulfillment is infinitely simpler; it is a private matter, crystallized in a perfectly autonomous vision. In a brilliant exposé on monomania *avant la lettre*, Kant explains how the madman,

d'histoire de la psychiatrie (Paris: Gallimard, 1994) that drew my attention to *vesania* (pp. 72, 82) and to Kant's relationship to obsession; I owe a great deal to this work.

3. Immanuel Kant, *Anthropology from a Pragmatic Point of View*, trans. Victor Lyle Dowdell (Carbondale: Southern Illinois University Press, 1978), 112–113.

who has convinced himself that his private thoughts are the norm, exists in a strangely rewarding universe, where "he has submitted to a play of thoughts in which he proceeds and judges in a world not shared with other people, but rather (as in a dream) he sees himself in his own little world."[4] Technically speaking, such a person has been "transported to a faraway place," and by virtue of this retreat from the real world, is suddenly capable of unifying the disparate into a systematic vision. "It is astonishing, however, that the faculties of the unsettled mind still arrange themselves into a system, and that Nature even strives to bring a principle of unity into unreason, so that the thinking faculty does not remain idle, even though it is employed, not objectively in the true cognition of things, but only subjectively for the continuation of animal functions."[5] It is not only that the unsettled mind makes itself at home within a system, but that this system seems so much more unified and resolved than that of its reasonable counterpart. The insane person's "thinking faculty," no matter how weak or diseased it is, still needs to organize meaning, to create patterns of thought, and turn fragment into totality. *Vesania* precipitates the movement from chaos to form, endowing the individual with a sharp sense of focus. Protected by an idée fixe, the afflicted individual goes through life with an astonishing amount of confidence, pontificating like a zealot, holding forth like a proselytizer.

Kant must have reveled in the paradoxical purposefulness of these rules that afforded their victim such a comforting sense of teleology. He must also have admired the radical shattering of these same rules, invalidated as soon as they erupted into the public realm. How could a series of actions that were perfectly reasonable when considered alone, suddenly be perceived as mad, even damaging, when brought into contact with others? Kant was impressed by the mad person's ability to perform a magical exchange between sense and "nonsense," turning the absence of reason into a highly desirable world apart. He credited this systemic form of irrationality with a privileged meaning: guided by a logic of alterity, the madman, by separating himself from general rules of thought, ensured both the vigor of his idiosyncratic rule and the unquestionable nature of his madness.

To Kant, this "rational" madness derived from a positive irrationality that enabled its "victim's thoughts [to] function in harmony with themselves." This rational "unreason," a category that is crucial to my under-

4. Ibid., 117.
5. Ibid., 114.

standing of obsession, is best summed up by Gladys Swain, whose highly original analysis of therapeutic madness will be most influential throughout this chapter:

This madness erects its own foundation, owing therefore nothing to reason. While holding itself high above reason, it makes itself reason's counterpart. It is through this madness that subjectivity becomes absolutely sovereign and the ultimate truth of folly is revealed. How can one doubt that for Kant this autonomous and rational Other is the final incarnation towards which all other forms of madness tend and in which their nature is revealed to all?[6]

This enviable interlocking of harmony and insanity is at the center of my reading of Baudelaire's prose poem "Mademoiselle Bistouri." Like the madman "who locks himself up in a circle of ideas that matter to him alone,"[7] the crazed streetwalker from *Le Spleen de Paris* allows us a glimpse into a madness whose ordered vision counteracts the estranging fragmentation of modernity.

The poem, however, would gain very little by being read as a mere elixir of therapeutic madness. Baudelaire's is a piece for two voices: the first is that of the unabashed *folle*, living for her medical idées fixes (she is fixated on doctors—real or invented—chats them up, takes them home, constructs her happiness around their alleged healing powers); the second belongs to the narrator, a *flâneur*, who, looking for a stimulant against his boredom, finds it in Mademoiselle Bistouri's monomania. The figure of the narrator is close to us: he is the perpetual witness of stories that never coalesce into a master narrative; he craves explanation and synthesis, but would be repelled if he were handed one; he wants to return to an idealized past and yet knows how laughable that would be.

Baudelaire's narrator, both blessed and cursed with Hegel's unhappy consciousness—pining after a lost golden age, while knowing that its restoration would be preposterous—is in the unique position of witnessing two realities at once: the categorical convictions of his mad interlocutor—she is confident that hers is the one and only truth—and his own muddled relationship with the real. Cursed by the godlessness of his disenchanted world, he is drawn to the figure who, through her insanity, fearlessly courts the absolute. Untouched by the relativism of modernity, Mademoiselle Bistouri is the painful reminder of his own modern illness, of the wound still fresh from the memory of a coveted absolute. *Le Spleen*

6. Swain, *Dialogue avec l'insensé*, 5. Translation mine.
7. Ibid., 6.

de Paris is not only the testament to this fissure, but a meditation on its double function. Bringing together Kant and Hegel's occasional views on madness affords us a remarkable tool through which to reflect on a duality that helps us grasp not only the productive contradictions within Baudelaire's universe, but our own implication in this process. As Hegel writes in *Encyclopedia of the Philosophical Sciences in Outline*, "Madness is a simple disturbance, a simple contradiction within a reasonableness that still remains absolutely present." The mad person, according to Hegel, does not "escape toward a space of subjective self-ruling where he would find full agreement with himself. He never leaves the sphere of communal thought. Neither does he find himself in the splendid isolation of a self-perpetrating mode of thinking. He stands opposed and in contradiction with himself, to the point that his state is in itself an ordeal and a blighted state of mind."[8] Hegel recognizes that such contradictions plague the sane and insane alike. Duality and disunity afflict us all. As Daniel Berthold argues, "we all act within a world of double meanings, of ambiguity, inversion, and reversal."[9] But rather than contributing to a general sense of ontological brittleness, these profound disturbances have a surprising effect on the insane. Madness "clings to itself and has its objectivity within itself;" it has the uncanny ability of "re-centering reality within the 'fixed idea' of its own interior life."[10] The idée fixe, while it disconnects from the ordinary anxieties of everyday life—work, the ability to socialize and to conform, the nitty-gritty aspects of domesticity—also acts as the cement that keeps uncertainty at bay. It postpones the inevitable recognition that there is no golden age after all. Hegel connected the compulsive nature of the insane to the restlessness of a decentered world. How do individuals, indeed, respond after having been robbed of the absolute? Can they survive in a world that has forsaken

8. Georg Wilhelm Friedrich Hegel, *L'Encyclopédie des sciences philosophiques en abrégé*, trans. Maurice de Gandillac (Paris, Gallimard, 1970), 376; quoted in Swain, *Dialogue avec l'insensé*, 9. The English version is *Encyclopedia of the Philosophical Sciences in Outline and Critical Writings*, ed. Ernst Behler (New York: Continuum, 1990).

9. Daniel Berthold-Bond, *Hegel's Theory of Madness* (Albany: State University of New York Press, 1995), 146. Berthold-Bond (now Berthold) goes on to argue that even though "at first glance, it might seem as though madness successfully solves the problem of alienation, since in displacing its connections with the external world, it achieves the desired state of self-reunification through a protective dream life which directly expresses its desires. . . . [T]he effort of madness utterly to remove external reality, completely to obliterate the laws of the ego and the reality principle . . . cannot be achieved" (147).

10. Georg Wilhelm Friedrich Hegel, *Philosophy of Mind*, vol. 3 of the *Encyclopedia of the Philosophical Sciences*, trans. William Wallace (Oxford: Clarendon Press, 1978); quoted in Berthold-Bond, *Hegel's Theory of Madness*, 149.

transcendence? Is it so surprising that those lost absolutes, so adept at keeping anxiety at bay, will have to resurface one way or another? Only now, they are manufactured from within, resurrected in the various idées fixes designed to bring relief to the doubt at the core of modernity. This short sketch of Kant's and Hegel's views on the structuring attributes of madness point to two scenarios: on one side we have Kant's vision of an autonomous, comfortingly impervious madness, and on the other, Hegel's understanding of insanity as a communal malady, a condition that indirectly strikes us all, acting as the tragically unifying emblem of our fallen condition. Baudelaire's poem brings alive these two postulations: Mademoiselle Bistouri's unreason is a prison with golden bars, one that attaches itself maniacally to the obsession that can only lead to illusory certainty.

It was Esquirol who first pointed out that "to the alienated man, it is the unity of the self that is lost."[11] But to Baudelaire's *flâneur*, the nomadic urbanite *par excellence*, this loss absorbs the despotically dependable idée fixe of Mademoiselle Bistouri and turns it into art. By witnessing a madness that has become the marker of his own forgotten wholeness, he can produce a work that simultaneously embodies his forsaken dreams and his fallen condition. Madness can divulge that uncanny kinship between ourselves and the demons that we have trained ourselves to exorcise. Is it not madness, as Marcel Gauchet claims, that provides us with a mirror through which to behold the self we have so carefully suppressed?

The madman is mad, yet at the same time he is like me. . . . What does such a seemingly excluding insanity teach me about who I am? Not: I am mad like the madman (or the madman is normal like me), but, "in what way might I be mad? In what way am I profoundly mad, beyond that which keeps me sane?"[12]

Gauchet's words call to mind what occurred when the philosopher Karl Jaspers saw Van Gogh's works in Cologne in 1912. The impact, Blanchot reported, was so powerful that it was as though somebody had provided him with a glimpse into "the ultimate sources of life," resurrecting "the

11. As Marcel Gauchet points out in his introduction to Swain's *Dialogue avec l'insensé*, Esquirol's understanding of human identity rests on debunking this notion of unity; to understand our human condition we also need to be able to articulate its opposite. So what might appear to be excluding the human (madness) is in fact what brings us nearest to it ("Ce qui nous semble exclusion en vérité rapproche," ibid., xxxv).

12. Marcel Gauchet, "A la recherche d'une autre histoire de la folie," introduction to ibid., xxxiv.

hidden motor of [his] being."[13] What if, as Gauchet suggests, madness resembled the surplus of possibilities that we have managed to repress in
our own natures, a surplus that teaches us about who we might have
been? Blanchot reminds us that this surplus was precisely how Zimmer,
the woodworker who took care of Hölderlin when he went mad, described the poet: "He is no longer mad at all. In fact, if he ever was mad,
it was because he knew too much. . . . [H]e just cannot rid himself of his
great amounts of knowledge."[14]

It is not that Baudelaire's narrator is awed by the streetwalker's knowledge or talent, but rather by her self-assured relationship with the world.
She is the person that he might have become had he not expelled the surplus and the aberrant from his life. Shunning any degree of self-censor-
ing, she triumphantly lives up her idée fixe, using it in ways others might
resort to a walking stick or a compass. It helps her carve her own geog-
raphy of being, making the sinuous streets of Paris strangely familiar and
unthreatening. Without Mademoiselle Bistouri and her radical way of
embracing her own fantasy world, the narrator would have been deprived of this productively distorted mirror-image of himself. In the context of Baudelaire's Paris, an exploded space where the open-ended is
painfully reflected in the loiterer's melancholic sense of incompleteness,[15] we can appreciate the appeal of a folly that moves the subject from
indeterminacy to sovereign subjectivity.

But let us look at the intriguing scenario. Our narrator is wandering the
outskirts of Paris. He is approached by a woman who meets all of Esquirol's criteria of monomania: shamelessly pursuing her sinister medical fixations (she is titillated by bloodied medical clothing and surgical
scalpels), she assaults every man she encounters, convinced that he is the
doctor for whom she has been waiting. Mademoiselle Bistouri collects
hospital interns with the single-mindedness of a bibliophile or a philate-
list. But unlike these ordinary collectors, hers is an idée fixe that ends up
revealing to the narrator of *Le Spleen de Paris* his own therapeutic relationship to art. Both protagonists can function only in an *anti-monde*, a
counter-world, akin to that of Nodier's fantastic fictions. It is a world
where the act of collecting provides an emotional coherence that prosaic
experience can never hope to offer. Baudelaire, unwittingly following

13. Maurice Blanchot, "La Folie par excellence," introduction to *Strindberg et Van Gogh*,
by Karl Jaspers (Paris: Minuit, 1953), 12. Originally published in *Critique* 45 (1951): 99–118.
14. Ibid., 29.
15. Ross Chambers, *Loiterature* (Lincoln: University of Nebraska Press, 1999).

Kant, goes well beyond Esquirol's medical classification in his presentation of the idée fixe. He uses the Kantian notion of madness as supreme unreason, but takes it a step further: in the hands of his Parisian prowler, it becomes wholly restorative. Once the narrator realizes that Mademoiselle Bistouri exploits her monomania in the way he does his literary subjects, it is she who suddenly turns into the doctor-therapist, shedding light onto *his* storytelling pathology. Just as her delusions have granted her a taste of Platonic bliss, a haven grounded "anywhere out of this world," he, in his turn, can brazenly make art out of the encounter, turning her into one of his poems, into a meditation on his own obsessive and self-forming need to relinquish life for art.

The ominous words "You're a doctor, aren't you?" will force the narrator to admit that, beyond anything he might say or do, he will always appear as doctor in the eyes of the madwoman. This false portrayal of his true identity reflects the principle of artistic representation. Art plays the same headstrong role as Mademoiselle Bistouri, always trying to pass one thing off as another, forcing the reader to substitute an imaginary world for the real one. The world of folly and the world of writing cannot help fraternizing. How could one not be fascinated by somebody's absolutely unerring relationship to reality? How often, indeed, do we encounter individuals who seem spared from existential malaise and incertitude, seemingly fulfilled by their eccentricities? In fact, thanks to her obsession with doctors, all her other doubts have been dispelled, replaced by a mythology that brings with it an extraordinary sense of plenitude. It is difficult not to compare this mechanism to the bliss described by Pierre Janet when he "permitted" his patients to divest themselves of their identity by investing it with his own—that of doctor-healer turned divinity.[16] If this mechanism is all about certainty, about the removal of ambivalence in an urban setting built exclusively on memories and lost ideals, then our mademoiselle has embraced the very monomaniacal principles that Nodier set up as an alternative to debilitating modernity: "[The monomaniac] is this poor logician of the real world who has made for himself

16. See Catherine Clément's *La Folle et le saint* (Paris: Seuil, 1993). This is how Clément describes Madeleine Le Bouc's relationship to Pierre Janet: "Janet is the incarnation of divinity (*l'organe de la divinité*), while God still remains *God-her-master*. Within Madeleine's willed servitude, Janet occupies the position of stage manager (*directeur délégué*), prefect, grand vizier, prime minister, and object of secondhand love (*amour par procuration*)," 66; my translation. Mademoiselle Bistouri also loves her "little doctors" secondhand. They represent the irresistible fusion of love, therapy, and omniscience.

a bitter pleasure in sacrificing the mortal for the immortal, and the perishable and odious present for an eternal future."[17] The petty complications of everyday life, its disappointments and shortcomings, are replaced by powerful fantasies. But does this not explain how this isolation, this ability to turn the world into a fortress of certainty, can provide a haven for the poet? The poem is a cure in the disease: like Janet's patients, like Nodier's *illuminés*, our narrator learns how to make use of his folly and the folly of others to give meaning to his world. He quickly learns how to build a perverse equilibrium from the crumbling foundations of his mad encounter.

Medical studies on obsession have shown us to what extent compulsive natures—whether they suffer from hypochondria or extreme forms of jealousy—lean on their obsession to structure their worlds. Without the debilitating rites they submit themselves to, obsessive people would experience an intolerable sense of loss and disorientation. Baudelaire explores this paradox by contrasting urban hesitation (with its endless weighing of options) and obsessive organization (with its radical embrace of one single possibility). Certainty and uncertainty meet by chance. "As I arrived on the outskirts of the suburb, under the gas lamps, I felt an arm slip itself gently under mine, and I heard a voice at my ear say: 'You are a doctor, sir?'"[18] The serpentine arm that slips itself under the narrator's is as intangible as its accompanying whisper—"You are a doctor" (*vous êtes docteur*). The sentence, at first interrogative, rapidly becomes a declaration, forcing a defensive response from the narrator: "No; I am not a doctor, let me *by*." But Mademoiselle Bistouri will not take no for an answer, interjecting her declarative response, creating a situation by the very nature of her certainty: "But yes! You are a doctor. I see it clearly. Come to my place. You will be quite pleased with me, come now!" Couched in the telegraphic style of the prose poem, this language stresses the utter lack of connection between the narrator's response and the madwoman's means of pursuing her ideal. Spurred on by her certitude, she pays no attention to his rankled reply and continues to build on her illu-

17. Nodier, "Rêveries psychologiques de la monomanie réflective," in *L'Amateur de livres*, ed. Jean-Luc Steinmetz (Paris: Castor Astral, 1993)," 54; my translation.

18. Charles Baudelaire, "Mademoiselle Bistouri," in *Œuvres Complètes* (Paris: Pléiade, 1961), 300. The poem belongs to *Le Spleen de Paris* and all references are from this edition; my translation. "Mademoiselle Bistouri" has been translated as "Miss Scalpel" by Edward K. Kaplan in *The Parisian Prowler: Petits poèmes en prose* (Athens: University of Georgia Press, 1977).

sion. She wishes him a doctor, so he will become one. He ends up yielding out of a curiosity that will bring him closer to his voyeuristic objective. So Mademoiselle Bistouri persists: "Come to my place. You will be quite pleased with me, come now!" Her declaration—"You are a doctor"—begins a whole narrative process. "I love mysteries passionately," the narrator retorts, "because I always hope to solve them. I therefore allowed myself to be led by this companion, or rather by that unexpected enigma." Let us note the parallel between the two characters. They will make use of each other to complete the most unreal of missions. One will follow his hunger for mystery—the world is, in sum, a place where paperbacks and detective novels play themselves out. The other realizes her passion for the man-doctor. One might ask how Mademoiselle Bistouri's monomania, a state that excludes all dialogue with the other, could become the motor of the poem. Indeed, she never establishes a dialogue with the world, for her words correspond to a purely interior universe, governed by its own laws. Hers is therefore a "state" of monologue, altogether similar to Kant's state of autonomous folly. But this monologue, instead of being presented through her idée fixe alone, is incorporated into a veritable hermeneutics where the narrator-interpreter is changed by the monological "text" he dissects.

Baudelaire's prose poem allows us a very close look into the intimate workings of the idée fixe. After leading the narrator to her house, she resumes her refrain: "Make yourself at home, my friend . . . that'll remind you of the good times of your youth—There now! Where did you get those gray hairs? You weren't like this, not long ago, when you were still L . . .'s intern. . . . I recall it was you who helped him in serious operations. . . . —Oh, me, I get around. I know that kind well."[19] As we have seen, the narrator is confronted with an absolute monologue. The questions and responses are formulated by a steady voice absolutely convinced of the veracity of its message. This voice becoming increasingly familiar and intimate, resumes her chorus, asking once more:

"You're a doctor?" [Vous êtes médecin, monsieur?]
    That incomprehensible refrain made me leap to my feet "No!" I yelled, furious.
"A surgeon, then?"
"No! No! Not unless it's to cut your head off."[20]

19. Baudelaire, "Mademoiselle Bistouri," 301.
20. Ibid.

Her fixation is compared to a chorus, to a litany, an incomprehensible refrain. Oddly enough, it is that impossibility of getting anything through to her that is at the root of the narrator's fascination. Her quasi-mystic certitude, her way of imposing her beliefs onto his world, becomes a narrative aphrodisiac. Her fixation has the power of Scheherazade's yarn. Nothing can stop her from living out her idea, and nothing can save him from its hypnotic effect. Her mind, and this is where Kant's fascination for *vesania* originates, manages to transform any piece of information into that single thought. How does this affect the narrator? As he follows her, still convinced that he is ultimately pursuing his own train of thoughts, he gradually loses himself in her world, her fixation triggering a productive form of estrangement. He begins to behold the madwoman not simply as a language to decipher, but as an incomprehensible phenomenon, a clashing chord impossible to integrate into his familiar world. It is because she is an enigma "impossible to resolve" that she becomes his sudden muse. The enigmatic aspect of Mademoiselle Bistouri, the "unintelligible" quality of her speech, produces a shock that breaks with the tedium of everyday life. She confirms Pierre Janet's belief that obsession is the paradoxical remedy against the unexceptional and repetitive nature of the prosaic.

Like Nodier's lunar character, Jean-François, Mademoiselle Bistouri collapses as soon as she is asked about this prosaic realm, about her interactions with "real" people. As he tries to engage her in a perfectly normal discussion, the narrator soon realizes that his questions are causing a psychological meltdown in their recipient. But rather than discouraging him, this fantastic degree of unreality is precisely what diverts him from his own languor. As he continues his interrogation, he inquires about "the other doctors," and what happens when *they* "fail to understand" her; no sooner does he refer to an objective, exterior reality than she takes on a "very sad air" and mumbles, discouraged, "I don't know . . . I don't remember," blanking out altogether. Clearly belonging "out of this world," she becomes a strange reflection of Baudelaire's own poetics of wishful displacement. But unlike the Baudelairean persona, struggling hard to find a no-man's land he never has to inhabit for long, she has effortlessly withdrawn from the present to occupy a space that will remain alien to all but herself. This permanent sense of displacement, as natural and unpremeditated as Baudelaire's, is intellectualized and anguished, and is what drives the narrator to look again at his own trajectory.

A certain jealousy emerges. Why can't he live with her intensity? Looking into himself, he does just what Gauchet suggests, opening himself to his own potential madness, trying to ferret out a disorder that might have some of Mademoiselle Bistouri's tantalizing single-mindedness. What he finds is the following: contrary to what his *flâneries* might suggest, his days are also organized around a fixation, because as much as Mademoiselle Bistouri spots doctors in every corner, he lives for his own maniacal mysteries, for enigmas that will give an immediate purpose to his loitering life and dissipate his melancholy. In fact, his self-professed compulsions are what get the conversation going:

> But, I said to her, following, in turn, my own fixation, "Why do you think me a doctor?"
> "Because you are so kind and so good to women!"
> "What singular logic!" I said to myself.[21]

The two characters reach a curious equilibrium in that they begin to fulfill each other's fantasies. Thanks to Mademoiselle Bistouri, the narrator begins to relate to her folly not as a "monstrous aberration," but as a "significant moment in the journey of human history."[22] She enables him to relive the bliss of absolute faith. As her monomania shatters his well-tested views, it restores by proxy a pristine plane upon which obsolete beliefs and certainties can continue to be played out, even if it is only for the time of a poem.

But where does Baudelaire's empathetic stance on madness take us? Is he serving up his troublesome *folle* as a counterpoison to modernity's disappointments? The unexpected agent of a totalizing worldview, she sparks empathy in her beholders, providing them with a retreat from a world that is stoically resisting any form of utopianism. Who can remain indifferent to her gaze? According to Gauchet's theory, only the truly insane, the dangerously disconnected, only those who do not identify with the universal fragility of selfhood, will distance themselves from such a plight. But let us consider the terms of such an insanity. How does "madness" manifest itself in the poem? It jumbles medical and mystical discourse, resorting to an autonomous logic that both appeals to and alienates the narrator. Witness Mademoiselle Bistouri's gory confession: "So then! Would you believe that I have a strange desire I dare not confess to him?—It's just I wish he would come to see me with his doctor's bag and smock, even with a little blood on it!"[23] Collector of doctors, she

21. Ibid., 302.

22. Hegel, *L'Encyclopédie des sciences philosophiques*; quoted in Swain, *Dialogue avec l'insensé*, 22.

23. Baudelaire, "Mademoiselle Bistouri," 302.

finds in them the torture of yearning and the healing of hope. Their pro-fession stands for the double-edged gratification of sacrifice, horror, and redemption. With their black bags and butcher's smocks, doctors are at once the incarnations of power and the mirrors of the spectator's own morbid desire to find release in suffering. The fascination they exert on her bounces back onto the narrator and then onto the reader. She has be-gun a delusional *ronde* that reflects an all-around need for escapism. The good doctor, as solacing as he is phantasmagoric, fills the intolerable *manque-à-être*, the absence of being, that turns the world into a meaning-less abyss. Busy and bloodied by his devotion, the physician restores the world to a semblance of order. By multiplying these healers, by filling the streets of Paris with their white gowns, Mademoiselle Bistouri re-enchants the world.

It is the narrator, however, not Mademoiselle Bistouri, who is meditat-ing on these fictions. As we have seen, what mesmerizes him is her abil-ity to live out her desire for the immutable. Like Kant's madman, she raises her condition to that of an absolute by transforming the irrational into a world altogether devoid of weakness. This is obvious in the way Mademoiselle Bistouri clings to a few fixed moments from her youth—when she used to haunt X, Y, Z, some of her favorite medical interns. She throws these names as evidence to the narrator, effortlessly blending her past with her present, fusing her blurry memories and this newfound conquest. Like the novelist, who merges fact and fiction, fantasy and re-ality, she confidently composes and inhabits a universe of both real and fictitious associations.

For Kant, such certitude can occur only in the realm of aesthetics. It is the sole domain that escapes the laws of positive verification. If the whole world agrees that arabesques on wallpaper or exotic sea creatures are beautiful, it is not because it can be proved, but because real aesthetic judgments function as an independent world that depends on faith, not hard evidence. Baudelaire unmasks the internal logic of madness by painting Mademoiselle Bistouri as an expert of the unreal, a free spirit who lives up to her fantasies for their own sake. Leafing through old pic-tures, she says, "Do you remember? . . . I knew it! Look! There's Z., who denounced the protestors. . . . [W]hen we meet again, you'll give me your portrait, won't you darling?"[24] Her fixation is so powerful that it func-tions like a jealous lover whose determination to surprise a rival sucks up everything in its path. What reaction does this elicit in the narrator? By

24. Ibid., 301.

playing the very same game, by putting himself in the madwoman's place, as though eager to infect himself with her disease, he attempts to grasp the world through her absolutist eyes. Here we see precisely what Swain and Gauchet recognized in Hegel's philosophy of madness: a great stride away from any simplistic polarity between sanity and insanity.[25] The poem's narrator, starting out with a clear-cut sense of hierarchy (he is in charge, she is in trouble), slowly breaks out of this dichotomy, gradually allowing Mademoiselle Bistouri's madness to revamp his outlook on the world. Because of the narrator's own ambiguous position, his simultaneous attraction and repulsion for his subject, he strikes a middling position, neither condemning nor encouraging what he witnesses. By yielding the floor to this *femme à docteurs,* this doctor-addict, he liberates his dormant single-mindedness, reviving an increasingly drained dialogue with art.

What is it about obsession that it can trigger and sustain such a dialogue? Baudelaire, himself victim of innumerable disorders, would certainly have endorsed Nerval's conviction that sickness and writing could not so easily be separated. Recall the chilling letter in which Nerval castigates the doctors who coerced him into admitting both his insanity and its cure by their hands. He could be released from their asylum only if he recognized the extent of his disorder and the impact of their treatment. The doctor, as Nerval sees him, is incapable of establishing a dialogue with his patient; he is tied to his own complacent categories. Doctors embrace their role as omniscient priests while patients must give into their diagnoses, acquiescing to whatever prognoses, if they wish to be spared excommunication. Medical science, to Nerval, reduces to silence those who exceed the habitual scope of meaning; doctors enclose themselves in absurd terminology (theomania or demonomania) to define the states that escape them.

Confess! Confess! They cried, as was done long ago to sorcerers and heretics, so to be done with it, I came to allow myself to be classified by an affliction defined by the doctors and called indifferently Theomania or Demonomania in the *Dictionnaire Medical.* With the help of the definitions included in these two articles,

---

25. Swain (*Dialogue avec l'insensé,* 17) is careful to point out that it was Hegel who broke out of the clear-cut conception of the mad versus the sane, seeing the world not as the battleground between two extremes, but rather as a stage where each individual lives with both possibilities within himself or herself. Madness, in other words, is not a faint possibility at the periphery of our being, it is right there, splitting us in two, always threatening to tip the balance.

science had the right to conjure away or silence the prophets and seers announced by the apocalypse, in whose number I dared count myself! But I resigned myself to my fate, and if I fail in my calling, I will accuse Doctor Blanche of having crushed the Holy Spirit into incomprehensibility.[26]

Let us note that the doctor in question (the famous Doctor Blanche, who not only cared greatly for Nerval and other artists of the time, but was also a great pioneer in the humane treatment of mental disorders) is portrayed here as the classic Foucauldian repressive agent. It is he who reduces the "Holy Spirit" to a rational phenomenon; it is he who classifies, orders, and hides his ignorance behind scientific jargon. Baudelaire's narrator refuses such clear dichotomies. Certainly he would side with Nerval's romantic celebration of the poet as *illuminé*, as marginal, but he would want to recognize polyphony in the encounter, grateful to his monomaniac for giving him the other side of things. This portrait of the narrator as a young doctor conveys two intertwined messages: it revels in its encounter with madness, while resisting the temptation of painting himself as the norm, the sane one. Baudelaire's narrator is careful not to have the last word, removing himself from the all too powerful position of omniscience. In fact, what transpires from the poem is the uncanny continuity between the narrator's alleged reason and Mademoiselle Bistouri's ostensible irrationality. We are far from the misuses of madness practiced in Breton's *Nadja*. Rather than being overwhelmed by his muse's "surplus"—Breton bargained for more than he could take, unable to absorb Nadja's dangerous eccentricities—Baudelaire's spokesman embraces the monomaniac's compulsion, understanding it as a variation of his own literary idée fixe.

Why, then, is the narrator so surprised that this woman can cure the heterogeneity of the world with her obsession? Is he not her fellow-monomaniac, spying on the passers-by, making up stories about their lives? How could he not graduate from amused and distant voyeur, to the assiduous student of her madness, a madness that will end up mirroring his own quest for a literary absolute? Madness becomes the foundation of his new epistemological dimension. From cynical dandy, watching the world as if it were a painting, he ends up becoming the subject of her wild imaginary canvas. In fact, always on the lookout for inspiration, seeking a life that mimics art, he recognizes in her hallucinations the power of the

---

26. Gérard de Nerval to Mrs. Alexandre Dumas, November 9, 1841; quoted in the introduction of Nerval's *Les Filles du feu*, ed. Béatrice Didier (Paris: Folio, 1972), 424–425.

imaginary, the force of an inner life that supersedes by far the constraints of the material world. All Baudelaire's scorn for his century's love affair with mimesis, with the hardness of facts, is expressed in the admiration for a monomaniac, whose world is entirely revamped by obsession.

Hegel conveyed a similar preference (the precedence of the spiritual over the mimetic) in his concept of *Geist:* art, because it pertains to the spiritual, will always be infinitely superior to nature. Nature is but an inert mass that does not depend in the least on our creative powers. All it does is remind us of our limits, of our fallen condition, of our imminent return to dust. It is here that the relationship between art and madness is particularly striking: just as the Hegelian "essence of truth" bears a privileged relationship to art, Mademoiselle Bistouri's madness, with its private system of beliefs, also bridges the human to the essential, to that very realm that keeps eluding the melancholic types of *Le Spleen de Paris.* Driven by her double vision, intoxicated by her godlike doctors, she accesses the truth as effortlessly as it dodges the narrator. While his understanding of the real comes with unbearable torment, hers is simply a by-product of her fantasy world.

"Mademoiselle Bistouri" is the striking example of a madness that forces the other to rethink his or her definition of the real. It is the story of a monologue that metamorphoses into dialogue. Its narrator, who condescends to follow a lady of the night, gets far more than he bargained for. Mademoiselle Bistouri acts as the narrator's double, mirror of their common fixation, endless reflection of his relationship to writing. Like him, she transforms real into unreal; like him, unable to stand the banality of daily life, she remakes the world, giving life to the specters she calls her doctors. The discovery of this symbiosis is remarkable in that it reduces the distance between subject and object, transforming a situation of potential exclusion into a mutual epiphany.[27] Addressing himself to God at the end of the poem, the narrator wonders whether it is not He who has given him "the taste of horror in order to convert his soul, like the cure at the end of the blade."[28] Asking God to take pity on madmen and madwomen, he recognizes that their raison d'être will always remain

27. Recall Gladys Swain's remarkable reading of this reversal. Comparing Esquirol's medical advances to Hegel's philosophy, she discovers a startling synthesis. Hegel, indeed, finds it imperative to "help each individual identify with madness. . . . Even though each of us merely possesses a virtual relationship to such a shattering state (*état limite*) of contradiction, it nonetheless represents the privileged moment in a process through which consciousness emerges," Swain, *Dialogue avec l'insensé,* 22.

28. Baudelaire, "Mademoiselle Bistouri," 303.

an enigma. "O Creator! Can monsters exist in the eyes of He alone who knows why they exist, how they *were made* and how they could *not have been made*?"[29] Somewhere at the heart of the enigma is a conversion. The same scalpel that unified Mademoiselle Bistouri's world becomes the double-edged instrument of his revelation. Infected by her monomania, the jaded narrator converts his situation into wonderment, seeing himself anew through the lens of her madness. From the monologue of an esthete living in haughty self-imposed isolation from the world, he graduates to a dialogue with a madwoman who will teach him who he is.

29. Ibid. Baudelaire's italics.

5 *Middlemarch*

Abstraction and Empathy

> The Imagination is very powerful in creating another
> nature, as it were, out of the material that actual nature
> gives it. We entertain ourselves with it when experience
> becomes too commonplace, and by it we remold experience.
> . . . Thus we feel freedom from the law of association . . . so
> that the material supplied to us by nature in accordance
> with this law can be worked up into something different
> which surpasses nature.
>
> Kant, *The Critique of Judgement*

> The most beautiful . . . I mean the spectacle of that strength
> which employs genius *not for works* but for itself *as a work;*
> that is, for its own constraint, for the purification of its
> imagination, for the imposition of order and choice upon
> the influx of tasks and impressions.
>
> Friedrich Nietzsche, *Daybreak*

In a letter to the poet James Russell Lowell, Poe complained of a strange illness that often beset him. He called it "constitutional indolence," a disease that drove him from excessive slothfulness to astonishing industriousness. During the indolent phase of his affliction, "he rambled and dreamed away whole months . . . unable to produce any writing."[1] Indolence, that great enemy of discipline and direction, hunts down obsessive personalities, tempting and enticing them into a world

---

1. E. A. Poe to James Russell Lowell, June 2, 1844, in *The Letters of Edgar Allan Poe*, ed. John Ward Ostrom (Cambridge, Mass.: Harvard University Press, 1948), 1:256.

they cannot endure. Work, conversely, acts as their benevolent tyrant, reining in their moods with its unbending schedules. No wonder, then, as Nietzsche mused, that work is so slavishly practiced, revered even as an antidote to despair. Unlike indolence, "work is the best policeman . . . it keeps everyone in bounds and can mightily hinder the development of reason, covetousness, desire for independence."[2] Nothing is more central to monomania than this *grateful* surrender of independence. Obsessive individuals fear independence for a very good reason: it leaves them to their own thoughts, their own meandering desires. Work, because it provides a codified environment, because it watches paternalistically over its victims, is the best cure against the terrible feeling of having wasted one's time. "But while work protects us from the demon of daydreams, indolence, with its share of 'reflection, brooding, dreaming, worrying, loving, hating,'"[3] has a frightening way of making us introspective. Pierre Janet's patients, with their *horror vacui*, their frenzied desire to be rescued from their inner void, were the living proof that introspection ends up being the great mastermind of desperation.

Middlemarch happens to be an extraordinarily lucid discussion of these fears. Why would a character as vibrant and enchanting as Dorothea Brooke recoil so violently against leisure, embracing instead the lifeless order of pedantry? Eliot draws with chilling accuracy her character's fear of the useless, of the ornamental (a clear offspring of indolence), indeed of all the superfluities that might detract from *meaning*. Why does anything that cannot be turned into a serious book or a weighty maxim fill her with *horror vacui*? Dorothea is infected with a brand of mystical Calvinism that makes her balk at the ordinary. The vague feeling of shame and unease that overcomes her when she watches the familiar motions of her sisters can be conquered only if she finds an urgent mission, a goal as abstract as it is ethereal.

Middlemarch is that rare novel that diagnoses single-mindedness as an escape from life's quotidian perils. Like her monomaniacal soulmates, Dorothea teaches us how the prosaic can become so intolerable that it needs to be revamped into idyllic unreality. Eliot's remarkable analysis of this urge to sublimate is helpful to anyone trying to understand the relationship between idealism and authority. Until Casaubon's death, Dorothea's frantic desire for indoctrination becomes the guiding idée fixe

2. Friedrich Nietzsche, "Those Who Commend Work," in *Daybreak*, bk. 3, no. 173, trans. R. J. Hollingdale (Cambridge: Cambridge University Press, 1982), 105.
3. Ibid.

of her life, the dogma that promises to restore meaning to a world that has forgotten how to make the Absolute its main focus. Unlike many of the monomanias this book examines, Dorothea's malady of the ideal is arrested before it destroys its victim. Despite this happy outcome, it still provides the reader with unusual insights about the uses and misuses of obsession.

Why select *Middlemarch* for this inquiry? There is a plethora of novels that deal with obsession in a more direct way. It was more than common for the young nineteenth-century heroine to become obsessed with the idea of love and to fall into what used to be called the tender trap. This tender trap was a feeling of intoxication that turned the most unappealing, profligate, and deceitful of men into the embodiment of charm and wisdom. This miraculous man was to take over the task that had been performed until then by the female imagination—to remold experience into something dazzling and continuously dramatic.

It is impossible to underestimate the sheer energy that went into these pre-marriage years of daydreaming. The fantasy of a better life, even though it was a strictly internal process, was a full-time activity and compensated for the limitations of reality, affording the ingenue a bottomless array of stories told and retold, stories that shaped and organized an otherwise uneventful existence. This is why it is hard to imagine how disorienting it must have been for women to shift from this level of sublimated energy, of mobilized emotions, to the plateau of disappointed married life. The expectations were no longer the private, lovingly nurtured dreams imagined by an ardent disposition; they were suddenly subverted and redirected to the one man who was to become the great entertainer, the charmer who could dispel all types of boredom and offer instead fantastically entertaining substitutes. Alas, our novelists tell us, it is a rule that these impresarios of bliss, once having signed their marriage contract, magically mutate back from princes into boors, leaving their sorrowful wives to wonder who will take charge of their dreams and who will now remold their experiences into a life worth living. Love, which from all accounts was the all-consuming idée fixe, the energizing mission that occupied every hour of the day, had failed, in the end, to turn life "into something different which surpasses nature."

In many ways, what is so strikingly original about George Eliot's *Middlemarch* is that its main character, Dorothea Brooke, who also has every intention of overcoming the commonplaceness of nature, avoids these predictable channels. Even if she does select a man as the solution to her dissatisfactions, this man bears no resemblance to any fictional ideal. It is

as though Dorothea has read all the recipes for romantic love and has decided to replace them with punitive alternatives. Why pick a picture-per-
fect Prince Charming when you could marry a dreary and dried-up
scholar? Why indulge in the quirkiness of experience when you could
have your whole life planned out around one single idea, an idea that is
not only not your own, but turns out to be so specialized, so opaque, that
it can never be shared? The sheer fact that Dorothea convinces herself that
she loves Casaubon for the very limitations he imposes upon her takes us
back to our main object of inquiry: what is the advantage of limiting one's
life rather than letting it expand? What draws Dorothea to rigidity and
gloom? Why does she devoutly sanction Casaubon's pedantic monomania? Such disastrous errors of judgement happen every day. Petrified parents puzzle over their children's incomprehensible preferences. How
could they be so blind? How could they want to devote the rest of their
lives to a man or a woman with no discernible qualities? Is this not because of the curious human urge to be devoted to something or somebody? To give oneself up signifies that one is no longer in charge.
Consider how many individuals bask in relationships where they are
dominated and dictated to. They will guiltily admit, when the ties are finally broken, that they found some type of liberation in the very act of being "repossessed." Eliot demonstrates how an imagination heated by
mystical books and high-minded ideals will easily fall prey to such self-
annihilating urges. Rather than exploring the masochistic roots of such
impulses, I turn to Eliot's work because it illustrates how abstraction can
be an antidote to the vulnerability brought about by empathy. *Middlemarch,* which I will pair with Wilhelm Worringer's *Abstraction and Empathy,* analyzes with chilling precision the fear of a life that opens itself to
the unscripted.

Worringer's essay, devoted primarily to the origins of abstraction in art,
gives a remarkable reading of the counterintuitive urge that draws certain individuals to difficult artistic works that prevent a visceral identification between work and public. In times of strife and stress, Worringer
argues, cultures have always rejected the figurative and the mimetic (too
similar to what is being experienced in real life, too close to the bitter
realm of the everyday), embracing instead a reality that does not resemble our own. What accounts for the strange urge that makes us crave the
frigid lines of a canvas or a novel without a plot?[4] Worringer explains this

---

4. Rae Beth Gordon's remarkable *Ornament, Fantasy, and Desire in Nineteenth-Century
French Literature* (Princeton: Princeton University Press, 1992), 23, quotes the following in-

"urge to abstraction" as a way in which fragile natures compensate for their fear of loss and decay.[5] Abstraction, or for that matter anything that smacks of the transcendental, becomes a defense mechanism against the unpredictability of life; it contrasts gloriously with the sporadic human penchant for empathy, which to Worringer, is a mark of life-affirming confidence.

Combining Worringer's theories of abstraction and Eliot's often brutal portrayal of pedantry and scholarly narrow-mindedness enables us to reconsider certain misguided extremist choices as forms of ascetic escapism. In Dorothea's scheme of things, scholarship (the more obscure, the better) is a flight from the superficiality of the everyday; in Casaubon's, it is an escape from the shallowness of his own selfhood. In both schemes, abstraction is an extremely useful alternative to the examined life. Both characters base their routines on something outside of life, something secure enough that it will always convey an authority that nobody can argue with, let alone interpret. Neither Dorothea nor Casaubon ever need to question the goal that has united them. The great book that Casaubon claims to be writing, *The Key to All Mythologies*, masquerades as pure authority, so weighty and irrefutable, that Dorothea believes that it will fill all the gaps in her life. Indeed, it will become her life. She looks up to Casaubon as the receptacle of this sapience, believing that any man who has wisdom instead of plain blood running through his veins will offer a life of pure meaning, thus protecting her from her "girlish" self-doubt. This quest is a variation on the courtly love pined for by romantic heroines. Its roots, however, reside in an even greater fear of the void. Dorothea falls in love with Casaubon because, and not despite the fact that, he embodies a life-denying persistence. She mistakes his rigidity for visionary courage, his obtuseness for integrity.

Her error is easy to explain: what seems to distinguish Casaubon from his peers is that his only involvement is with the spirit and that his life appears to be thoroughly devoid of pettiness. What he has brushed aside, in her eyes, are all the superfluities that end up amounting to nothing.

sight by Gombrich: "If the flickering visions seen under the influence of hallucinogenics are normally suppressed by our conscious mind, it is perhaps due to our need to visually order the world." E. H. Gombrich, *The Sense of Order: A Study in the Psychology of Decorative Art*, 2nd ed. (Oxford: Phaidon Press, 1994), 123. Gordon gives us an extremely enlightening analysis of complexity and decorative excess and their relationship to chaos. Gordon, *Ornament, Fantasy, and Desire*, 23.

5. Wilhelm Worringer, *Abstraction and Empathy*, trans. Michael Bullock (1908; New York: International Universities Press, 1980).

This horror of the void (filled by Dorothea's fictional sisters with sunsets and enflamed declarations) is the direct cause of her unnatural need for abstraction. Dorothea, after living a life replete with the fear of wasted time, endorses with a vengeance Casaubon's illusory power. Absolute master of his sophomoric knowledge, he seems blissfully protected from doubt and indeterminacy. His expertise masks any porosity in his own feelings and fears, infecting Dorothea with a similar (albeit short-lived) sense of salvation. It is this need for salvation that leads both characters to the same idée fixe.

But why is it so important to have one's life *mean* something? What is so threatening about letting it take its own meandering course? Rejecting the natural shape of time and putting the intellect in its place would seem to enable Dorothea to circumvent that unsettling space where daydreams might reveal secret wishes, wishes that could ultimately lead back to the much-feared insignificance of life. *Middlemarch* is the rare novel that scrutinizes abstraction as a substitute for intimacy. Dorothea, eager citizen of a Platonic republic of restraint, selects the man whose very inability to love is seen as a solution to her existential quandaries. The desire for intimacy, an intimacy much anticipated by less cerebral nineteenth-century heroines, is replaced here by a series of intellectual frameworks, all taking place in a world compulsively cleared of its sensuality. This willful shunning of pleasure, this obsessive focus on specialized forms of learning, illustrates Worringer's theory of abstraction by playing out violent reactions to empathy.

At the outset of the novel, Dorothea conceals her ardent and empathetic nature behind Casaubon's abstract principles, displaying that dread of space that Worringer reads as a visceral fear of experience. "Whereas the precondition for the urge to empathy is a happy pantheistic relationship of confidence between man and the phenomena of the external world, *the urge to abstraction is the outcome of a great inner unrest inspired in man by the phenomena of the outside world;* in a religious respect it corresponds to a strongly transcendental tinge to all notions. We might describe this state as an immense spiritual dread of space."[6] Dorothea's dread of space, her phobia of the futile, has her rise violently against the "external world," finding Casaubon its perfect alternative—a model of transcendence. By saving her from the doldrums of domesticity, he turns the dangerously open society of Middlemarch into a life of obsessive rituals and hermetic habits. Eliot depicts with extraordinary accuracy the somewhat inexplic-

6. Ibid., 15; my italics.

able phenomenon that makes individuals organize their lives around rigidity and authority. All Dorothea knows about the grim scholar she is about to marry is that he sees life as a superfluity. Like Worringer's abstracted individual, who stands so "tormented by the entangled interrelationship and flux of the phenomena of the outer world," Casaubon uses scholarship to take "the individual thing out of its arbitrariness and seeming fortuitousness [and] eternaliz[e] it by approximation to abstract forms."[7] Leading the alleged life of the mind enables him to discard anything that would force him to reflect, to hesitate, allowing him instead the freedom of solipsism. Dorothea conflates this isolation with strength and integrity. She confuses his misanthropic strategies with intellectual passion, unable to comprehend that his ferocious discipline conceals a tremendous fear of the world.

If Worringer's theory of abstraction is an uncanny version of Casaubon's flight from the world, it is the struggle it elicits in Dorothea that will be most instructive in this chapter. Dorothea uses her husband's bookishness as a model that will serve as a defense against her own enormous vitality, her all-embracing capacity for empathy. Eliot documents how certain natures (impressionable, fanatically prone to reading) understand their own empathetic drive as a threat, a dangerous harbinger of personality fragmentation. This fragmentation usually culminates during rushes of empathy; at those moments, the individual embraces the world, overcome by feelings that blur the distinctions between right and wrong, true and false, making it almost impossible to distinguish between one's own self and that of others. Eliot portrays empathy as a spilling out of emotion, an ability to live several lives at once. Clearly, empathy is the tool of the writer herself, a tool that cuts both ways—productive, but also destabilizing. Dorothea compensates for her openness by trying (unsuccessfully) to suppress it. Only by submitting to a rigid reordering of experience (little does she know that Casaubon's ink has never been dipped into anything close to the human) will she be able to preserve the illusion of a world order, one where her plural vision can be restricted to one single idea. She serves gratefully Casaubon's narrow scholarship in the hope of turning her own life into pure thought.

This pointed rejection of the prosaic in favor of a higher plane of learning consumes Dorothea to the exclusion of everything else. Worringer would see in this single-mindedness the desire to live a framed life, one secured by one single foundational principle. Individuals who adopt ab-

7. Ibid., 16.

straction (whether in art, in religion, or in any essentialist mode of representation) seek powerful substitutes for "organic" life. The natural and the organic are threats, dangerously capable of controlling us, making us lose our hold on the world. Abstraction, on the other hand, does the opposite, granting us an evenness that simply does not occur in everyday life. We crave such consistency in moments of crisis, when we stand "so lost and spiritually helpless amidst the things of the external world, experiencing only obscurity and caprice . . . that the urge is so strong . . . to divest the things of the external world of their caprice . . . and to impart to them a value of necessity and a value of regularity."[8] To Dorothea, her surroundings are all caprice, whereas the act of painstakingly copying yellowing manuscripts returns her to meaning. It is a virtuous form of labor, in no way like the pastimes that fill her sisters' days. A theoretical life-hater, Dorothea equates the life of necessity and regularity with moral virtue. She would have been a great follower of Adolf Loos, having no trouble equating the frills of domesticity with moral decay.[9] Only work, she believes, will safeguard her from menacingly full-blooded situations, where emotions are shared, discussed, and enjoyed.

Casaubon's life incarnates the anti-narrative; he has no story, and unlike Will Ladislav, whose life is a series of messy mishaps, Casaubon appears to have survived as an unblemished brain, as pristine as a closed book. Unlike her familiar world of provincial intrigues, heavily structured around biological imperatives (courtships, marriages, births), Dorothea sees in Casaubon a superbly imposing sterility. His mind, never distracted by sordid current affairs, will be solely devoted to the unraveling of truth. Distraction, however, is unavoidable, and Dorothea's temptation will become the short history of the great schism between abstraction and empathy. Which will be her fate?

In German, *empathy* and *compassion* (*Mitleid* and *Einfühlung*) suggest the weaving of the self into the suffering of another. For Dorothea, these sentiments take on the threatening qualities of a seducer, trying to pry the virtuous heroine away from her chastity. In one of her first heated con-

---

8. Ibid., 18.

9. "To seek beauty only in form and not in ornament," writes Loos, "is the goal toward which all humanity is striving." Adolf Loos, "The Luxury Vehicle," in *Spoken in the Void: Collected Essays, 1897–1900*, trans. Jane O. Newman and John H. Smith (Cambridge, Mass.: MIT Press, 1982), 40; quoted in Gordon, 25. Gordon further comments on the fact that ornament and evil have always been linked through "the operative intermediaries of excess and seduction"; she adds that the "valorization of plainness in manner and attire" is a "symbol of restraint and orderliness" (ibid., 24). By rejecting what cannot be categorized under "work," Dorothea views her sisters' free time as sinful and dangerous to the soul.

versations with Will Ladislav, the latter remarks upon the "fanaticism of sympathy" she displays.[10] He has detected the gap between ideology and impetuousness; she cannot merely be sympathetic to a cause, it must consume her absolutely, becoming her monomania. In a panic, Dorothea stutters that it is because she wants "to make life beautiful—I mean everybody's life."[11] What ensues is an analysis of the pain caused by empathy. She admits to Will that paintings and museums have become intolerable: "it spoils my enjoyment of anything when I am made to think that most people are shut out from it" (252). Her natural impulse—to reject anything that would exclude "most people"—contradicts dramatically the abstract course that she takes in life. How paradoxical that she would marry a man who is as impermeable as she is porous. Eliot's point is that this is in the logic of things: while Dorothea instinctively opens her spirit to others, her equally powerful intellect deflects this propensity into its opposite. She closes herself to flux by locking herself behind the bars of mentorship. Because her nature is "altogether ardent, theoretic, and intellectually consequent" (51), she wills herself to trade relationships with the living for the promise of immortal transactions with the dead. Casaubon's quixotic *The Key to All Mythologies* is the repository of this barter. What appeals to Dorothea about this all-encompassing project is the very fact that it is not grounded in the real. It "accuses all the mythical systems or erratic mythical fragments in the world" as degradations of "a tradition originally revealed." Dorothea is innocent enough to believe that once she has "mastered the true position and taken a firm footing there, the vast field of mythical constructions" would not only become intelligible, but "luminous with the reflected light of correspondences" (46). Casaubon's far-fetched theories are all the more tantalizing to Dorothea in that they have no specific use. One could argue, along Worringer's lines, that it is the very opacity of the project that is enticing. In his mentoring, similarly, Casaubon provides his absolutist student with a complete escape from a recognizable, narcissistic self. His work, then, becomes her cure—temporarily, at least. Her blind endorsement of his project stems from the very specific urge at the center of Worringer's theory, which is "to wrest the object of the external world out of its natural context, out of the unending flux of being, to purify it of all its dependence

---

10. George Eliot, *Middlemarch*, ed. W. J. Harvey (Harmondsworth, England: Penguin Books, 1965), 252. All quotations are from this edition, followed in the text by page numbers only.

11. See also Barbara McGovern, "Pier Glasses and Sympathy in Eliot's *Middlemarch*," *Victorian Newsletter* 72 (1987): 6–8.

upon life, of everything about it that was arbitrary, to render it necessary and irrefragable, to approximate it to its absolute value."[12] The vocabulary of purification goes hand in hand with Dorothea's need to find the absolute value of things. She allows herself to believe in something (and this is why she has the typically puritanical aversion to art) only if it contains some form of moral and pedagogical imperative. Whatever is bred from (or for) pleasure, from raw passion, or from a source attributable to the self, is to be avoided.

When skeptically cross-examined about Casaubon, Dorothea's defense is based on "reason," not intuition. She portrays him as "a modern Augustine who united the glories of doctor and saint" (47). His legitimacy, she insists, stems from his being somewhat unexplainable, from his entertaining a commerce with something even bigger and more eminent than himself. Eliot is mercilessly witty in her report: to Dorothea, Casaubon will teach her "to see the truth by the same light as great men have seen it," enabling her "to devote herself to large yet definite duties" (67). Dorothea has no idea what these duties will be, but they have a Kantian ring to them in that they embody purpose for its own sake. But more than a desperate urge to embark on a selfless mission, Dorothea's is also a plight that reveals the dangers of submission. Recall her wishing she might have married Milton:

[She would have gladly married] John Milton when his blindness had come on; or any of the other great men whose odd habits it would have been glorious piety to endure. . . . [T]he really delightful marriage must be that where your husband was a sort of father, and could teach you even Hebrew, if you wished it. (32)

The blinder, the better! The more she can give, endure, the less she will have to weather her own selfhood. Marriage, then, is a test of one's sacrificial flair. It is not about one man, but about any man who will command such pious self-effacement. The very fact that Milton is blind and could never see how delightful *she* is, constitutes her notion of delight. Marriage is not merely about meaning and order but is a project of self-betterment and self-annihilation.

Dorothea turns these pedagogical fantasies into the idée fixe that will become her prison. Earlier in this book, we have spoken of figures who cannot function in the world unless they turn it into an inanimate idea.

---

12. Worringer, *Abstraction and Empathy*, 17.

Whether the lines of a canvas or the sentence in a paragraph, these structures impart to their practitioners a powerful sense of boundaries. Flaubert referred to such mechanisms as ways of cleansing one's surroundings. "When the exterior world disgusts you, weakens you, corrupts you and cripples you, if you are honest and delicate, you will be driven to seek somewhere within yourself a cleaner place to live."[13]

This pristine place can be found only in absence or abstraction.[14] Oddly enough, Flaubert's host of characters, very much in the same fashion as Dorothea's role models, do not occupy real space—their qualities are past or future, but never engaged with the present. This fear of real space has a great deal to do with Eliot's analysis of the tension between the theoretical and the real, between abstraction and empathy. The will to live anywhere out of this world, to quote Baudelaire's prose poem discussed earlier, starts out as Dorothea's idée fixe. It is an ideal that does not impinge on any familiar sense of space, but is rooted, in Worringer's words, in a person's being "spiritually helpless amidst the things of the external world." Reality, to Dorothea, is synonymous with suffocation, so to free herself from it, she must passionately embrace the most abstract of ideas and live in the most otherworldly of environments. "The greatest activity would be [t]o reconstruct a past world, doubtless with a view to the highest purposes of truth. . . . This elevating thought lifted her above her annoyance at being twitted with her ignorance of political economy" (40).

Note that this truth she fantasizes about is never specified but is a mystical effusiveness, much like her uncontrollable spells of empathy, one that "lifts" her above the mediocrity of human interaction into a rarefied atmosphere. The space she yearns after is a home for her soul, not her body. On a solitary wandering with her dog (revealingly named Monk), she muses on the fact that only a staunch sense of order would counteract "the indefiniteness which hung in her mind, like a thick summer haze" (50). This melancholic fog (not dissimilar to Emma Bovary's) corresponds to the panic of moving in an excess of space. To be confined be-

---

13. Flaubert to Louise Colet, September 4, 1852, in Gustave Flaubert, *Œuvres complètes*, ed. Jean Bruneau (Paris: Pléiade, 1980), 2:151.

14. Michel de M'Uzan explains that this longing for otherworldliness usually coincides with a malaise, an uneasy relationship with open space; this malaise turns into a violent trance (*saisissement*) which then leads to a state of being that eventually brings about a new order: "This state, experienced anxiously, can be classified as a 'phénomène de dépersonnalisation,' an exaltation that resembles the initial moment of artistic or mystical inspiration." Michel de M'Uzan, *De l'art à la mort* (Paris: Gallimard, 1977), 6; my translation. This trance (*saisissement*) follows a disagreeable period of floating; the individual wants to escape an unstable, anarchical emotional situation and enter a far more defined space.

hind four secure walls would dispel this fear. When she first sets eyes on Lowick, Casaubon's dark and dreary mansion, Dorothea immediately senses an ordering principle. Unlike her sister who balks at the unwelcoming grounds and the morbid house, she reacts without trepidation: "Dorothea, on the contrary, found the house and grounds all that she could wish: the dark book-shelves in the long library, the carpets and curtains with colors subdued by time, the curious old maps . . . had no oppression for her. . . . A piece of tapestry over a door also showed a blue-green world with a pale stag in it."[15] The narrator notes that while all these features summon up immediate dread in Celia (she contrasts Lowick's darkness to "the white freestone, the pillared portico, and the terrace full of flowers" she is familiar with), they are singled out by Dorothea with a great deal of emotion, as she marvels at their being dissociated from domesticity. The coldness and lack of emotion conveyed by the house summon up extraordinary feelings of liberation. Instead of the dreaded domestic prison she is accustomed to, Casaubon's house seems designed for thought alone. She almost hugs the books and the maps, looking most kindly at the beat-up aspect of the curtains, tapestries, and carpets. Still unaware of the role to be played by the *pale* stag (another wink from Eliot), the young woman reveres her future husband through the very ugliness of these items. Dorothea is quick to praise Lowick's sparseness as the counterpart to the indecent "classical nudities and smirking Renaissance-Corregiosities" that her uncle collects. Casaubon is not one (as it will appear all too soon) to indulge in decadent Italian trips; *his* voyage is altogether spiritual.

Certainly one of Saint Augustine's more successful students, Dorothea would consider ornament an insult to the life of the mind. Beauty is a mere excuse for a lazy and self-absorbed mind to avoid contemplation. Eliot gives us a picture of her future house as an expanse that pointedly does not accommodate the body. As much as the "Corregiosities" of her uncle called forth frightening fantasies, inflaming the imagination, Casaubon's world could be a museum or an archive: "almost everything he had said," reports the narrator, "seemed like a specimen from a mine, or the inscription on the door of a museum which might open on the treasures of past ages" (55). Eliot makes us smile as she describes her character falling in love with somebody who speaks like a museum label. How

---

15. This tapestry brings to mind the tapestry hanging above the heroine's bed in Maupassant's *Une vie*. As in Eliot's portrait, it symbolizes shifts in perception between the time of courtship and marriage.

can one single sentence command such authority? Here Eliot paints Dorothea as a fortuitous phenomenologist: she fills in the blanks and reads between the lines to find truth. The narrator refers a number of times to the blankness that permeates the house tour; Dorothea is a virtuoso when it comes to seeing what is absent. "She filled up all blanks with unmanifested perfection . . . accounting for seeming discords by her own deafness to the higher harmonies. And there are many blanks left in the weeks of courtship, which a loving faith fills with happy assurance" (99–100). The image of Dorothea as the faithful warden of Casaubon's empty mind suggests a long prison-sentence. The ambiguous "might open" in the quotation above points early on to the dangerous lack of foundation in Dorothea's hopes. But in truth, and this is what makes Eliot such a great reader of temperament, Casaubon does initially correspond to Dorothea's yearning for an intellectual authority.

Eliot masterfully describes this dream of an impersonal life. The retreat into form is an effective antidote to narcissism; Casaubon's wisdom, Dorothea hopes, will replace her old self with a new selflessness. Her gain, therefore, coincides with loss, but one that she starts out cherishing. The foreign quality of her experience fills her with awe, and she interprets it as the first steps in her educational training program. She hears Casaubon's words as though filtered through thick museum walls: strictly informative, they can attach themselves to her new present, and she can receive them as an assignment to be completed.

In the first part of the novel, Dorothea's relationship to the space she is about to occupy is emphatically disconnected from her personal needs. Not once does she envision her future home as something to mold or to change. Upon visiting Casaubon's somber mansion, Dorothea plays the part of the preservationist in that she will protect at all costs the order she is excluded from. Hers will not be a space of living, but of learning, and therefore she embraces the impersonal nature of the grounds. Just as she had admired Casaubon for his "unchanging and eternal soul," she loves the house's unchanged and outdated quality. This sense of permanence could not be further from Will Ladislaw's definition of the poetic mind: "To be a poet is to have a soul so quick to discern that no shade of quality escapes it . . . a soul in which knowledge passes instantaneously into feeling, and feeling flashes back as a new organ of knowledge" (256).[16]

---

16. See Carol S. Gould's essay, "Plato, George Eliot, and Moral Narcissism," *Philosophy and Literature* 14 (1990): 24–39. Gould argues that one of Dorothea's most shocking life lessons is when she finally grasps that knowledge is not the dried-up still life that Casaubon

The poet's quick wit and ability to convert knowledge into feeling is all about change. It has the spontaneous unpredictability that frightens Dorothea, who holds on desperately to Casaubon's supposed immutability. Any alteration she might inflict upon the great man's lifestyle would therefore be sacrilegious. Even the time it takes to tour Lowick she finds mortifying. A grave disruption, a terrible waste of time, it makes Dorothea painfully aware of Casaubon's tyrannical timetable. Anxious to get on with her new role as scholar-wife, she clearly indicates her indifference toward the rooms and sofas, shrugging off the mundane. As it turns out, the courtship itself is a terrible burden to the great man. "The hindrance which courtship occasioned to the progress of his great work— the key to all Mythologies—naturally made him look forward the more eagerly to the happy termination of courtship" (87). Eliot executes a brilliant transition between Lowick, idyllic pasture of intellectual pursuits, and Lowick the bleak prison. The dark bookshelves that Dorothea had admired (undoubtedly as buttresses against Celia's Italianate porticos) will progressively close in on the heroine. Consider this astonishing description of Dorothea's impending depression while she is still in Rome and at the very beginning of her honeymoon: "Dorothea had not distinctly observed but felt with a stifling depression, that the large vistas and wide fresh air which she had dreamed of finding in her husband's mind were replaced by ante-rooms and winding passages which seemed to lead nowhither" (227–228). Eliot's description rekindles the first description of Lowick. Neither fresh air nor vistas were yet of any importance to Dorothea, since they would be amply provided for by Casaubon's "airy" intelligence. Back then, not only did Dorothea have no use for the physical, but she attached herself only to its absence.

Eliot describes the self-delusions of early love with a twist. By using the word *faith* alongside courtship, she stresses the dangerous confusion between love and an abstract sense of the transcendent. Dorothea relentlessly pursues role models who are either long dead (Milton, Locke, Pascal, or Augustine) or the living dead (Casaubon); she becomes their disciple, abrogating her self, and turning to icons to satisfy her thirst for permanence.[17] Her devotion is that of the meek disciple taking orders from the hidden

---

embodies, but a human exchange "enmeshed with sympathy," where "the other has a vantage point distinct from one's own," ibid., 34.

17. Dorothea is comforted by the fact that nobody could ever suspect her of marrying Casaubon for his appearance. Like her model, Saint Augustine, she hopes to divorce herself from the body, but unlike Augustine she longs to hold in a purified embrace not God, but wisdom.

god. Like the Old Testament worshiper, Dorothea's faith is strong enough to sustain itself without tangible signs of reciprocity. Weathering Casaubon's indifference will prove the test of Dorothea's commitment to pure thought. Like his uninviting property, he proudly purports absolute contempt for things worldly. A house, like a library, should contain only instruments of knowledge. To clutter it with decoration would be a crime against thought itself. No wonder, then, that Dorothea is shocked that her uncle and sister imply that her future house could benefit from improvements. How can perfection be tampered with? How dare they even place Casaubon's house within the category of conventional architecture? Lowick, she makes clear, does not belong to real space.[18] To her future husband, Dorothea admits being "much happier to take everything as it is," and rebels against any talk "of altering—I like to take these things as they are" (100). She treats her house as a place of worship. She shudders when her uncle suggests the purchase of hangings, or "that sort of thing," counteracting his offer by selecting what he would deem most life-denying, most inorganic.[19] Her prejudice against adornment is a violent endorsement of essences against appearances. This explains why her perception of Casaubon blends with her ideas of all ascetic figures. "Here was a living Bossuet, whose work would reconcile complete knowledge with devoted piety; here was a modern Augustine who united the glories of doctor and saint. . . . [S]he found in Mr Casaubon a listener who understood her at once. . . .'—He thinks with me . . . or rather, he thinks a whole world of which my thought is but a poor two-penny mirror. And his feelings too, his whole experience—what a lake compared with my little pool!'" (47).[20]

18. This invention of abstract space, the flight from the amenities of the everyday, follows the standard patterns of asceticism. In one of his many examples of monastic behavior, Peter Brown describes the wish to flee the world in order to establish a counterworld. Many examples from his analysis echo Dorothea's exchanging one world for another. The Egyptian monks, writes Brown, left "a precise social structure for an equally precise . . . social alternative. The desert was a 'counter-world,' a place where an alternative 'city' could grow." Peter Brown, *The Body and Society: Men, Women, and Sexual Renunciation in Early Christianity* (New York: Columbia University Press, 1988), 217. Dorothea believes that Casaubon will offer her a "precise social structure" to counteract the unstructured shape of her youth.

19. Dorothea's severity takes us back to Mondrian's rigid formalism or to Malevich's Suprematism. The latter used to argue that if man demands nothing of the world it will not disappoint him. In other words, if you do not seek the world as your home, then you will never turn to it for solace. Solace will come from divorcing yourself from the world and from creating a counterworld that will approximate permanence. Kazimir Malevich, *Suprematismus—Die gegenstandslose Welt*, trans. and ed. H. von Riesen (Cologne: DuMont Schauberg, 1962), 68.

20. See Francis C. Blessington, "The Portrait in the Spoon: George Eliot's Casaubon and John Milton," *Milton Quarterly* 20, no. 1 (1986): 29–31.

Describing her thinking as "a poor two-penny mirror" leads her to hang on Casaubon's every word. It is *he* who will and *must* cure her of her alleged mediocrity. He will turn her life into something like the kind of twelve-step program so popular today. While eulogizing her husband, she throws in the very words (feelings, understanding) that are absent from their marriage. Her tirade derives its pathos from her perceived inferiority, turning the disparity itself into the pillar that will, she believes, support her dreams.

As Worringer points out, the fragile self is particularly prone to dispel its restlessness by searching for "a point of tranquility and a refuge from appearances."[21] Incongruously enough, that point corresponds to Casaubon's absence of affect, an absence that will finally reveal itself in the terrible gap between their bodies and minds. The sentence begins with "he thinks with me," and turns into "he thinks a whole world of which my thought is but a poor two-penny mirror." The appeal, then, is a function of his being separate from her. They have no *common* ground, and that is Casaubon's great achievement. Dorothea can project encyclopedic knowledge, saintly visions, and even medical expertise onto this vast forehead. What is in place, then, is a brutal misreading where absence turns into absolute presence, converting the formless and trite into a permanent spiritual home. Casaubon's physical and moral impotence paradoxically start out serving Dorothea's ideal. His sense of order, his stern intellect, will prevent her life from unraveling like one of her sister's embroideries, making it solid and noble. Eliot describes with glee these misconceptions, reporting Casaubon's great ability to convert his limitations into slander. When he fails miserably as a passionate lover, he justifies himself by denigrating both poetry and masculinity. "Hence he determined to abandon himself to the stream of feeling, and perhaps was surprised to find what an exceedingly shallow thrill it was. . . . He concluded that the poets had much exaggerated the force of masculine passion" (87).[22]

Dorothea, entirely absorbed in her idée fixe of a perfect life of knowledge, does not see through Casaubon's impotent rationalizations. During her melancholic honeymoon in Rome, she reads her husband's passionless style as a mere offshoot of her own intellectual deficiencies. She persists, therefore, in interpreting every sign according to one single grid. He

21. Worringer, *Abstraction and Empathy*, 16.

22. Casaubon scoffs at passion the way philosophers dismiss sentimentality as a flaw in reasoning: sentimentality distorts reality rather than setting it straight. See the article by Robert C. Solomon, "In Defense of Sentimentality," *Philosophy and Literature* 14 (1990): 304–23.

is the master, she is the student, and the configuration must remain this very way. "I should not wish," admits Dorothea, "to have a husband very near my own age. . . . I should wish to have a husband who was above me in judgement and in all knowledge" (64). Casaubon, and this is perhaps the only instance in which he shows some intuition, senses her will to focus on a single project—himself. In the dreadful marriage-proposal, he smugly acknowledges her single-mindedness. "I am not, I trust, mistaken in the recognition of some deeper correspondence than that of date in the fact that a consciousness of need in my own life had arisen contemporaneously with the possibility of my becoming acquainted with you. For in the first hour of meeting you, I had an impression of your eminent and perhaps exclusive fitness to supply that need. . . . I have discerned in you an elevation of thought and a capability of devotedness" (66).

Casaubon's pitiful prose and roundabout style communicate one thing: self-interest. Besides sounding like a translation from an obscure dead language, awkwardly resurrected by an untalented pen, his declaration declares everything except love. The thrust is that he has found in Dorothea not a soulmate, but somebody with the "exclusive fitness to supply" his needs. Even though he is unable to separate her quixotic temperament and her "capability of devotedness," he senses in her the fixed and unswerving qualities that would blind her to anyone but himself.

Like Don Quixote, with whom Eliot opens her second chapter, Dorothea is locked into an equation that informs all her actions and thoughts: Casaubon is the guide, she, the mere follower. There is no flexibility to this pattern, and this is what makes Eliot draw the analogy with Cervantes' deluded hero, Don Quixote, who until the end turns every situation into a fanciful encounter with the noble creatures of his dreams. When asked whether he sees a "cavalier who cometh toward us on a dapple-gray steed, and weareth a golden helmet," Sancho retorts that it is nothing but "a gray ass like my own, who carries something shiny on his head." To which Don Quixote, paying no attention to Sancho's rebuttal, responds with his usual idée fixe: "Just so, and that resplendent object is the helmet of Mambrino."[23] This "just so" is symptomatic of the monomaniacal mind; everything, including Sancho's straightforward protests, is used to the same end.[24] Similarly, Dorothea's quixotic nature seeks the "just so" in every aspect of her married life.

23. Cervantes, *Don Quixote*; quoted in Eliot, *Middlemarch*, 38.
24. As we have seen, the just-so syndrome is central to Baudelaire's "Mademoiselle Bistouri." The eponymous character, utterly unable to engage in any form of dialogue with her interlocutor, pursues her initial idea with a pathological fixedness.

Dorothea appears to emulate those pagan ascetic figures who relentlessly prayed in order to escape real space and time. In his remarkable book on asceticism, Geoffrey G. Harpham declares that "pagan asceticism is founded on the idea of self-mastery and self-possession, a form of control available only to a few, and gained only through extensive learning, discipline, and culture."[25] Dorothea tries ardently to control her environment by reducing it to the minimum. The following quotation typifies Dorothea's rigid integrity: "In the ascetic self the personal is the trivial, it is that which must be sacrificed in the interests of form. It is the corrupt, the wavering, the kinetic, the *historical.*"[26] Harpham further notes that the ascetic's deepest wish is "[to] become signs—and not spoken signs, but durable signs 'written in heaven' in a script which, defying the nature of script itself, is intimate with the divine essence."[27] Questions of intimacy and spirituality remain painfully unanswered. Casaubon ends up paying as little attention to Dorothea's spirit, her will to learn, as Dorothea did to Lowick. Both ignore the particulars of their new situation. The idée fixe works as a hermetic barrier against self-knowledge. It shields the couple from ever having to scrutinize their personal motives and emotions.

These parallel lives are contiguous but never intimate. At first, Dorothea seems delighted that Casaubon shows utter disregard for her womanhood, since she is the one who wants to be considered as a disembodied abstraction. She has renounced her flesh and blood to become a pure sign of knowledge. Loving her as a woman would be the betrayal of Casaubon's ineffable being. His blindness would have to turn into insight, and what he would see might even transform him into flesh and blood. But because Casaubon never considers her as a human being, indeed, has never considered her at all, he has somehow given her the impression that she is finally being treated as a spirit. Since her aim is to escape from her flawed self, only an individual who disregards this self could be worthy. Her version of chivalric love does not entail absence in the sense of *amour de loin,* but absence from the demeaning and trivial tasks of everyday life. "There would be nothing trivial about our lives. Everyday-things would mean the greatest things. It would be like marrying Pascal. I should learn to see the truth by the same light as great men have seen it by" (51). Dorothea is drawn to Casaubon because he is a "great man." He does not exist among the "everyday-things" of his contemporaries, but outside palpable reality. Dorothea

25. Geoffrey G. Harpham, *The Ascetic Imperative in Culture and Criticism* (Chicago: University of Chicago Press, 1987), 25.
26. Ibid.
27. Ibid., 10.

finds irresistible a speech pattern so riddled with quotations, so firmly embedded in the distant past, that it resembles a foreign language. She has found the only figure who will tear her out of her dismal historical present. "Hemmed in by a social life which seemed nothing but a labyrinth of petty courses, a walled-in maze of small paths that led nowhither,"[28] Dorothea is set free. Her freedom, though, corresponds to that melancholia that Worringer describes as a "strict exclusion of life": "The less mankind has succeeded, by virtue of special cognition, in entering into a relation of friendly confidence with the appearance of the outer world, the more forceful is the dynamic that leads to the striving after this highest abstract beauty."[29] Worringer stresses that the persistent failure to establish a genial relationship with the world causes the individual to retreat from what is recognizably human. Resistance will replace friendly confidence, and what is farthest removed from the human will become synonymous with beauty. Dorothea takes this to such a degree that she automatically converts the ugly into the beautiful and the silent into a purified language of Platonic harmony.

Eliot analyzes Dorothea's devotion to truth and wisdom as the counterpoison that will eliminate "triviality" from the world (55). Dorothea not only disregards the scholar's physical imperfections, but actually considers them a sign of transcendence. The wit of the following response to Celia's exclaiming "how very ugly Mr Casaubon is" says it all: "'Celia! He is one of the most distinguished-looking men I ever saw. He is remarkably like the portrait of Locke. He has the same deep eye-sockets.'" To which Celia retorts: "'Had Locke those two white moles with hairs on them?'" It is amusing that in the rubric "On Being Arbitrarily Conscious of One's Ideas," from *Anthropology from a Pragmatic Point of View*,[30] Kant assures his readers that far more couples would be happy if they were able to *abstract* themselves from each other's physical flaws. "Many people are unhappy because they cannot engage in abstraction. Many a suitor could make a good marriage if he could only shut his eyes to a wart on his sweetheart's face or to a gap where teeth are missing." Dorothea goes even beyond Kant's wildest dreams, for not only can she abstract herself from her husband's "two white moles with hairs on them," but she actu-

---

28. There is a great deal more to say about Eliot's spatial metaphors. Mazes, labyrinths, closed windows, and small paths are used throughout the novel to strengthen Dorothea's theoretical resolves. We will examine later how these images conjure the pull either toward empathy or toward abstraction.

29. Worringer, *Abstraction and Empathy*, 17.

30. Immanuel Kant, *Anthropology from a Pragmatic Point of View*, trans. Victor Lyle Dowdell (Carbondale: Southern Illinois University Press, 1978), 14–15.

ally reads these imperfections as proofs of profundity and otherworldliness. Locke's "deep eye-sockets" indicate *gravitas* and intellect, proving that every attribute corresponds to a quality of mind, to a trait that is uncommon and triviality-adverse.

Just as physical beauty is trivial, so is any type of emotion that gives immediate sensual elation. Dorothea, the self-proclaimed Augustinian, is horrified when an innocent riding exercise procures her some pleasure. Her delight turns into the same horror that attacked Saint Augustine when he caught himself admiring a lizard: his natural curiosity he took for his shallowness as a Christian. Likewise, Dorothea views her riding bliss as "an indulgence . . . she felt that she enjoyed it in a pagan sensuous way, and always looked forward to renouncing it" (32). Eliot slyly suggests that this is an ever-repeated pattern (she *plans* to renounce *life* the way others might renounce chocolate). By surrendering to the ugly, to Casaubon's sinking eyes and hairy moles, she achieves a cathartic self-renunciation. She can look right through her husband's moribund features, reaching right for his soul.[31] The infatuation, then, is with absence, and accepting the abject with rapture enables Dorothea to cut her ties with reality as the "common" individual lives it.

After Casaubon's timely death, and once Dorothea chooses empathy (and passion) over abstraction, the situation is delightfully reversed. When her sister wonders at how it "all came about," that is, how she and Will fell in love, Dorothea can no longer make the type of pedantic enumeration she used to thrive on. Celia's question renders her speechless. Rather than expound great theories about transcendence, all she can do is smile, then fall silent, and eventually pinch her sister's chin. Her desire to theorize, to validate her love through abstract categories, has evaporated.

> "I cannot think how it all came about." Celia thought it would be pleasant to hear the story.
>
> "I daresay not," said Dorothea, pinching her sister's chin. "If you knew how it came about, it would not seem wonderful to you."
>
> "Can't you tell me?" said Celia, settling her arms cozily.
>
> "No, dear, you would have to feel with me, else you would never know." (888)

It is Celia, this time, who uses the word "think," and Dorothea the word "feel." The turnabout is radical. Dorothea happily admits that thought

---

31. Harpham reminds us that "for the Christian ascetic, pagan beauty was thematized as the demonic, while the disfigured was figured as the desirable, the admirable, the holy" (Harpham, *Ascetic Imperative,* 27).

has nothing to do with her feelings for Will Ladislav, and what is more, her present experience defies narration. So Celia's failure to grasp her sister's choice, and Dorothea's speechlessness, are all about accepting that life is a puzzle, not a carefully argued theorem.

The novel is an extraordinary voyage from abstraction to empathy, from the ideal to the real. Only the act of feeling with (*einfühlen*), putting oneself in the place of someone else, will produce understanding. This is no complicated theory of hermeneutics, but simply a return to a world that is worth living in because it escapes classification and gains little by being constricted by straitjackets. Unlike the practitioner of the idée fixe, whose flight from the self becomes a full-time job, the return to empathy in *Middlemarch* is the anti-Platonic acceptance of mimesis. Finally, Dorothea sees life as it is, with its imperfections, and not as it should be. Rational explanations, rigid resolutions, do little, she finds out, to solve the polyphonic quality of life. Dorothea has transcended Flaubert's plasticizing of reality. There is no need to turn Will into a book to make him legitimate or acceptable. Eliot cures her character of the severity of her mystical disposition, freeing her life from the coercion of the idée fixe. Dorothea's marriage to Will brings to a close Eliot's reflection on the incompatibility of abstraction and empathy.

This acceptance, however, does make the reader ask how the thirst for symmetry and immutability lead so effortlessly to the acceptance of the everyday. The conventions of fiction writing made Eliot end the novel before any of life's inadequacies could resurface in Dorothea's world. Like Tolstoy, who, in *War and Peace,* used Pierre's unwavering loyalty to silence Natasha's doubts, Eliot provides her heroine with a life that promises to cure her soulful disorders. If it seems doubtful that Dorothea could be content with watered-down versions of both abstraction and empathy, it is clear that Eliot wanted her heroine to enter "into a relation of friendly confidence with the appearance of the outer world." This way, the reader would find in art what in all likelihood is absent from life: a sense of closure and completion. Asceticism is at last allowed to recede, and Dorothea can finally view the world as through a wide-angle lens; all the elements that were locked out because they failed to pass the test of principle can now enter. Dorothea's continuous need to outstrip the real with the ideal can finally stop when she realizes that it is perhaps in the very incomplete nature of experience, in the trivial manifestations of the familiar, that lies not the key to all mythologies, but the key that will unlock the radiance of everyday life.

6
Musings on Hypochondria

Thomas Mann's Magic Thermometer

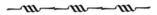

My body is that part of the world which my thoughts are
able to change. Even *imaginary* illnesses can become real
ones. In the rest of the world my hypotheses cannot disturb
the order of things.

Georg Christoph Lichtenberg, *The Waste Book*

Ever since I have been ill . . . I have longed and longed for
some palpable disease, no matter how conventionally
dreadful a label it might have, but I was always driven back
to stagger alone under the monstrous mass of subjective
sensations, which that sympathetic being "the medical
man" has had no higher inspiration than to assure me I was
personally responsible for.

Alice James, *Diary* (May 31, 1891)

After years of skeptical doctors' reports, 1891 brings Alice James the
illness she had been begging for: a painful, unequivocally cancerous tumor.
One critic brilliantly labeled this lump the "solid emblem of a perverse kind
of achievement."[1] As James records in the May 31, 1891, entry of her diary,
this illness would finally bring a rich sense of achievement, and her tone is
exultant: "My aspirations may have been eccentric, but I cannot complain
now, that they have not become brilliantly fulfilled."[2] What drives Alice
James to beg for and to welcome this devastatingly "real" disease? Why

1. Ruth Bernard Yeazell, introduction, *The Death and Letters of Alice James* (Berkeley: University of California Press, 1981), 2.
2. Alice James, May 31, 1891, entry in *The Diary of Alice James*, ed. Leon Edel (1964; Boston: Northeastern University Press, 1999), 206–207.

would she trade her ineffable ailments for something palpable, even fatal? Perhaps because unlike melancholy and whatever other names were given to her conditions—neurasthenia, hysteria, and nervous sufferings that were always at odds with concrete diagnosis—a "real" illness has a name, definition, and possible cure. Legitimately couched in black ink, bound in medical encyclopedias, real diseases tell full-bodied stories. James pines for such definiteness, which is why her newly discovered tumor is a great revenge over her usual fare, that "monstrous mass of subjective sensations." Cancer will be taken seriously and solidly by her medical and lay audiences. Up to that moment of blissful diagnosis, her pain had been intolerably vague and slippery, destroying her, but without the pomp and circumstance of a serious and legitimate illness. Her state had been decidedly unstately, doomed to be called a mood rather than a malady, the mere shadow of a loss not even real enough to be properly remembered.

James teaches us something fundamental about the crippling effects of a life legislated only from within. The craving for diagnosis amounts to being let out of oneself, finally recognized by an authority. The long-awaited illness finally places Alice James within society. She no longer needs to make up the rules of every day to come, because the rules are now dictated by her condition. Without the firm contours of illness, James's identity was beaten down by a vaporous double, sticking to her like boredom. Now she has the robust tumor to be ruled by. She is liberated by the authority of her executioner. It is the grateful surrender to authority that makes James's reaction so striking. The doctor's authority is a specialized language, one that stops the endless doubting and questioning. The grim verdict that rules out a cure is anything but grim to those whose fear of the formless far superseded that of death. To live without the order of accepted knowledge is akin to being engulfed by one's own lack of substance, one's own unreality.

There is a great deal to learn from the "almost" sick person's obsessive need to convert this indeterminacy into something real and undeniable, even if it is at the cost of life. The "almost sick" gets very little status from his or her illness. By giving a real name to James's condition, the doctor recognizes the plight that will help her feel reincarnated, owned by something more real than her own anguished thoughts. So within the confines of her pain, she is demanding a tangible home, one that will endow her suffering with respectability.

Obsessive personalities flee from the amorphous.[3] Whatever feels liq-

---

3. As David Shapiro describes in *Autonomy and Rigid Character* (New York: Basic Books,

uid to them (as opposed to solid), whatever is sensed like a skin of quick-silver, summons up fears and phobias. Winnicott explains that such indi-viduals are terrified by the void; they will do anything to control and "reorganize" it by dutifully setting tasks for themselves. Anorexics, for instance, make their lives revolve around self-imposed trials (how long will I hold out against hunger), turning absence (their hunger, the absence of food) into presence (the plenitude of being in full control of their hunger).[4] The original fear of breaking down is replaced by the pride in not having succumbed to temptation.[5] The hypochondriac's schedule, likewise, is regulated by a ritualized routine. One could see symptom-seeking as a measure to counteract *horror vacui:* the inner desert is now filled with ailments that compensate amply for the painful inner void. To a certain extent, these obsessive types cannot survive if they are not up-held by a firm structure. They turn to deadlines and predictable tasks to counteract these floundering instincts. This is not to say that they do not fritter away their days, recording symptoms invisible to the outside world, but this chaos has an ordering principle. Besides the obviously in-tolerable nature of their all-consuming worries, of their love-hate rela-tionship with obsession, there is a solacing side to their routine. It is this aspect—the pleasurable regression of always being able to find stability in the very act of worrying—that turns it into a coping mechanism, an es-capist aesthetics that teaches us as much about art as it does about illness.

This chapter tackles the individual for whom disease functions as an aesthetic principle, restoring order to a disorderly universe. Reading re-

1981), obsessive types turn the amorphous, the "relaxed," into work. Because they dread sensations of floating, of finding themselves at loose ends, they ritualize activities into obli-gations. "It is not that these people are always occupied with work in the usual sense of job or project. Virtually all of life *becomes* work to them. Reading a book, listening to music are transformed into purposeful projects, projects of self-improvement, measured or valued ac-cordingly. The living of life itself becomes work, like the running of a business, with mental records of its productiveness" (83). Pretending that everything is a job that must urgently be tended to gives these individuals a strong anchor. It is easier to turn everything into a pur-pose, a contract that must be completed by a certain time. Such small aims divert them from the greater meaning of life, easing the pressure of meeting more abstract, perhaps even spir-itual, aims.

4. One recalls the description of this reversal in Éric Bidaud, *Anorexie mentale, ascèse, mys-tique: Une approche psychanalytique* (Paris: Denoël, 1997), 145: "Anorexics make the void com-pact . . . turning it into the paradoxical figure of plenitude. They fetishize it."

5. D. W. Winnicott, "Fear of Breakdown," *International Review of Psychoanalysis* 1 (1974): 103–107. "The difficulty is that the patient fears the awfulness of emptiness, and in defence will organize a controlled emptiness by not eating or not learning, or else will ruthlessly fill up by greediness which is compulsive and which feels mad" (106–107).

ports about hypochondriacs who obsessively live through imaginary ill-nesses, feeling almost useless when they have no symptoms to report on, I found striking the performativity between afflicted and affliction. The example I turn to is Thomas Mann's *The Magic Mountain,* because the novel's main character (by no means a medically confirmed hypochon-driac) is a striking example of how medical diagnosis can help provide a place in the world. Illness comes to Hans Castorp as a shock (he is merely visiting his sick cousin when he himself is diagnosed), but is received with noteworthy elation. I examine this joy-in-sickness as a particular form of hypochondria. As in Alice James's case (illness as a liberation from psychological homelessness), Hans Castorp finds a new identity among the sanatorium's elite clientele through his fever, flushed cheeks, and change in demeanor. His condition gives him the key that will allow a privileged relationship with his fellow "inmates." Sickness enables him to communicate in a more direct, more complete way with the sanato-rium's residents; it makes him acceptable, first to others, then to himself. Why? What can we learn from the conversion of something negative, dangerous, even potentially destructive, into something made positive through its ability to instill an ordered identity?

Let us first remember some of the mechanisms found in a number of obsessive melancholics: Flaubert never hid his desire to turn the ani-mate, the vacillating, into the inanimate. He turned to art because, in his hands, it became a mastered universe, closed and controlled. Art was ap-pealing because it protected against the onslaught of unpredictability and change; the horizontal peacefulness of the perfected sentence, like a line from a Mondrian painting, shielded him from the ups and downs of ex-perience. For the constitutionally fragile, for the melancholic, the aes-thetic experience, and more specifically the moment of artistic creation, is both the outlet for and the regulation of lawless inspiration.

One can pursue these acts of regulation frantically. We can picture our particular type of hypochondriac as an aesthete who keeps turning his or her body into a work of art. More than that, he or she has become both the museum guard and the rare object. "Handle with care" could be the label attached to this body. The single-mindedness with which the hypochondriac scrutinizes him- or herself may be the ultimate idée fixe and succeeds in turning the self into the cause and effect of all experience, endowing the body-hypochondriac with the status of a museum, of a state treasure that is jealously guarded against foreign intrusions. This mausoleum of aches and pains eventually takes on a life of its own, be-coming an autonomous world, governed by its own implacable and seemingly rational laws. If we return to the quotation opening this chapter, we notice that Alice James treats her ill-defined disease as a pariah; if only it could speak and tell its tragic story! The serious hypochondriac, however, treats his or her ailment as the plot of the century. In this manner, he or she has enormous advantages over the legitimately sick (who is controlled by, not in control of, the disease) or the depressive (who is painfully cognizant of the scattered nature of his or her symptoms). Unlike the unsettlingly vague status of Alice James's illness, and unlike the debilitating condition of the very sick, the hypochondriac can be blissfully protected by the idée fixe. He or she wakes up and falls asleep to an overpowering obsession—How is yesterday's ailment going to develop today?—that endows life with a formidable sense of gravitas and purpose. It is not as paradoxical as it seems to claim that illness can be used as a pretext to disengage from life, while engaging in a gripping tale of drama. The passion for symptom tracing, the endless poking and probing one's body for signs of a disease that has yet to declare itself, reveals an extraordinary ability to be abstract, to see the world in an entirely new way, one that seems to outrank everybody else's.

It is this sense of superiority, perhaps, that sustains the hypochondriac. If in general, and well beyond the fear of contagion, we are often threatened by other people's diseases, this is especially true in the case of the *malade imaginaire*. Somebody else's illness, serious or not, inevitably steals our wearily won center stage. Even if we have been trained to say otherwise, we don't really like to believe that what is happening in somebody else's body is quite as real as what is brewing in our own. Only our own ailments are real. Even though they might brand us, reveal our weaknesses, they are part of us, and like our passions, they bring to the surface a dormant, infinitely enthralling part of our being. Ask somebody about his or her love life, inquire about somebody's illness, and notice what deep distrust overcomes you. Self-proclaimed passion or firmly asserted pain often sounds like boasting. People go to such lengths, the small-minded voice in our head hints, to make themselves sound interesting; other people's complaints, the nagging inner voice continues, are mostly psychosomatic, while ours are never taken seriously enough.

If the adversities that befall our fellow humans are as suspect as their amorous ecstasies, they are nonetheless unexpected indexes of the way people turn their own bodies into autonomous worlds, into sovereign realms that need infinite tending, sometimes even to the exclusion of all other forms of activity. Hypochondria is bound to become a profoundly antisocial activity. Similar to anorexia or obsessive-compulsive disorders, it involves private rituals that compensate for all the "dangerous" variables that inevitably disrupt one's life. The attentiveness with which hypochondriacs tend to their bodies (there is a Voltairean aspect to their worlds-as-gardens) functions as a compensatory activity: it signals that the world can be perfected and controlled by their ability to monitor the variables of experience. Disease, when it is deconstructed, is no longer the predator, the enemy, but an ally, witness to our powers of observation, to our ability to control. Hypochondriacs always believe they can see what their doctors have overlooked; theirs is always a superior diagnostic. If they select isolation, if they take themselves out of the public realm into a self-imposed quarantine, it is so they can contemplate their bodies in silence. This cloistering gesture is not dissimilar to the monk's, self-sequestered in his cell. Life is no longer about action, but about contemplation. In fact, the hypochondriac behaves toward his or her body like a scholar with a rare manuscript, recording and footnoting every anomaly, later to be presented to, hopefully applauded by, the authority in the field. The hypochondriac and the certified pedant are close relatives, because they both are bound to details and meticulous investigations. What strikes anybody else as a mere footnote or a common cold—a dripping nose is nothing but a dripping nose—turns into a full-fledged drama, a narration in its own right, a bodily Bildungsroman that deserves exegesis.

The need to collect and compile symptoms is the first hint of this archeological hunt. The hypochondriac's behavior has a great deal in common with the collecting impulse, since it is not necessarily the object's significance that is important, but the fact of owning it. It seems that collectors and disease seekers accumulate what might have gone dispersed and scattered. The hypochondriac's body, for one, is erected into a museum of symptoms. The most unseemly bodily fluids have become delicate and rare elixirs, and the most obscure glands take on the weight of an epicenter. However, these excavations occur for their own sake. There is a morbid delight taken in these acts of compilation that will never amount to anything global. The time it takes to amass, to gather, and to diagnose is time gained against the anxiety of self-legislation. The mind is working as hard as it can (keeping busy with new ailments, fresh preoccupations) to overcome the dangerous restlessness that threatens it continuously. Like the compulsive buying of new books that will remain unread, collecting ailments is a therapy against the ordinary weight of time. If the "real" patient, the patient Alice James pined to be, straightforwardly craving a speedy recovery, is so antithetical to the hypochondriac, it is because the latter wants to arrest time, to stretch it out, while the other wants it to hurry up. The obsessive patient is too absorbed by his or her own body plots to face greater anxieties (the pointlessness of life, death, disappointment) that are conveniently being deferred. Amidst the unendurable fixations and compulsions lies a soothing shortsightedness that embraces the minutia in order to avoid the big picture.

Like the scholar, the hypochondriac resides in an ivory tower, impermeable to the ills of the world, bent inward not outward. George Eliot's Casaubon might as well have been measuring the size of his carbuncles instead of perusing yellowing manuscripts. Indeed, what mattered to the irksome pedant was the perfect mastery of his method. The trademark of the idée fixe, as we have seen earlier, is the compulsion to displace reality by blocking out whatever does not immediately fit the obsession. Similarly, Canetti's monomaniacal scholar in *Auto-da-fé* walls himself in with pillars of books to stave off the threats of real life and quixotically replaces chaos with order. These plights are about turning the infinite into the finite.

A cough here, a fever there, become wonderfully gratifying signs; they indicate within the body's disorder that there is some kind of logic, even a possible explanation. The new ailment, like the new book about to be added to the shelf, becomes the object of intense focus, one that will bring the subject into greater intimacy with his or her self, eventually providing an extra layer that will keep the world at bay. The unconscious function of layering, of delaying one's access to the world, is a key feature in the dissociative tendency of these idées fixes. They provide or restore orderliness: whatever appears before the eyes of the obsessive type must be converted into something geometrical. Delaying and regimenting through geometry betrays the profound inability of these types to exist in open spaces, which are threatening because they offer too many options. Space, like time, must be tamed, controlled, and possessed. This is why the page, the canvas, and the human body are so enticing: they are natural boundaries against uncertainty; they promise to contain rather than to disperse. But what is it that the hypochondriac wishes to preserve and contain? Isn't hypochondria all about losing one's health? How can you recover something precisely when you are about to lose it? One of the great paradoxes of hypochondria is that as soon as you believe illness is about to rob you of your well-being, you gain something else instead.[6]

6. As Susan Baur puts it, "Hypochondria usually stabilizes a family as well as disrupts it. It is as if the interlocking roles of hypochondriac–indispensable strong person or hypochon-

Disease, we have seen, is simultaneously disruptive and stabilizing; it offers you a new form of identity. So as the "good" body decays, another body takes its place, one that you yourself have reconstituted mentally, limb by limb. This type of disease resembles the thread of Ariadne; it slowly leads you back to your lost core. Hypochondriacs are meticulous phenomenologists; they use their bodies as foreign matter, as raw materials from which they will extract the kernel of their identity. Their laboratories are the hospital room, the library, or the office space—all womblike with their sterilized efficaciousness. As laboratories require experts, hypochondriacs are intent on making themselves the absolute experts of their own bodies. By the end of their voyage into illness, they are the holders of fancy diplomas, masters in their own terribly obscure fields. They will become remarkably well informed as to the causes and effects of their afflictions, learning a new language that will be useless outside of this specific and specialized condition. It is very important that this language be quasi-autonomous. They have perfected, indeed, this rather awesome terminology in order to give weight to their condition, even before it has been named or identified.

Hypochondria is a strange medley of symptoms. While it pushes the world to the margins, it also demands absolute attention from this same world; if the latter does not take heed, does not acknowledge the legitimacy of the condition, it will be coldly rejected. Hypochondriacs, hence, are masters of spatial management, their own and that of others; they let into their universe only those who will pay proper tribute to their bodily woes. The connection with monomania is clear: it checks its own idée fixe against the dubious *idées reçues* of the healthy about the sick—a difficult transaction full of misgivings and suspicion. Who, indeed, will recognize the urgency of the hypochondriac's situation?

—⁂—

Falling ill can sometimes be like falling in love. Hans Castorp in *The Magic Mountain* scrutinizes his body as lovingly as he would that of a beloved, discovering in himself unsuspected angles and curves, exhilarating strengths and weaknesses. If it has been said of love that it is the emotion most conducive to epistemological inquiry, the same can be concluded about hypochondria. As much as the lover interprets every sign

driac—devoted but manipulative nurse force most of the family problems onto a single circular track or, more precisely, into a self-regulating feedback loop." Susan Baur, *Hypochondria: Woeful Imaginings* (Berkeley: University of California Press, 1988), 73.

in the beloved, eager for clues about the progress or the decline of the romance, the hypochondriac turns himself or herself into a stethoscope, infinitely attentive to every fluctuation of the bodily routine. Even though Mann's character is granted what Alice James craved (tuberculosis is an illness with prestige: it has a name and a history), the onset of his tuberculosis offers us rare insights into the mechanisms of obsessive behavior. The "Thermometer" chapter is an extraordinarily accurate delineation of the love affair that can flare up between patient and disease. My analysis makes a contribution to the extensive Mann scholarship by presenting the "Thermometer" chapter as a case study in the paradoxically therapeutic powers of illness. Illness, when it is recognized, when it is greeted with the approving nod of an expert, can resemble a creed. Mann describes a veritable closed society, where the insiders relish a rare sense of privilege. To be ill on the magic mountain is not a handicap but the key to an elite club where members revel in their difference. This tells us a great deal about the relationship between illness and recognition. Without the stamp of approval placed on his symptoms, Hans Castorp is a mere outsider. In a broader sense, this means that for an individual who has no solid identity, illness can provide a category within which a new sense of self can develop, shielded from the heterogeneity of society's random judgments. If you are told you have consumption, you are branded as consumptive, but at least your beholder might stop there and leave it at that. *Classifying* is another word for forgetting, a welcome form of solitary confinement for those hiding behind their idée fixe. As injurious and limiting as this labeling may seem, it affords the very sense of recognition that Alice James was pining for.

On the Magic Mountain, it is not unusual for a cold to turn into a catarrh, shortly followed by deadly pneumonia. Particularly interesting in Mann's narrative is not just these types of singular transformations, but the confidence they provide in their recipients. Hans Castorp, once his fever has been acknowledged and named, begins to cut a real figure in the padded confines of the sanatorium; his triumphant fever radically changes his sense of self. Mann masterfully documents this response, showing how a doctor's diagnosis can radically alter one's rapport with the world. The patients on top of the mountain seem to be nursing rather unexceptional ailments (some of them hardly appear ill at all).They manage, however, to turn their slightly fevered bodies into autonomous worlds, separate universes upon which mysterious scenarios begin to unfold. Being ill is a beginning, not an end. The ethereal world of the sanatorium leaves behind prosaic matters (holding a job, raising a family) to occupy itself with bizarre conventions—the proper positioning of one's thermometer (upright under the tongue) becomes all-consuming. To maximize the chances of an exact reading is as important to the patient as the strategizing before a major battle. The world is suddenly filled with the need for perfect symmetry. What is central is not world events, but the monad-like quality of the sanatorium, with its tight rituals and its glorification of malady. You need to take your temperature for exactly seven minutes. If you don't? The reading might be the same, but you have betrayed the trust, you have cheated the ritual. The patients of the Berghof, like inpatients from any hospital, have their lives turned into predictable, routine events. At seven comes the first round of temperature taking, at seven-thirty the syrups, at eight breakfast, at nine the lab work. Regardless of their inherent significance, these are rites that convert the randomness of day into a near-religious ceremony. What with Doctor-God, Nurse-Priestess, and the pharmaceutical Eucharist, the hospital is organized like a church. It unifies its parishioners, teaches them a common language, and finally has them congregate at the same time to make sure they are communing in a selfsame reality. The hospital-church is teeming with sycophants, false prophets with their miracle cures, and new arrivals, freshly converted to the art of malady.

It is this experience of unmitigated conversion that turns the thermometer addict into a monomaniac: suddenly, the newly sick is capable of a radical change of allegiance, becoming fanatically receptive to situations that have nothing to do with "life," but merely with the life of the disease. The illness, suddenly an all-consuming idée fixe, displaces any previous creed or practice. Perhaps it is this power of displacement, sweeping the stage clean for a new ideology, that closes off the hypochondriac from the world, thereby providing him or her with a new order, a new harmony. He or she, indeed, begins developing a callous take on life, an indifference, even a blindness to the lives of others. Those who do not share the symptoms are discarded as trivial and commonplace.

Before launching into Mann's treatise on thermometers, I will merely add that patients who follow with such relish their bodily temperature have become natural detectives, putting together the missing details of a plot. These half-baked Aristotelians, indeed, are eager for the story's beginning and middle, but they care very little about its end. Unlike real detectives, they are indifferent to the outcome of their precious findings; the only clues that interest them pertain to their own private realm. The signs of bodily malfunction become an idée fixe comparable to that of Kierkegaard's "The Unhappiest One" or the disturbed narrator of Poe's

"Bérénice." The patient treats his own body with the same reverence as a lover's. But rather than loving something loveable, the love is aimed at the diseased, at that very thing that slowly alters the core of being. More than the simple passage from intersubjective to narcissistic love, striking in the patient are the newfound powers of concentration that enable him or her to turn the heterogeneity of experience into one single event, the progress of the illness. The body begins to radiate with new meaning. Having a fever up there on the Magic Mountain is what distinguishes the philistine from the expert, the atheist from the believer.

Hans Castorp, who has been spending a few weeks at the alpine sana-torium of Davos resting while visiting his cousin Joachim, is planning his departure back to Hamburg. But before he can get under way, "it looked, in fact, as though Hans Castorp would return home in possession of a first-class cold."[7] Castorp's first reaction is annoyance. How incongruous that a sanatorium would bring this upon him! His cousin retorts: "'Very vexatious and most unfortunate. Colds, you know, are not the thing at all, up here; they are not *reçus*. The authorities do not admit their existence. . . . [I]t is a little different with a guest—you have a right to have a cold if you want to. . . . I doubt if anyone will take enough interest in it'" (165). Hans Castorp's cousin Joachim has two reasons for being annoyed. He knows that whatever is not strictly tubercular is not taken seriously up on the mountain. But more vexatious still is that the credibility of his own private sanatorium will be questioned if his visitor returns to the healthy in worse shape than when he arrived. He is not concerned so much with Castorp's ailments, as he is with their social ramifications. It is a faux pas, a blunder, to catch a cold. They are not "*reçus*" he mumbles in French, stressing most emphatically that cold bearers are pariahs in the select so-ciety of the seriously sick. He speaks of the "authorities," "official atti-tude(s)," having the "right," "things to do down below" as opposed to "up here." He speaks as though overheard by the Big Brother of Health Control. He is submissive, even subservient, as far as the party line is con-cerned. One is ill only if the authorities have signed at the bottom of a doc-ument. His cousin moves in a gray zone, one where illness is not yet declared and therefore has no objective value. Castorp, on the other hand, is experiencing his transition to malady very differently. He is becoming conscious of his body, its inflammations, the changes in its temperature.

7. Thomas Mann, *The Magic Mountain*, trans. H. T. Lowe-Porter (1928; London: Penguin, 1969), 163. All references to *The Magic Mountain* are from this edition and are followed in the text by page numbers only.

"He felt the onset of catarrh, with oppression in the frontal sinus, and inflamed uvula; he could not breathe easily through the passage provided by nature. . . . His voice took on overnight the tonal quality of a hollow bass" (165). Suddenly, an impressive array of technical terms is being thrown around. Frontal sinus or inflamed uvula give a much more real quality to his nose or throat. His body abruptly becomes the stuff of medical encyclopedias; he, consequently, turns out to be a potential case study for the advance of medicine. Castorp even begins to speak differently, almost pompously: he now expresses himself "with dignity . . . dividing his remarks into categories" (171). He has become quite the pedant, lecturing for a public of experts and placing himself as an exemplum, perhaps even the subject of a future case study. He even speaks of himself in the third person. Like the dandy, that elusive figure, he has no trouble with dissociation: "And it will be interesting to see an examination," he tells his cousin, when the latter suggests he come along to his own monthly checkup. Even though it is indeed Joachim's privileged time with the specialist, Hans Castorp, who will be the show-and-tell star of the day, feigns scientific detachment. Castorp is striking the pose of the aloof bystander, when in fact, the day of his diagnosed fever is no ordinary day.

Hans Castorp later recalls that Madame Chauchat was wearing a golden yellow sweater that day—with large buttons and embroidered pockets. He remembers Claudia Chauchat's new sweater not because it is so memorable, but because of the radically new way in which she looks at him. Her gaze functions as a christening that anoints him with new powers: "She looked at himself [sic], unmistakably and personally . . . as though to say: 'Well, it is time: are you going?' And the eyes said thou, for that is the language of the eyes, even when the tongue uses a more formal address. . . . Was it possible she knew he was to be examined at two o'clock?" (176). She has finally returned his glance. Disease has made him worthy of her; this posturing is later confirmed by Hofrat Behrens, one of the high priests of the sanatorium, who admits: "I had my suspicions—I can tell you now—from the first day I had the . . . honour of making your acquaintance; I made a pretty shrewd guess that you were one of us" (180). There is definitely something restrictive, authoritarian even, about Behrens' inkling. "You are one of us" is a key concept in the world of obsession; it is a leitmotif echoed by the other patients when they find out that Castorp might be graced with a pair of deficient lungs. When he turns down his daily Kulmbacher beer, eyebrows are raised, and the "attention of his table-mates was attracted; they wanted to know the cause of his caprice" (171). Castorp puts on a long face and proclaims that "he would drink no beer to-day; he would drink nothing at all, or at most a swallow of water" (171). Two things are at work: the undivided attention of the other inmates, and a violent, very noticeable break in ritual. The beer, an important element in the daily ceremony, is turned down, apparently for no good reason. The cause of his caprice, he modestly answers, is that "he had a little fever—really minimal: 99.6" (171). The whole scene occurs in a very Dostoyevskian, scandal-bound fashion. Castorp pretends to find the whole scene ludicrous. He downplays the situation, *modestly* letting everyone know how much fever he has, only to relish the impact. He stages his declaration with a great sense of pace and timing: to his cousin's surprised inquiry at finding him lying inert on a chair, he "sat awhile without answering. . . . Then he said: 'Well, the latest is that I have some fever.'" Letting more time pass, so the remarkable news sinks in, "Hans Castorp let him wait a little for the answer, then delivered himself airily as follows: 'Feverish, my dear fellow, I have felt for a long time—all the time I have been up here, in fact. But at the moment it is not a matter of subjective emotion, but of fact. I have taken my temperature'" (170). Similarly, when the dining-room guests ask him about his temperature, he feigns amusement, eager to underline that it is they who are overreacting. A complicated pose is at work: Castorp needs first to stress that it is *they* who are overreacting, while he is still a controlled and bemused beholder of their whimsical worldview. There is indeed something of the pantomime in the following passage. Mann portrays the players as Punch-and-Judy figures, gesticulating wildly, while trying to drag him, the mere spectator Castorp, onto their stage. "Then how altogether ludicrous it was to see them! They shook their fingers at him, they winked maliciously, they put their heads on one side, crooked their forefingers beside their ears and waggled them in a pantomime suggestive of their delight at having found him out, who had played the innocent so long" (172). Note how Castorp's very identity is put in doubt. Cast in the role of the accused, he is chided for having "played the innocent so long." Innocent of what? Of concealing his true nature, living under false pretenses, in sum of living *up here* as though he were *down there*. Being ill is the first step toward recognition. The insiders are saying to the outsider: "Admit it, you've been one of us all along." They are telling him to cast away his pose, his elusiveness, and conform to the spirit of the group. Once the outsider is accepted, invited into the inner circle, then everything outside that circle seems irrelevant and hollow. Meaning happens from within the circle, and it is by a firmly established group, an already formed faction, that Castorp is invited in. Compliments proliferate. The women are especially delighted: as the Schoolmistress puts it, it is a scandal. Frau Stöhr admonishes him flirtatiously: "So our respected guest has some temperament too. . . . He is in the same boat with the rest of us after all" (172). In other words, illness is equated with passion and character, whereas health is bland and banal. Even the Great-aunt "gave him a meaningful glance and smile," while pretty Marusja, "who had barely looked at him up to now, leaned over and stared" (172). In the sanatorium, unlike *down there,* in the streets of Hamburg, illness is status. Illness is a form of stardom; you might make a modest debut, but then graduate to win the Most Serious Incurable Disease award.

The budding invalid, like the first-time comedian, has stage fright. Not used to being stared at, he needs to readjust his dialogue with others: unnoticed in the past, he is now scrutinized, dissected, thereby forced to reevaluate his own relationship to body and world. Earlier in the day, upon discovering that he has a temperature, Hans Castorp feels looked at and readjusts his gaze to an imagined audience. "Now and then he smiled—it was precisely as though he smiled *at* somebody" (170). He has internalized, and projected back onto himself, the other patients' aspirations. This somebody he is smiling at is not from his past, but inaugurates his entrance into a future that is somehow already codified and solacing. It is a world where judgments are suspended and where logic seems to function backwards. This reverse logic sets in when the rather daunting Directress barks at him for not having a thermometer. I transcribe the exchanges only:

"Have you measured? Why not . . . perhaps you never do take your temperature?"
"Oh, yes, Frau Director, when I have fever."
"My dear child, one takes it in the first instance *to see whether one has fever.*" (166)

The logic is indeed twisted. Castorp, the plain-clothed civilian from Hamburg, meets the uniformed Directress, with her curiously abstract reasoning, only to discover that the world of the Magic Mountain is ruled by mysterious tricks. He, as he claims, would only take his temperature to confirm an already obvious sickly state. She, on the other hand, takes it because there could always be a fever looming, waiting to be discovered. To Castorp, the body will tell you when something runs amok; to the expert, the body is just a machine, too ignorant to tell us anything, animated by mysterious forces that only mercury can adequately measure. There is nothing random in the world of the Magic Mountain. As Fräulein von Mylendonk, the Directress, explains, those who "belong below" (166) shouldn't even be meddling with the experts' insights; they should simply give in to the bewitching nature of illness.

A great deal is at work here. First, it should be noted that illness functions as a form of enchantment; it casts a spell on its victim, operating a series of metamorphoses that end up transforming the present into an alternate world, an island of insularity that functions according to its own laws. As mentioned earlier, this magic works in much the same way as an elixir of love. It is quasi-mystical, triggering irrational responses that radically alter one's relation to the real. It is this pattern that suggests the connection between hypochondria and monomania. Monomania is the act of turning the world as a whole into a fragment, a secret universe from which one's particular essence will be extracted. Clearly, the world of doctors and patients, hospitals and sanatoriums, provides microcosms where ordinary thermometers are turned into cult objects and doctors into gurus. The magic in the German word *Zauber* suggests a reenchantment of the world; the old "I" is placed under a spell, prepared to be transfigured. Recall how Castorp's first encounter with his brand-new thermometer combines romance and mystical experience: "Smiling he took up the red case and opened it. The glass instrument lay like a jewel within, fitted neatly into its red velvet groove. The degrees were marked by red strokes, the tenths by black ones; the figures were in red and the tapering end was full of glittering quicksilver" (167). Castorp does more than check the nature of his recent purchase. He looks at it as an object in and of itself, a jewel that could continue to lie in its case, with no other function than to be beautiful. Everything in the description suggests that he would rather postpone its use and enjoy its aura a little longer. The entire chapter unfolds as a strictly regimented courtship between Castorp and the thermometer. The priestly authorities of the Magic Mountain expertly handle the transition between disease and faith; they lead their patients into the mystical, making them believe that the thermometer is literally sent by the gods, a miraculous sign almost appearing on its own: "So she has sold me a thermometer. . . . But I didn't need to take the trouble to buy it; it just fell into my lap" (168). It is important that the thermometer just lands on Hans Castorp's lap. He will use that first miracle to justify subsequent ones as inevitable. Mann makes it clear that Castorp does not take his temperature, but that he is *taken* by the thermometer. His fever has religious overtones, because like a calling, it occurs outside of his will, threatening to eradicate his old self. Like a spiritual revelation, it is not something deliberate, but transcendental. He does not acquire faith, it acquires him. In other words, his illness brings him spiritual grace and understanding. "He took the article out of its case, looked at it. . . . His heart beat strong and rapidly" (168). The ritual has begun. First, you contemplate the object, then you are consumed by it. The scene revolves around the hiatus that marks the before and after of the revelation. It is when Hans Castorp finally takes possession of the thermometer, carefully putting it "in his mouth, the mercury beneath the tongue," that his idée fixe, his budding monomania, is launched. What are the symptoms? Obsessive forms of behavior surface in odd artistic manifestations, often accompanied by an intense rejection of the outside. When Castorp's cousin Joachim tries to leave the protective walls of the sanatorium, the freedom of health proves disastrous. Having pined to leave the Magic Mountain, and to return to the world of action and politics, he eventually returns to the sanatorium to die.

Castorp's extraordinary eruption onto the stage of the Berghof can be read as a petition in favor of disease over health: cure me by making me ill, he seems to be saying; lock me up so that I can be free. Castorp is not unlike Huysmans's Des Esseintes, who by turning his house into a windowless museum, a pre-Proustian corked-in universe, can be sure to erase all traces of contemporary life. This enables Hans Castorp to turn every event into a timeless conversation or an aesthetic principle, both undisturbed by extraneous infiltration. Better to live in an absolute world, albeit confining and claustrophobic, than in an imperfect and haphazard one. His desire to be without air is part death wish, part nostalgia for a womblike existence, all of which materialize in the thermometer: "He closed [his lips] firmly, that no air might get in" (168). The ritual has begun. As instructed by the ferocious temperature queen, Fräulein von Mylendonk, there is only one proper course of action: "straight under the tongue, seven minutes, four times a day, *and shut the lips well over it*" (168). Were air to interfere with the body heat, affecting it by micro-degrees, then one would never know what one's absolute temperature really is. Nothing is indeed more intense, more serious than to know *what is absolutely, exactly*. Such knowledge becomes the all-consuming aim. Why? Perhaps because such an "objective" criterion is a rarity in everyday life. Such unquestionable diagnoses are so few and far between, that having one's entire being sized up and distilled to perfection in a tiny speck of mercury creates a strange sense of bliss. Somebody knows me out there, and nobody can question the thermometer's conclusion. The inside and outside are suddenly perfectly fused, so for a fraction of time the world does not seem quite so alien or arbitrary. Here we are returning to one of the main themes of this book: namely, that the idée fixe is a drive to convert disparity into unity, and is intimately bound with the idea of a return to a euphonious universe. The thermometer is the microcosmic refraction of this perfectly controlled and rational world. It is no wonder, then, that the little glass cigar, as it is tenderly nicknamed, becomes such a gem. It is the precious gauge that promises perfect insight into Castorp's deeper self. The bliss it provides corresponds to its degree of irrefutability. In contradistinction to the world, with its unsettling polyphonies, there is nothing in the least equivocal about the reading of a thermometer.

What is happening here in terms of the idée fixe is that, while the subject is focusing all his energy on this oddly serious ceremonial of temperature taking, a larger narrative is unfolding. Besides the comical side of the self-absorbed hypochondriac, who behaves with his health the way the miser behaves toward his money—counting over and over his banknotes—there is a seriousness of purpose that underscores Castorp's naive surrender to the science of health. Somewhere, beyond the glass of the thermometer, there is a promise of truth and happiness. If Hans Castorp passes the test—hence his nervousness about taking his temperature the wrong way—he will no longer be an exile, but part of a blessed constituency. Still an intruder in the world of the sick, he will continue to behave like one until he is granted permanent citizenship in the universe of tuberculosis. So far, he can only react like an exile who mechanically conforms to half-understood rules. Why this passivity? For no better reason than that of being overawed by an imperative dictated from above. Castorp still observes a set of codes that are meaningful only by association; they are abstract, and seem to develop on their own, autonomously, leaving their subjects delightfully dependent and overreliant on authority.

Being ill, and cultivating one's own illness for the purpose of becoming the focal point, is a measure of last resort when nobody is looking anymore. It is best understood through the tension between inclusion and exclusion, difference and sameness, and is an astonishingly powerful motor in the workings of hypochondria, and by extension, of monomania.[8] Looking back at Alice James's wish ("I have longed and longed for some

---

8. "Being sick," writes Baur, "is one way of agreeing to be helpless . . . the vulnerable person simultaneously obtains the protection and attention he craves. . . . He substitutes illness, a blameless form of failure, for his sense of general worthlessness. Put another way, he desperately maintains his belief that he would be strong, independent, and lovable if only he were not sick" (Baur, *Hypochondria*, 5). In *The Magic Mountain*, illness is the direct source of integration.

palpable disease"), we can equate disease and identity. The patient vam-
pirizes her disease, living off its symptoms and exalting in the very cause
of her future destruction. Her condition has proved that like her body, she
also is out of the ordinary, deserving expert scrutiny. The hypochondriac's malady reads: I am sick, therefore I am. Conversely, the quest to
be accepted, to become *one of them*, to be intimate enough to share their
most lurid symptoms, indicates the daunting power of the illness as status symbol. After it has initially disrupted the rhythm of ordinary life, illness puts in place a series of healing mechanisms, generating a more
meaningful, richer counterexistence. It turns fragment into whole and
alienation into acceptance.

Mann's sanatorium shares the labyrinthine quality of Kafka's castle.
There are doors that cannot be opened and rituals that have to be accepted
as such, even though they are in fact quite senseless. In this autonomous
world of order, there are all kinds of totalitarian voices that resonate with
uncanny power, subtly brainwashing the credulous visitor. If the overtones of power and discipline, contained in the rhetoric of Mann's doctors and head nurses, are so unsettling, it is because they coincide with
the inmates' desperate need to conform, even to obey. As the temperature
ritual indicates, Castorp often confuses a slightly ridiculous routine with
an awe-inspiring observance: the ruling party of medical authorities,
with their grateful disciples and their fearful patients, have managed to
give symbolic meaning to some of the more unremarkable facts of everyday life. They can transfigure something as commonplace as a thermometer into a paragon of desire.

Castorp thus organizes his world around a symptom that might never
have surfaced without the approval of an eventual public. His illness,
then, is conditional upon its being considered as such. It is declarative
first, therapeutic after. It coincides with a higher healing process, one
where self-consciousness and cure are fused. Castorp can heal only if he
surrenders to the image he believes others have of him. As in traditional
analysis, there is no hope of recovery until the patient has begun verbal-
izing his or her symptom. The difference here is that the verbalization is
a projection of the desire of the other; in true Lacanian fashion, Castorp's
illness is *la maladie de l'autre*. Castorp can rest easy once he has been caught
in the delightfully escapist web of the sick.

Mann describes Castorp's conversion as a radical splitting of personality. While he protests, claiming he wants neither the inmates' attention
nor their diagnosis, he is already fully attuned to their perception of who
he is to become. Castorp's initiation to what might be called the au-

tonomous realm of the body is initially a jagged process. His resistance corresponds to the power of the attraction. By stating that he coughed *half of the night,* he provides the very details that will fuel his audience's interest, thereby confirming the gravity of his condition. The fuss made by Castorp is a Rousseauist tactic. The opening lines of Rousseau's *Rêveries*—do not read me, because you will not understand—most effectively grab the reader, making him or her want to take up the challenge: "No, no. . . . You are all mistaken, my fever is the most harmless thing in the world; I simply have a cold, my eyes run, and my chest is stopped up. I have coughed half of the night; it is thoroughly unpleasant of course" (172).

The disclaimers are pro forma, and his protestations are superlatives in disguise. In the same breath, he dismisses his fever, while adding that he coughed all night. He knows that his cough is a crucial ingredient to his new persona, but is still hesitant to surrender to this embryonic self by identifying with it right away.

Specialists who have examined obsessive forms of behavior—bibliophilia, compulsive art collecting—that cause the subject to relinquish everything in order to possess the coveted object, claim that the obsessive type finds in his or her fixation "an emotional coherence" that stems from turning "what once had to be passively endured" to something they are able to collect and control. Whatever trauma this act of collecting goes back to is now "overcome through active countermeasures."[9] Collecting paintings or collecting symptoms is a genuine pastime, an identity-forming hobby that keeps nothingness at bay by offering a never-ending supply of concerns.[10] The collector, and this is true of the patient with hypochondriac tendencies, is an avid reader of symptoms. Like the reader of mystery novels, he or she identifies violently with his or her collection, gathering clues, postponing diagnoses, and mostly turning the disease into a religion that will provide a new existential core.

Mann's great insight is that, while this baroque liturgy is at work, a far more significant event is taking place. Hans Castorp is slowly turning his

9. Werner Muensterberger, *Collecting: An Unruly Passion* (New York: Harcourt Brace, 1995), 43.

10. This is how an anonymous collector describes his passion: "I am a sponge. . . . I get a feeling for [a particular historical] period. I want to read [certain documentary source materials]. . . . It is like a lust. It is like a burning force. I go into this or that store and try to scoop the whole thing in. I go with my hands along all those things. I cannot be discriminating. I have to have it. . . . It's a hedge against nothingness. . . . There is always something new, a never-ending supply. All those books. I am an expert. . . . Taking in the whole world, having a membrane around the world" (ibid., 45).

body into a world apart. His sense of time and place is gradually shifting from the particular to the universal, and his relationship to experience is passing from the material to the immaterial, from the mutable to the absolute. The thermometer is a crucial moment of meeting between the two worlds: the time it takes for the mercury to travel from left to right on the see-through scale corresponds to the passage from this world to (so it appears to the inmates of the Berghof) the privileged and insular world of essences. In paradoxical fashion, the loss of liberty that accompanies the onset of disease coincides with another type of freedom, one that could be described as the willful surrender to a totalizing universe. Castorp's experience of the sanatorium is an adventure in essentialism, for to quote Marcuse's definition of this phenomenon, it entails "the abstraction and isolation of the one true Being from the constantly changing multiplicity of appearances."[11] For a brief moment, when all eyes are focused on Hans Castorp, it is clear that he has turned his healthy past into a negligible episode of his development. And when the guests put down their silverware to contemplate him with newly approving eyes, what they behold is somebody who finally embodies *their* Truth: he has become their essence, the vindication of a lifestyle where illness becomes the most solemn manifestation of true art.

11. Herbert Marcuse, "The Concept of Essence," in *Negations: Essays in Critical Theory,* trans. J. J. Shapiro (London: Penguin, 1983), 43.

7 Elias Canetti's *Auto-da-Fé*

The Scholarly Malady

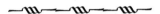

For nothing contributes so much to tranquilize the mind as
a steady purpose,—a point on which the soul may fix its
intellectual eye.

> Mary Shelley, *Frankenstein*

The tablecloth-lunatic is dazzling white. . . . Some people
come to her to get order. She is irresistible. She says little,
but whatever she says has the dogmatic force of an entire
church. It is not certain that she prays, she is her own
church. When she celebrates the dazzling white, one is
plunged into shame for living so long a life of filth.
Compared with her, everything is filth, denials are futile . . .
It is as though one had all her tablecloths inside, strictly
folded, never spread, on a dazzling white heap, forever,
forever.

> Elias Canetti, *Earwitness*

Knowledge has freed us from superstition and beliefs.
Knowledge makes use always of the same names,
preferably Graeco-Latin, and indicates by these names
actual things. Misunderstandings are impossible.

> Elias Canetti, *Auto-da-Fé*

Elias Canetti's one-time model and mentor, the great Viennese
satirist Karl Kraus, was once compared to a Don Quixote who had been
robbed of his Sancho Panza.[1] Kraus's quest for the absolute, his in-

---

1. It is Claudio Magris who thus describes Kraus in "The Many People That Make Up a

domitable pursuit of Truth, turned out to be lethal: having never found a down-to-earth companion, a Sancho who could rein in his extremism, he was eventually destroyed. Fortunately for us, Canetti, the great Bulgarian-born, English-bred, and Viennese-educated author, managed to channel his own quixotic nature through writing. Crafting a novel about a monomaniacal character (the sinologist Peter Kien) actually rescued him from the potentially lethal power of books. With eerie acuity, Canetti taps into the syndrome we have been following throughout this book. Why do we get seduced by absolutes? Throughout this study the question of ordering the world into a firm principle has been central. Flaubert's ability to turn life into a perfect sentence, Eliot's canvassing of Dorothea's will to asceticism, Janet's mystically obsessed women—all have in common the impulse that drives them to cure ambiguity with order, ambivalence with ideology. When it comes to Canetti's sinologist, all the symptoms present in the previous chapters seem to manifest themselves with an even greater urgency.

Canetti's novel reaches far beyond the universe of the compulsive scholar. His case study helps us grasp our own uncanny ability to float in and out of hidden power structures. What draws us to endorse so compulsively, so contradictorily, the most outrageous political views or the most irrational of relationships? Canetti muses on the alchemy of these compulsions, taking us to the heart of an escapism blind to its own teleology. Kien, like Eliot's Casaubon, uses his knowledge not to grasp the world but to flee from it. Pathologically dependent on a system of classification, he frantically buries himself in the act of possessing and organizing his books to dispel life's complexities. To him, as one critic noted, the essence of a work or of a text "consists in structure, unity, the dynamics of a form of creativity."[2] This dynamics places meaning secondary to the therapeutic value of structure itself, allowing method to overrule any quest for truth.[3] Canetti's works are filled with monomaniacs, creatures haunted by an idée fixe. As Claudio Magris put it, these monoma-

---

Writer: Canetti and Cacania," in *Essays in Honor of Elias Canetti,* trans. Michael Hulse (New York: Farrar, Straus and Giroux, 1987), 277.

2. Manfred Schneider, "The Cripples and Their Symbolic Bodies," in *Essays in Honor of Canetti,* ed. Hulse, 31.

3. Schneider explains the obsessive impulse not as a drive to achieve something particular, but as the act of reorganizing what has been jumbled. "Kien's soul is his work, he labors obsessively over it, [it is] his personal myth. . . . This myth . . . is a dynamic power whose energies are unknown but whose structure remains constant: it is a kind of spending of physical powers in the service of a second, symbolic, and complete body," ibid., 32–33.

niacs' devotion to truth, their allegiance to one single guiding principle, entranced and repelled Canetti from the outset of his writing life.[4] *Auto-da-Fé*[5] was originally going to be one volume of an eight-part cycle entitled, in Balzacian fashion, *The Human Comedy of Madmen*. Each part would document a particular form of obsession. Initially named *Kant Catches Fire* and then *The Bookman*, *Auto-da-Fé* pivoted around Kien (formerly named Kant) and his idée fixe—the library that had become the center of his world. Kien's single-minded devotion to his library, his conviction that life ends beyond the printed page, might well be the most extreme and yet instructive form of monomania encountered in our case studies. Why instructive? Canetti's preoccupation with forms of power, with the preternatural ability with which individuals surrender to fanaticism, is rooted in his own bookish entanglements. In one of the most ekphrastic examples of life imitating literature, Canetti recounts how he himself, after completing *Auto-da-Fé*, was almost destroyed, having turned into a nearly incapacitated offshoot of his own literary creation. To those around Canetti, it was increasingly evident that Kien's monomania was becoming his own. As he narrates in his memoir *The Play of Eyes*, Veza, his companion at the time, "had lived in fear that I would never find my way out of my novel. She had seen how deeply I had entangled myself in it and how much it had taken out of me."[6] What concerned Veza most was Canetti's identification with the radical forms of behavior he had staged in the book. She worried about "[his] reclusiveness . . . [his] admiration for individuals that were completely different . . . [his] desire to break off all ties with a degraded mankind." She saw an individual increasingly drawn to Platonic "purity," to an otherworldliness that he was enthusiastically, and by no means critically, correlating with mania. Indeed, not only was he adopting his character's aloofness—"when I did see [Veza], I was monosyllabic and morose"—but he had also taken to viewing "the manias of some people [he] knew as perfect works of art."[7]

This exchange with Veza occurs right after Canetti has killed off the main character of the novel. Kien and his library have just been engulfed in a sea of flames, consumed by fire and by the laughter that pours out of the mad sinologist. Canetti has murdered his hero, but it is he who claims

---

4. In 1974 he wrote *Earwitness*, a curious overview of fifty types of monomanias.

5. It was published in German as *Die Blendung* (*The Blinding*), but was also known as *The Tower of Babel*.

6. Elias Canetti, *The Play of the Eyes*, trans. R. Manheim (New York: Farrar Straus Giroux, 1986), 13.

7. Ibid.

to be perishing, sentenced to depression by his own fictional decision. It is his turn to succumb to the profound mental breakdown that affected Kien throughout. With the destruction of the perfect world that Canetti designed for his professor, there was no longer any way to funnel his own need for order. Now that his creation was complete, he had lost Kien's idiosyncratically perfect work of art. The symmetry between art and life was gone. The writer was left with the real world, and it paralyzed him:

Kant Catches Fire, as the novel was then titled, had left me ravaged. I could not forgive myself for burning the books . . . I felt that the same thing had happened to me. I felt that I had sacrificed not only my own books but also those of the whole world, for the sinologist's library included everything that was of importance to the world. . . . All that had burned, I had let it happen, I had made no attempt to save any part of it; what remained was a desert, and I myself was to blame. For what happens in that kind of book is not just a game, it is reality. . . . Catastrophe had taken root in me and I could not shake it off. (4)

The lines between art and life have eroded. Canetti is "ravaged" because he has burned Kien's precious library. He has gotten rid of the perfect paradise of books, that very haven that would restore meaning to a problematic life. He blames himself because he has "let it happen," and made "no attempt to save any part of it." Oddly enough, Canetti has co-opted Kien's inability to distinguish between fact and fiction, thought and world. The claim that such a "book is not a game," but "reality," underscores the unsettlingly close relationship between the symbolic world of art and life. Salman Rushdie was to note that Canetti had "donated both his sense of privacy and his priceless library to the central character of *Auto-da-Fé.*" He tells of Canetti's house in Hampstead. "Inside this house, I'm told, is to be found a library of staggering proportions; books rising in Himalayan splendor from floor to ceiling, books occupying every available inch of wall space, a Babel of books."[8] At the same time that Canetti praises mania as a privileged, highly aestheticized realm, he senses that this realm has begun to consume him. He holds on to it by gradually having fiction spill into his present. "The desert I had created for myself began to cover everything. Never have I felt the threat to the world in which we live more intensely than after Kien's death."[9] Writing had provided Canetti, as it had Flaubert, with a marvelous sense of invi-

8. Salman Rushdie, "The Worm of Learning Turns, Swallows Its Tail, and Bites Itself in Half," in *Essays in Honor of Canetti,* 83.
9. Canetti, *Play of the Eyes,* 4.

olability; art, no matter how gruesome its subject, always transmuted potential into fact. Conversely, instead of being an array of liberating possibilities, life, with its openness, its range, was a threat, a destabilizing fall into indeterminacy. The great promise of writing was that it could manipulate all this murky instability into something irrefutable. Writing, like Kien's systematic studying, offers a redemptive counterworld. But there is a disquieting twist to this scenario, for when Canetti finally completes his work, instead of being solaced by the conclusive nature of his character's death, he finds his sanity in jeopardy. Now that his madman is gone, he develops a strange infirmity, as though he cannot tolerate the blunted afterlife of creation. His wife Veza, the Sancho of this tale, finally explodes, berating him for living a life that has become an unbearable novel. "Once she lost control and cried out: 'Now that he's dead, your book character has taken possession of you. You're just like him. Maybe that's your way of grieving for him.'" It is unclear how much of this diatribe is staged. Canetti basks rather ostentatiously in his own art-induced crisis. The sickly interdependency between book and self is nonetheless profound. It takes us right to the core of the novel. What happens when you think you have taken absolute control over your life and then, suddenly, you realize that this control is entirely fictitious, even dangerous? Kien's plight—the loss of supremacy over his intellectual empire—turns out to be Canetti's. The act of writing is one of godlike control; it has the cathartic sense of closure that life denies us. What Veza feared most in these curious developments (or what Canetti despised most in her judgment) was that he would be terrified by the very closure he had instated. Closure would induce a terrible *horror vacui*, but any rewriting would be counterproductive in a different way: it would diminish the absolute power of fiction and relativize the relationship between writing and life: "[Veza] was infinitely patient with me, but I resented her relief over Kant's death. . . . [S]he feared above all that I'd changed my mind, that the last chapter wasn't right, that for one thing the style jarred with the rest of the book, so I'd *torn it up*. Kant had come back to life, the whole thing was going to start over again."[10] The autobiographical script Canetti describes and sets in motion is about both this nightmarish osmosis between life and art and the deep-seated psychological roots that compel individuals to construct airtight lives in the first place.[11]

10. Ibid., 10.

11. This has been described as literature's ability to counteract the collapse of the symbolic. Literary representation simulates an orderly worldview that is absent from life as we

The story of Peter Kien, his psychiatrist brother George, and his tyrannical wife Therese, is about the relationship between abstract truth and its impossible translation into experience. One of the great achievements of the book is to document the workings of a utopian space that we have all craved but that is bound to unravel into the greatest of nightmares. Canetti presents masterfully one of the most intoxicating of human desires: the temptation to substitute the triteness of the everyday with something irrefutable, something that endows our lives with a sense of unequivocal resolution and pure bliss. Whether it is the building of a perfect library or the consummate mastery of an argument, *Auto-da-Fé* makes us realize how dependent these fantasies are on obsessive attachments. Obsession, once again, reveals itself as a double-edged sword; it is restorative and destructive at the same time.

Canetti makes it all too clear that any obsessive drive stems from the belief in an illusory reward—the reward of a new immortal self. Such a promise is hard to resist; next to such geometry, all other purposes rapidly pale. Kien might very well repel us, but not before arousing a certain complicated envy. The peace of his universe, the unambiguous confidence in his scholarly findings, are precious assets that we rarely achieve in our own lives. A world without the clutter of repetitive tasks, without the petty obligations of routine, cannot leave us wholly indifferent. And because Kien's is a world turned entirely onto itself, it operates at first, something that also applies to the reader's fantasy, as a rescue operation, one that defends against the inevitable formlessness, of life, the relentless disintegration of relationships.[12] It is not surprising, then, that Canetti had invested himself to such a degree in his hero's therapeutic pathology. Likewise, the very act of reading *Auto-da-Fé* cannot leave us indifferent to our own ways of courting unreality.

Scholarship, even though it can track relentlessly the course of human life, can be a fierce escape from the human. Kien's dogged blindness to the world around him forces us to ponder the self-ruling desire behind a

---

know it. As Kristeva puts it, "aesthetic and particularly literary creation, and also religious discourse in its imaginary, fictional essence, set forth a device whose prosodic economy, interaction of characters, and implicit symbolism constitute a very faithful semiological representation of the subject's battle with symbolic collapse. . . . The literary representation possesses a real and imaginary effectiveness that comes closer to catharsis than to elaboration; it is a therapeutic device used in all societies throughout the ages." Julia Kristeva, *Black Sun: Depression and Melancholia,* trans. Leon Roudiez (New York: Columbia University Press, 1989), 24.

12. See again Kristeva, *Black Sun,* for her description of the depressive affect as a defense against parceling, "a strategy that returns a measure of cohesion to the self."

life devoted to learning. How can one wish to excavate a culture and yet use it as an ironclad shield against experience? Kien, for one, cannot fathom human frailty; in fact, the only people he can interact with are potential clones of himself—future sinologists. Children, he muses, "ought to be brought up in some important private library. Daily conversations with none but serious minds, an atmosphere at once dim, hushed and intellectual, a relentless training in the most careful ordering both of time and space" (12). Note how the mundane and the everyday are to be hidden from the child, forced to abandon the nursery for the library, and taught the ferocious art of space and time management, designed to minimize time spent away from books.[13] Knowing each volume's place, counting, checking, and stubbornly overseeing is the only form of intimacy he should ever have to learn. In Kien's system, the child will actually be brought up in the library. Kien, the great strategist of library art, knows that the outward order of volumes corresponds to a far greater ordinance: the correspondence of truth and knowledge. So the maniacally ordering impulse that propels Kien to order and reorder his books is not simply the therapeutic ritual that one might encounter in obsessive personalities; it is also Kien's encouraging way of talking to his "troops" before he consults them in earnest.[14] As soon as he returns from his walks, from his visits to bookstores, he rushes back to his brood to check anxiously on the status of his shelves. He treats the rows as schoolchildren, disciplining them lovingly into straight and unchanging lines.

It is the linear nature of this library that puts Kien in the category of obsessive systematizers. Like stamp collectors, who are said to feel deeply the gaps in their sets, Kien also has a phobic relationship to what is not there, a deep disgust toward the "absent" book, the interrupted perfect line.[15] Not only does nothing stand out *physically* from his shelves, but the

13. There is no question that only boys and men have been included here. Woman could only wreck Kien's pristine environment. Therefore I use mainly the masculine pronoun in this chapter.

14. I shall return to this later in this chapter. The collection of essays, *Essential Papers on Obsessive-Compulsive Disorder,* ed. Dan J. Stein and Michael H. Stone (New York: New York University Press, 1997), is an exhaustive presentation of this condition from the tenth century to the present. One of the earliest discussions about obsessive-compulsive disorder is that of the Persian Muslim medical writer Najab Ud din Unhammad, who "described a ruminative state of doubt. Unhammad called the condition *Murrae Souda* and felt it stemmed from the excessive love of philosophy and law." Michael H. Stone, "Introduction: The History of Obsessive-Compulsive Disorder from the Early Period to the Turn of the Century," in Stein and Stone, *Essential Papers,* 19.

15. Karl Abraham, "Contribution to the Theory of the Anal Character" (1921), in *Selected Papers* (New York: Basic Books, 1953), 1:370—92; quoted in Stein and Stone, *Essential Papers,*

shelves are themselves monotonously straight and uniform: "Nowhere did a table, a cupboard, a fireplace interrupt the multicolored monotony of the bookshelves" (23). Space has been contained, compressed, concentrated into these fiercely rigid containers of knowledge. Recall the dark rooms in Casaubon's house; darkness, like monotony, guards the eyes from temptations. There is nothing to look at, nothing to covet, save the venerable books.

If we examine this curious relationship between uniformity and sanity, we find the following. Whereas a "healthy" mind will dread monotony, trying to escape at any cost a patterned and repetitious train of life, the compulsive collector can envisage meaning only through the constraints of predictability and control. Just as the stamp collector loathes the gap, Kien cannot endure any crack in his perfectly ordered universe. Any rift or fissure will rip open his hidden self, revealing him as what he dreads being: human, all-too-human. Canetti describes his character "holding on" to truth, single-mindedly exchanging plurality for singularity. At all costs, the rift must be solidified into one body, for unifying two divergent elements will save the mind from decadent dispersion, turning it back into a blissful *esprit de synthèse*.

Kien abhorred falsehood; from his earliest childhood he had held fast to the truth. . . . Knowledge and truth were for him identical terms. You draw closer to the truth by shutting yourself off from mankind. . . . His ambition was to stick stubbornly in the same manner of existence. Not for a mere month, not for a year, but for the whole of his life, he would be true to himself." (15–16)

What does Kien mean by falsehood? It is anything that is multifaceted, subject to interpretation. The liar, like the novelist, or even the passer-by ("every passer-by is a liar. . . . They change their faces with every moment" [15]) is a master of manipulation. He tells at least two stories at the same time. Kien's *Emile*, if he were ever to write a treatise on education, would be based entirely on memorization. An anti-Montaigne if there ever was one, Kien understands how memorization will protect the child from

---

84. Abraham demonstrates very convincingly that the obsessive personality has a rich relationship to viewing his or her own possessions. He stresses, for example, "the pleasure in looking at one's own mental creations, letters, manuscripts, etc., or completed works of all kinds," 84. There is an intensely satisfying relationship in running one's eyes across the smooth bookshelves or on the impeccably fluffed-up pillows, etc. These "tamed" objects are confirmations that the world is in order. Abraham goes on to discuss anal fixations, but what concerns us here is the utterly gratifying pleasure derived from an uninterrupted orderliness.

making up his own mind. With every memorized page, the reader would receive another sheet of pure reason, one where there is no need to sort true from false. It is the sorting out that destabilizes the world. Decision making belongs to a different moment in time, one that Kien's reader should have no need for. Kien "sticks stubbornly" to habit because this will keep him the master of any decision making, sole judge allowed to rule out the necessity of human interchange. It is not surprising, in the words of William Donahue, that Kien selects such "abstruse Oriental texts"; this guarantees that "all semiotic power emanates from the master interpreter who fixes for all time a heretofore incomplete or corrupt text." Not only that, but "as long as no one can challenge his claim to the title of the 'world's foremost sinologist,' he meets with little opposition."[16]

Kien's self does not exist outside of his ritualized gestures; it is merely measured against a host of mechanical actions that end up confirming not that he is a person, but that he is a person only because he has completed a self-imposed task. This suggests that to be awarded a self it suffices to repeat identical gestures every day. Sameness, then, is the ruling ingredient of identity. Selfhood is a closed book; it cannot be viewed in terms of a give-and-take situation; it allows no growth, no expansion, and no change; it remains singularly static. No wonder that the outside world is conceived of as "a lie" (in the Platonic sense). To such rigid characters, it can be only a lie; truth is unmixed, unchanging, not prey to chance, but the result of a self-imposed design. This regimented view of the world makes new experiences not merely superfluous, but threatening. Anything that cannot remain identical must be done without.

The library is beguiling; its contents mimic scores of conversations with the world, each book sending Kien to another corner of the planet without ever having to leave his desk. The books pose and answer riddles only he can properly unravel, casting him as the unchallenged master and servant of knowledge. Canetti explores this desire for unilateral mastery. What is it about being a scholar (Kien is *the* great unchallenged sinologist) that turns isolation into a singular form of omniscience? Is it that books do not talk back and that unlike our human interlocutors, they enable us to use them to fill in our own mental deficiencies and gaps? His books do not merely become part of him, they shield him from any self-examination. The remarkable description of his library is one of the most chilling

16. William Collins Donahue, *The End of Modernism: Elias Canetti's "Auto-da-Fé"* (Chapel Hill: University of North Carolina Press, 2001), 62.

episodes in the book. This self-willed prison is his refuge from Therese's gradual takeover of his life. Note the contrast between the immaterial library and the rest of the world: "It was as if he had barricaded himself against the world: against all material relations, against all terrestrial needs, had built himself an hermitage, a vast hermitage" (67). Up to the last dramatic scene, when Kien piles his books against the door, burying himself alive, the library is analogous to an army, an almighty fortress. It delivers him from "all material relations," most dramatically against Therese and her starched body. The library thwarts the very notion of exchange: human exchange, exchange of ideas, indeed anything that suggests interaction. Canetti goes on to describe it as being so vast that "it would hold those few things on this earth which are more than this earth itself, more than the dust to which our life at last returns as if he had closely sealed it and filled it with those things alone" (67). What is meant by "more than this earth itself?" How can the library, allegedly Kien's hubristic tower of Babel, exceed the earth that has inspired its contents? Precisely because the earth is repellent to Kien; it breathes like an animal; it cannot be controlled, shelved, or filed.[17] The library, conversely, has its own autonomous energy. But this energy is slowly being drained by Therese, the novel's great evil force, and George, Kien's brother and antithesis. Therese appeals to Kien because she is the embodiment of order. Her body, far from seducing with its curves, dazzles Kien because it is covered by a perfectly starched uniform. It displays no superfluous movement. Therese's genius is to have understood the way to Kien's heart; this self-contained creature treats his books as though they were deities.

Books can be antidotes to an unpredictable life. As Kien barks to his brother, the psychoanalyst, his books must never be confused with novels. They represent pure learning, not "feminine" stories. His books are about what does not change, whereas novels and memoirs are about flux and the fickle human condition: "They teach us to think ourselves in other people's places. Thus we acquire taste for change. The personality becomes dissolved in pleasing figments of imagination. The reader accom-

17. Judith Ryan points out that as educated people were becoming increasingly aware that they might simply be, in the words of Ernst Mach, "a bundle of sensations" (rather than stable, reasonable, and predictable beings), "panic began to spread. If there was no real distinction between subject and object, the familiar structures of language seemed to have been eroded. Many contemporaries felt virtually paralyzed, unable either to act or to speak." Judith Ryan, *The Vanishing Subject: Early Psychology and Literary Modernism* (Chicago: University of Chicago Press, 1991), 21.

modates every point of view. Willingly he yields to the pursuit of other people's goals and loses sight of his own. . . . Novels should be prohibited by the state" (42). Novels make us dissatisfied with the status quo; they blur the borders of our personalities, making it quite clear that our self is not a permanent condition. Kien inveighs against fiction because it returns us to an in-between state of being. Learning to understand every point of view is perverse, relativistic, and a sign of betrayal.[18] Kien speaks like the religious fanatic who cannot bear to hear about other religions. His violence also betrays an inexplicable fear of distraction and diversion. Having already proclaimed that he does not take holidays, that there are no Sundays in his life, he treats novels as the Sabbath of books—dangerous wastes of precious time.

Kien's brother George, the antithesis of Peter, is a lady's man, a gynecologist turned psychoanalyst. He explains to his brother that he does not learn by books but from others. He lets the experiences around him mold his present and has no fixed philosophy, only one that is as transient as the moods of his patients.[19] Kien interprets his brother's openness, his empathy, as a vulgar quest for sensations. Because he cannot live by knowledge alone, he becomes the predator of human sensations. The following outburst is directed against the power of stories that turn people inside out (the word "change" keeps surfacing), making them live vicariously. "Memoirs are not interesting. . . . [Y]ou are curious, I am not. You hear new stories every day, and now, for a change, you would like one from me. I renounce all such stories. . . . You live by lunatics, I by my books. Which is the more estimable? I could live in a cell, I carry my books in my head, you need a whole lunatic asylum. . . . The truth is you're a woman. You live for sensations" (436). Note the religious overtones: Kien has "renounced" stories. He could live in a cell like a monk. He could part

18. These were the anti-decadent theories of fin-de-siècle Germany. Recall Nordau's *Degeneration* (Lincoln: University of Nebraska Press, 1968). The book was originally published as *Entartung* in 1892; inspired by Lombroso's writings on crime, it proclaimed that the likes of Oscar Wilde and his followers should be examined for signs of degeneracy. Their artistry was the medical offshoot of physical decay: whatever smacked of talent was in fact sickness, brought about by bad digestion and nervous exhaustion.

19. "Thus he lived simultaneously in numberless different worlds. Among the mentally diseased he grew into one of the most comprehensive intellects of his time. He learnt more from them than he gave them. They enriched him with their unique experience; he merely simplified them in order to make them healthy" (398). Canetti stresses the pliancy of Kien's brother, who points out that his learning comes directly from experience, not from books. The slightly shocking mention that he was once a gynecologist—dealing in bodies, in the health of sexual and reproductive organs—serves again to differentiate the two brothers.

easily with the world since he carries his books in his head. Kien has contempt for his brother's predatory interest in other people; the latter feeds on his patients because his own blood is too thin to endure a contemplative life. Kien's contempt is directed against "weakness"; it is weak to need the company of others. One must survive by one's wits alone.[20]

By setting the two brothers as counterfigures, Canetti continues playing with the Sancho/Don Quixote models. The psychiatrist is rooted in the real, his brother uprooted by the ideal. It is George who analyzes his brother's eccentric lifestyle as a Kantian way of life. Kien has indeed created a parallel universe for himself, forcing the world to bend to his own daily routines. George likens his brother's ability to turn reality into a self-contained world to Kant's duty for its own sake. "Of course I shall never bring myself to that complete self-abnegation, to that attitude of work for work's sake, of duty for duty's sake, which Immanuel Kant—and long before other thinkers—Confucius, have demanded and which you have achieved. I'm afraid I'm too weak for that" (427). Interestingly, the psychiatrist flatters his brother by invoking his own inferiority. He cannot live a life of monkish self-denial, he cannot abstract himself from human constraints, and this makes him weak. It is difficult to forget that Canetti wanted his novel to be called *Die Blendung* (The Blinding). Who is being blinded here? How is it that Kien's blindness to the world is used as a model of strength? Canetti does not delve into Kien's past, so we are never quite aware of the roots of his flight from the world. We are so utterly locked into Kien's consciousness that there is no clue as to what his torture might have been. As was suggested at the outset, Canetti was the first to be drawn into his character's misanthropy. Kien's proceeding

---

20. Here I will quote David Shapiro. Rigid characters, to his mind, are individuals whose contempt corresponds to a covert respect for power: "an individual who respects power and the powerful above all and despises weakness and helplessness, who tyrannizes those beneath him and is submissive to, wishes to 'fuse' with, the powerful ones above." David Shapiro, *Autonomy and Rigid Character* (New York: Basic Books, 1981), 103. Shapiro's theory can be summarized briefly in the following way. Some individuals never manage to extricate themselves from early powerful influences (parents, mentors, etc.). A "healthy" subject eventually internalizes moral imperatives, making them his or her own, whereas the weaker character continues to perceive these imperatives as dictated from the outside. Consequently, instead of having a flexible relationship to power, he or she continues to impose harsh regulations upon himself or herself. The rigid person, Shapiro argues, "lives under the authority of his will, it is also true that he himself imposes that authority, that he respects it, identifies its aims and purposes as his own, and guards them even against his own feelings" (ibid., 73). Kien despises the fact that his brother takes his cues from the world; he is convinced that his own solitary confinement, his unwavering willpower, are proof of strength and power.

through life with blinders is his way of cutting himself off from the new and carving a space that cannot be occupied by others.

Psychologists who have worked on obsessive natures, on rigid and autonomous temperaments, have stressed such mechanisms of self-protection. Shapiro makes a compelling case when he singles out the "abstract attitude," that capacity to

regard a thing conceptually, as a member of a class or of various possible classes, and to consider it from various points of view, without regard for its incidental context—implies a detachment from that thing and an objective attitude toward it. Such an attitude toward what is external also implies a sense of the self's separateness from it and therefore an objective sense of the self.[21]

Nothing is more uncanny than this "objective" sense of the self. Canetti is interested in a mind that is capable only of envisioning things conceptually, objectively.[22] The most striking example of this occurs at the novel's outset. Kien appears on a sidewalk, outraged by a scene he happens to witness. One man is asking directions of another. His questions are met by absolute silence. Losing patience with his interlocutor's reticence, the man lashes out at the silent figure, insulting him and pushing him. Only at the end of this shadowy, Kafkaesque episode does Kien realize that the man was talking to him. As Shapiro notes, these "rigid types" are so engrossed in their deliberations, they have gone so far in their research-oriented lives, that they become oblivious of their selves, turning into ascetics of sorts. Kien has lost himself to knowledge, he has become so utterly disconnected from his own being that any encounter becomes a cerebral riddle-solving exercise. Armed with a thesis, an antithesis, and a synthesis, the Kien-like character turns the world into an anonymous canvas, one that has a subject but no subjectivity.

Canetti draws his reader into the odd perfection of this solitary disengagement. What emotion does he tap into to make the reader actually identify with Kien's despair when his life is disrupted? How can he lead us so effortlessly into this "perfect world" of silence and scholarship? Is Kien's blissful bookishness a variation of Flaubert's retreat into form, or of Worringer's blindfolding abstraction? The reader is suddenly hit by the

21. Ibid., 38.

22. As one reader of this manuscript has pointed out, it seems rather incongruous on the part of Canetti to have chosen a scholar of Chinese. Nothing could be more antithetical to Chinese writings (notoriously unsystematic and dealing with nothing but opposing interpretations) than this alleged objectivity.

same dread of chaos that plagued Flaubert. Canetti's power is to have sensed this longing for balance and status quo. What he has done is to lure us into a symmetrical peace that is impossible to achieve outside of art. So when George calls Kien a Kantian, he is really referring to his brother's ability to return to an undivided realm of absolute safety, a strangely innocuous universe from which desire is absent.[23]

Canetti was known for his ability to surrender his entire soul to a friendship; in one of the most moving chapters of *The Play of the Eyes*, he reveals to what extent he was not only prone to personality cults, but was content to lose himself in the other's "perfection": "What was it about Sonne that made me want to see him every day, that made me look for him every day, that inspired an addiction such as I had not experienced for any other intellectual? . . . And he seldom addressed me directly. By speaking in the third person, he distanced himself from his surroundings."[24] It turns out that he had initially mistaken Sonne for his role model Karl Kraus. Canetti explains not only that he became addicted to this man's pronouncements, but that he was seduced by the very way in which Sonne was capable of remaining somewhat immaterial. Like Kien, Sonne lived in the third person; he conveyed nothing about himself, but merely spoke through the Idea. "I knew nothing about Sonne; he consisted entirely of his statements, so much so that the prospect of discovering anything else about him would have frightened me. No particulars of his life were bandied about, no illness, no complaint. He was *ideas*, so much so that one noticed nothing else."[25] Canetti's infatuation with Sonne displays the same impersonal quality that was so important to Kien. Sonne is a head without a world; Canetti's friendship is not about loving an individual, but about loving an immutable essence. Ultimately, it is about the power that radiates from such certainty. Sonne does not live within the realm of particulars; he only trades in ideas. Canetti is relieved to know nothing about his mentor; and by never complaining about illness, Sonne never appears as a body, an individual cursed by physical weaknesses and frailties. He is as unreal as one of Kien's volumes, and

23. Kant's description of the beautiful corresponds to Kien's storehouse of knowledge; both elicit a loss of desire, an absence of willing. They absorb the self so that it coincides with a greater project, a neutral community that has absorbed selfish desires. Terry Eagleton has referred disparagingly to Kant's formal world as a realm of "cloistral security:" "The beautiful representation . . . is an idealized material form safely defused of sensuality and desire. . . . The subject can find rest in this cloistral security, but its rest is strictly temporary." Terry Eagleton, *The Ideology of the Aesthetic* (Oxford: Blackwell, 1990), 91.

24. Canetti, *Play of the Eyes*, 133.

25. Ibid., 140–141.

this is precisely what Canetti desperately seeks out. In his presence, Canetti finds certainty. He sees the absolute divide between right and wrong, good and evil, and sticks by it, relieved that Truth has descended upon him, imparted by this miraculous deus ex machina. "He saw a world divided into good and evil; there could never be any doubt as to what things were good and what things were evil. . . . [H]e painted a picture of stunning clarity which I was almost ashamed to accept as a gift in return for which nothing was asked of me but an open ear."[26] Sonne gives clarity to a darkened world. By basking in the rays of his wisdom (*Sonne* means sun in German), Canetti holds on to this man as his model, exchanging his nightmarish doubts for the blinding illuminations of this "perfect sage."

Returning to Kien's selfless life (or his lifeless self), it is striking how Canetti presents it as a therapy against the foreboding decisions that mar most people's existence. Kien reads and collects in order not to surrender to the weakness of mankind. He does just what Nietzsche, in an attack against Schopenhauer, interpreted as a cowardly retreat into aesthetic contemplation, labeling the latter's retreat from the world a convenient therapy against desire. Compare his interpretation to Kien's tragicomic wedding night:

Of few things does Schopenhauer speak with greater assurance than he does of the effect of aesthetic contemplation: he says of it that it counteracts *sexual* "interestedness," like lupulin and camphor; he never wearied of glorifying *this* liberation from the "will" as the great merit and utility of the aesthetic condition.[27]

What Nietzsche sees as escape from Eros, as endorsement of the aesthetic for its own sake, Canetti paints as the flight into the solidly bound universe of books. Kien is capable of translating all life into contemplation. His will orders the world into a battlefield where the division between good and evil, friend and enemy, are perfectly clear.

From the perspective of Kien's brother the psychiatrist, Kant and Kien have both been sedated by their ability to close themselves to experience. Both have taken refuge from the unknown, turning away from all dynamic and risk-ridden encounter. Theirs is not a dialogical, but a monological, if not monomaniacal, course. The quest for knowledge is not the quest for the new, it is a regressive voyage home, a nostalgic return to an

26. Ibid., 149.

27. Nietzsche, *On the Genealogy of Morals*, bk. 3, no. 6, trans. Walter Kaufmann and R. J. Hollingdale (New York: Vintage, 1969), 104–105.

unbroken self. George must admit that he will never achieve "that attitude of work for work's sake, of duty for duty's sake" (427). What he is
saying is that his relationship to the world will be empirical, to some degree self-interested, while his brother's has freed itself from the very notion of egotism. Kien lives a disinterested life; his judgment of taste is free
from moral judgment or, for that matter, self-interest. It is this freedom
from any personal connection to the object that enables him to overlook
its usefulness, and judge it on a formal basis alone.

In his description of the aesthetic object, Kant stresses the notion of *dispositio*—how it is the formal arrangement of that object that triggers in us
the idea of beauty. The shape of beauty is shrouded in a mystery that we
cannot account for, that we cannot locate in our own desires or motives.
It is the sense of inevitability—we are controlled by something that is pre-
ordained—that generates our awe. Likewise, Kien's reverence for knowledge is based on its ability to stand on its own, without him. When
looking for a fact, Kien is drawn to the texture of the printed page. He is
mesmerized by the power of writing as such: "Merely in order to find a
minute detail, which he knew by heart anyway, merely to check a reference . . . he read thirty pages. . . . But once his eyes fell upon anything
written or printed he could not pass it over" (31).

Kien is drawn inexorably to the printed. It is a consolation that derives
from the unalterable nature of writing. Writing is redemptive and restorative in that the writer uses it against the opacity of nature. It is possible,
as H. R. Jauss suggests, that through "the human process of abstraction"
the artist is capable of reconstructing the disturbingly raw material of the
world into a "constructive order whose totality is less complex than its
parts. . . . [T]he artist experiences his work as a blissful seizing of the possibilities of his own, finite world. . . . It perfects the imperfect world."[28]
Outside the confines of Kien's monumental library, everything is indeed
imperfect. Paradoxically, it is Kien who brings this imperfection onto
himself. A book is missing from his collection; never having misplaced
anything in all his years of collecting, he suspects his housekeeper. The
advertisement he places in the newspaper is what launches the catastrophic intrusion from the outside: "A man of learning who owns an ex-
ceptionally large library wants a responsibly-minded housekeeper. Only
applicants of the highest character need apply. Unsuitable persons will be

28. H. R. Jauss, speaking of Paul Valéry's essay on Leonardo, in H. R. Jauss, *Aesthetic Experience and Literary Hermeneutics*, trans. Michael Shaw (Minneapolis: University of Minnesota Press, 1982), 9–10.

shown the door" (26). Housekeeping is a matter of high morality. Kien displays a classic case of Manichaeism in which the world divides into bad (those who have no scholarly disposition) and good (those who do). The perfect housekeeper appears in the shape of Therese whose skirt is so perfectly starched that it seems to have become part of her. To show her respect and to win Kien's approval, she reads one of his books with gloves, having positioned it on "a small embroidered velvet cushion," and claiming to have read every page a dozen times to get "the best out of it" (45). More remarkable than her astonishing deceit is the manner in which Canetti portrays Kien's reaction. Creature of his idée fixe, living every second of his life for his collection, Kien turns everything into an extension of his obsession. Because Therese has tapped into his preservationist spirit, he considers her "the heaven-sent instrument for preserving my library. If there is a fire I can trust in her" (47). So he marries her, or rather, he marries the quality he believes will enable him to continue his life's calling. Shapiro gives an interesting variation of Kien's mad act: "The fixed purposiveness of the rigid person narrows his interest in the world and restricts and prejudices his experience of it. He looks only for data . . . with a checklist in mind of certain qualifications [marriage] . . . does not see that woman objectively; he sees a selection of traits and features whose sum is not a person but a high or a low score."[29] Fixed, rigid, restrictive, and narrow are some of the characteristics of the monomaniac. In the case of Kien, anything outside of his "data-base" must be rejected. He is blind to everything about Therese outside of his own "checklist." Were she a book, she could easily become one of the quotes from his manuscript, but she is as crooked as he is straightforward. The struggle between her materialism, her greed, and Kien's Platonism culminates in the rather hilarious description of their first night. Kien had piled his precious books on his divan, convinced that her respect for his library would protect him from any untoward advance. "He was a man, what was to happen next? Happen? No, that was going too far. First, he must decide when it was to happen" (57). Things do not happen on their own in the world of the idée fixe. They are willed, never occurring randomly. Note how rapidly his thoughts shift from his masculine reality to a decision-making reflex. Books, he hopes to make clear to his new wife, make physical intimacy entirely superfluous. His plan fails. Therese callously throws the books from the bed, and "a terrible hatred swelled up slowly within him. This she had dared. The books . . . ! Kien plunged out

29. Shapiro, *Autonomy and Rigid Character*, 75.

of the room in long strides, bolted himself into the lavatory, the only room in the whole house where there were no books, automatically let his trousers down, took his place on the seat and cried like a child" (57).

Viennese psychiatrists writing around the 1920s might have chuckled at Kien's retreat into the bathroom. They might have read it as the unmistakable result of his compulsive nature. Karl Abraham's groundbreaking article "Contribution to the Theory of the Anal Character" tackles a number of the issues revealed in this passage. To Abraham, Kien's retreat to the lavatory would be the replay of earlier demonstrations of control. Properly speaking, the anal phase is a phase of experimentation; the individual plays with the very notion of control, of self-imposed restraint by "holding back the excreta, and . . . evacuating it."[30] When Kien realizes that Therese has broken his pact, he physically loses control. He bursts into tears and "relieves" himself in the bathroom. Only in this neutral place, this book-free cubicle, can he revert to patterns that he has suppressed in everyday life. This rather simplistic interpretation helps us understand the way in which the scholar was used to being the sole commander of his body and soul. He absconded to the lavatory just as he had exiled himself in the library; both spaces are formidable retreats from the world, two enclosed zones that he has made his own.

Canetti's genius is to keep drawing on the peaceful quality of self-banishment. In *Auto-da-Fé*, library and lavatory seem to be places where people purge while collecting themselves. Kien's marriage to Therese, however, turns Kien's immaterial lifestyle into a daily battle where tables and beds start to take on a life of their own, actively undermining the scholar's enraptured studiousness. The two characters begin a war of *idées fixes*, both wanting what the other loathes. It is silence against speech, ideas against objects. It becomes impossible to pursue knowledge when furnishings become the guiding principle of Therese's universe. Canetti portrays with uncanny realism the devastation caused by domesticity. The calculating housekeeper intrudes on Kien's physical and mental space, wearing him down until he is driven away. As much as he needs nothing in terms of furniture, she requests (being the rightful wife) a table, a gigantic bed, and three rooms out of the four. Giving in to all her material requests, Kien only wants silence and a fraction of his living space in return: "From now on I shall keep the door into your rooms locked. I forbid you to step over my threshold as long as I am here. . . . He panted for silence as others do for air" (66). Kien has lost his sacred space.

30. Abraham, "Contribution to the Theory," 75.

Like his house, his self has been divided. Everywhere he looks, his "pure" train of thought is contaminated by material objects. "He needed a book and got up to fetch it. Even before he had it, that damnable bed crossed his mind. It broke the taut connections, it put miles between him and his quarry" (68).

Whatever is tangible around him is an interruption, a break in his perfectly linear train of thought. The tyranny of these objects makes him yearn for "*his* library which he would soon possess again: four lofty halls, the walls from floor to ceiling robed in books . . . work, work, thought, thought, China, learned controversies, opinion versus opinion" (382). Note how it is the disposition of his library, the four halls of uninterrupted shelves, that he really longs for. He can only get them back mentally, so what he does is to blind himself to his surroundings and rebuild his library in his head. It is the only way to avoid the following plight: "When Kien looked up from the writing desk, which was placed across one corner of the room, his view was cut off by a meaningless door. Three quarters of his library lay behind it; he could sense his books, he would have sensed them through a hundred doors" (67). The library, Kien's hermitage, is the sum of an absolutely concentrated existence. As he mutters to himself, a "scholar's strength consists in concentrating all doubt onto his special subject" (67). This anthropomorphized door needs to be removed. In order to do so, Kien starts living like a blind man in that he walks through his apartment, eyes closed, doing everything in his power to abstract himself from Therese's reality. "Practice in walking blind soon made him a master of this art. In three or four weeks he could find, in the shortest possible time . . . any book he wanted" (71). Kien is waging a war of sight against insight; to him, sight, when linked to material luxuries is what leads to intellectual dissolution. Blindness, it turns out, when it is willed and perfected, becomes the decisive weapon against the predatory nature of the real: "[It] is a weapon against time and space; our being is one vast blindness, save only for that little circle which our mean intelligence . . . can illuminate. The dominating principle of the universe is blindness. It makes possible juxtapositions which would be impossible if the objects could see each other. It permits the truncation of time when time is unendurable" (71). Kien's most astonishing intuition is that sight actually prevents us from seeing what is fundamental. Just as knowledge protects us from self-knowledge, blindness is a weapon against the world's randomness. Not seeing—a characteristic infirmity for the monomaniac, who lives according to a perfectly known path—is Kien's way of regaining what he has lost.[31] He uses the housekeeper's calculations to sharpen and to test his single-minded capacities.

She destroys the order and peace that helped him gain absolute composure over his environment. His immateriality stands directly against her greed. The contrast, however, is not as simple as it appears. Canetti turns Therese into a monomaniac in her own right. In the hope of getting his imaginary fortune, she tampers with his accounts, adding as many zeros as it takes to become a millionaire. "Her favourite letter was O. From her schooldays she had retained some practice in writing Os (You must all close up your Os as nicely as Therese, teacher used to say. Therese made the best Os).... For the remaining hours of the night she was busy increasing the sums of money she would inherit, by her skillfulness in writing Os" (116, 127). Therese's nighttime activities echo Kien's study habits. While he lives in his Kantian realm of pure reason, she builds a fictional universe where her happiness is contingent upon adding zeros, as though this could actually increase the contents of her husband's bank account.[32] She is as deliberate in her mission as he is, so that in looking for his hidden treasure, she "calmly and without haste . . . searched one section of the shelves after another, never missing anything" (30). Both characters are eerily thorough. Neither leaves any stones unturned. The result is an infernal meeting of mental constructs, utterly disconnected from process, and following compulsively a path that has been traced only in the solitude of their sick minds.

31. John Bailey notes that "Kien survives by haunting the state pawnshops, 'releasing' by purchase all the books which headless people have brought to pawn, and repacking them in his own head." He interprets this type of activity as our way of serving the world while "retaining our own solipsism." John Bailey, "Canetti and Power," in *Essays in Honor of Canetti,* 137.

32. As Manfred Schneider notes, Kant concluded the first part of his *Critique of Pure Reason* with the following refutation of Descartes' ontological proof of the existence of God. His scorn is clear in this scathing remark: "Thus the famous ontological (Cartesian) proof of the existence of a higher being by conceptual means is a total waste of time and effort, and a man might as little increase his stock on insight through mere ideas as the merchant would increase his fortune by adding a nought or so to his credit column." As Schneider judiciously writes, "in Kantian terms, Therese's writing of zeros amounts to an absurd assertion of the presence of God. Her conjectural hunt is both analogous and in contrast with Kien's work. Kien's absolute text . . . wipes out the name, works, and power of God, or, in Kantian terms: interest in speculation makes him replace the God that exists with a dual store of memory and text. The fortune hunter Therese . . . creates a real God for herself through her artificial manufacture of numbers, and to this real god she gives the name Mr. Puda—the 'superior young man.'" Manfred Schneider, "Cripples and Their Symbolic Bodies," 30.

Kien's books do come alive, though. Once he has turned his library into a battlefield, the books become soldiers, the letters jumping down from the pages to wage a war against the enemy. Kien, victim of calligraphic hallucinations, is commander in chief. "Now they were all at home together again. They were persons of character. He loved them. . . . [T]he library rose up again as of old, more inviolate, more withdrawn, so that the enemies appeared all the more ridiculous. How could they have dared to have quartered this living body, this whole, by closing the doors?" (89). Temporarily reunited with his books, Kien speaks about them as his faithful vassals. Just as he had advertised for a housekeeper endowed with the "highest character," he speaks of their moral integrity. The library rises as a congress, strong against the "enemies" (the outside world); Kien bravely defends the books sequestered behind those evil locked doors. He even asks himself whether they do not feel pain when separated from one another. "But what proof have we that inorganic objects can feel no pain? Who knows if a book may not yearn for other books, its companions of many years" (67). Kien is capable of empathizing with books, not with humans. He has managed to substitute animate for inanimate. The world is now entirely in his head and his only reality is solipsistic. In his musings about the capacity of books to feel, Kien makes clear that what he means by intimacy has nothing to do with human exchange, since intimacy is simply a matter of being spared unwanted communication. So rather than helping him connect with the world, books are the deadly weapons that protect him from what is other. We are reminded of Schelling's bleak sizing up of this impossible desire to remain purely self: "Either it remains still (remains as it is, thus pure subject), then there is no life and it is itself as nothing, or it *wants* itself, then it becomes an other, something not the same as itself, *sui dissimile*. It admittedly wants itself *as* such, but precisely this is impossible in an *immediate* way; in the very wanting itself it already becomes an other and distorts itself."[33] Schelling emphasizes that any form of desire projects the subject outside of the self. Any conscious shaping of the self inevitably betrays the identity we have clung to hitherto.[34]

33. F. W. J. Schelling, *On the History of Modern Philosophy* (Cambridge: Cambridge University Press, 1994), 116; quoted in Slavoj Žižek's "Selfhood as Such Is Spirit: F. W. J. Schelling on the Origins of Evil," in *Radical Evil*, ed. J. Copjec (London: Verso, 1996), 4; italics in original.

34. Žižek demonstrates that the "subject either persists in himself, in his purity . . . and thereby loses himself in empty expansion; or he gets out of himself, externalizes himself, by way of 'contracting' or 'putting on' a signifying feature, and thereby alienates himself, that is, he ceases to be what he is." (Kien, not as a scholar but as an individual, is caught precisely in this no-win situation. When he does manage to live in his own head, he is without a world,

Kien had found perfect oneness with his calling; self and books were interchangeable. But the very fact that Kien identifies with his volumes suggests that he is utterly devoid of a proper self. He can achieve self-identity only by breaking out of his single-minded trajectory; the protective idée fixe stands in the way of any such voyage. Monomania and the search for a true self are therefore profoundly antithetical.

Canetti lingers on his character's extreme thirst for isolation. Kien is an ascetic spirit; he lives the mystical language of Plotinus and would certainly agree that "[the soul] is pure when it keeps no company; when it looks to nothing outside itself; when it entertains no alien thoughts."[35] He also has endorsed Plato's hierarchy of universal over particular, absolute over mutable, internal over external, and immaterial over material. Kien uses his books as unmistakable instruments of domination, both intellectually and physically, and his revenge against the real world takes the form of his "commanding" his books to attack his aggressors, fending off anyone who might threaten his Platonic hierarchies. It is his ability to identify with his volumes that affords Kien a dominant-like position, not dissimilar to Flaubert's theory of omniscience. In a famous letter, the latter extols the power writing bestows on its practitioners: "It is very nice to be a great writer, to put people into the frying pan of a sentence and set them hopping about like chestnuts."[36] At the outset of the novel, Kien is king of his four-room universe. His authority goes unquestioned at congresses where his status as absolute master is never once challenged. Like Flaubert, he is everywhere and nowhere, dominating the event without even having to be present. His mastery comes from his dual status as presence and absence. Canetti probes this bizarre psychology of power in that Kien's intellectual domination occurs chiefly through the academic papers he has others deliver. He never appears in person and therefore his aura grows out of his exclusively written persona. Nobody has ever seen a photograph of Kien, because the scholar

---

useless outside the bounds of his scholarly production; when he is in the world, he loses his mind, so disoriented that he can no longer be who he is. Žižek quotes the pivotal passage in Schelling: "The subject can never grasp itself as what it is, for precisely in attracting it becomes an other; this is the basic contradiction, we can say, the misfortune in all being—for either it leaves itself, then it is as nothing, or it attracts-contracts itself, then it is an other and not identical with itself. No longer uninhibited by being as before, but that which has inhibited itself with being, it itself feels this being as alien." Schelling, *On the History of Modern Philosophy,* quoted in Žižek, "Selfhood as Such Is Spirit," 4.

35. Plotinus, *Enneads* 3.6.5.

36. Flaubert to Louise Colet, November 3, 1851; quoted in Marthe Robert, *En haine du roman: Étude sur Flaubert* (Paris: Balland, 1982), 144.

appears to keep public and private fiercely separate. Similarly, in terms of speech, he cannot endure anything that is not part of a purely scholarly vocabulary. Daily speech, for example, is perceived as a frightful waste of time because it needs to adapt to unexpected everyday situations. There can be no deviation from clear and distinct ideas in the closed universe of monomania, given that the monomaniac believes in Truth, holding on rabidly to the sacred separation of body and mind.[37]

One of Canetti's great insights is to present the obsessive mind as a zone that is neither private nor public. Kien rules over a purely quotational universe, with no real-life interlocutors to disturb the linear path of his erudition. He has gathered his selfhood into an airtight ball that is indistinguishable from his obsessive pursuit. At its peak, his monomania helps him turn his life into a firm equation, a safe place where there are no meandering paths. This confinement safeguards the perimeters of his identity. But when it ends up collapsing, his idée fixe shatters this stability in an utterly crushing fashion. In this staggering psychological portrait, knowledge and self-knowledge have nothing to do with one another. When they do eventually overlap, and when Kien is expected to look into himself, to surrender to another, he descends into madness.

Without his rigid rituals, without his knowledge that everything is exactly in its place, indeterminacy erodes the envelope of selfhood, revealing the void underneath. This inner void will eventually be reflected in Kien's own destruction of the library. On the verge of being saved from fire by his gruesome neighbors, he no longer can distinguish between reality and fantasy. He locks himself in with the raging flames and even his beloved books turn against him. "A letter detaches itself from the first line and hits him a blow on the ear. Letters are lead. It hurts. Strike him! Strike him! . . . A footnote kicks him! . . . More and more. He totters. . . . Lines and whole pages come clattering down on to him" (463). His universe is coming to an end, letter by letter. He is being assaulted by his own life's work, his Babel-like folly tumbling down on him. In a final gesture of paranoid madness, Kien realizes that his books are the enemy. No longer

37. Shapiro contends that pathologically rigid patients have the remarkable capacity to live out perfectly abstract lives. Their capacity to "regard a thing conceptually . . . and to consider it from various points of view, without regard for its incidental context—implies a detachment from that thing and an objective attitude toward it. Such an attitude toward what is external also implies a sense of the self's separateness from it and therefore an objective sense of the self," Shapiro, *Autonomy and Rigid Character*, 38. Kien has no capacity to contextualize what happens to him. He marries Therese precisely because he is so detached from her reality, entering her into a preexisting equation for happiness. He might say, "She will clean my books lovingly, therefore I should marry her."

one with his library, he turns viciously against it. The violence of his anger indicates a desperate return to a self that can exist only if it is radically at odds with everything around it. Kien is now brought back to the fold of a purely sterile selfhood.

The letters rattle inside the book. They are prisoners, they can't come out. They've beaten him bloody. He threatens them with death by fire. That is how he will avenge himself on all his enemies. . . . In front of the writing desk the carpet is ablaze. He goes into the bedroom next to the kitchen and drags out all the old newspapers. He pulls the pages apart, and crumples them, he rolls them into balls, and throws them into all the corners. He places the ladder in the middle of the room where it stood before. He climbs up to the sixth step, looks down on the fire and waits. (464)

By immolating his most memorable creation, Canetti demonstrates what happens when the constructed self finally dissolves, leaving behind a world of unfathomable loneliness.

    In his autobiography, Canetti relives his youthful infatuation with the sculptor Fritz Wotruba. He marveled at a man whose methods of sculpting sprung from the desire to convert the finite into the indestructible; like Kien, he used his art as an antidote against impermanence. "I had gone there with the prevailing opinion that what mattered to the sculptor was the *permanence* of the stone, which secured his work against decay . . . I realized that what mattered to him in the stone was its *hardness* and nothing else. He had to battle against it. He needed stone the way others need bread."[38] As a young intellectual, Canetti craved a way of battling the impermanence of objects with the permanence of art. The harder the stone, the more difficult it would be to carve, but the more victorious the sculptor would come out at the other end: "He struck powerful blows and I could see how much the hardness of the stone meant to him. . . . This was a deadly serious work with granite. I realized he was showing himself as he really was. He was so strong by nature that he had sought out the most difficult of occupations. To him *hardness* and difficulty were one."[39] Concentrating on the stone's hardness, the difficulty of converting it into form enabled Wotruba to escape from his own tormented selfhood. His triumph coincides with our monomaniacs' deep-seated urge: to replace self with work, subject with stone, and to obliterate the rift between life and art.

38. Canetti, *Play of the Eyes*, 97.
39. Ibid., 96.

8

The Cure in the Disease

Nina Bouraoui's Melancholic Imperative

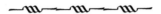

It might be lonelier
Without the Loneliness—
I'm so accustomed to my Fate—
Perhaps the Other—Peace—

Would interrupt the Dark—
And crowd the little Room—
Too scant—by Cubits—to contain
The Sacrament—of Him—

I am not used to Hope—
It might intrude upon—
Its sweet parade—blaspheme the place—
Ordained to Suffering—
It might be easier
To fail—with Land in Sight—
Than gain—my Blue Peninsula—
To Perish—of Delight—

> Emily Dickinson, "It might be lonelier"

These plaintive lines tell a strange story: that of the sufferer's re-
liance on her pain.[1] Loneliness turns out to be Dickinson's most faithful
companion, the only keeper of her solitary, but intact world order. Far
more reliable than hope, with its broken promises and coarse manifesta-

1. A version of this chapter, "Maghreb and Melancholy: A Reading of Nina Bouraoui,"
appeared in *Research in African Literatures* 34, no. 3 (August 2003): 84–100. "The cure in the
disease" is a loose translation of Jean Starobinski's coinage (and book title) *Le Remède dans le
mal: Critique et légitimation de l'artifice à l'âge des Lumières* (Paris: Gallimard, 1989).

tions, the pain of solitude provides unexpected perks, leaving its victim with one certainty: the suffering, at least, is hers. Everything else can be taken away—credibility, reputation, love—but nobody can ever rob her of her own grief. While so much of this book has been about the counter-intuitive strategies that are put into place when individuals feel their hold on reality slacken, this chapter tests the following hypothesis. Could it be that melancholy, like the peculiar brand of monomania we have been examining, provides solace through the very pain it incarnates?

One of the great queries in Nina Bouraoui's *La Voyeuse interdite* is how writing, and more precisely, the writing up of melancholy, can assume the function of a cure. Bouraoui adds a crucial dimension to what theoreticians of melancholy (from Aristotle to Freud, through Starobinski, Kristeva, and Agamben) have considered the fundamental relationship between loss and the work of art. In this case, the connection between pain and writing helps in diagnosing and treating a threefold case of exile (linguistic, psychological, and political). This momentous and courageous book helps us meditate on the role of depression as a counter-culture, powerful and secret enough to become art.

Nina Bouraoui's short novel *La Voyeuse interdite* was published in Paris in 1991 and can be added to the increasing number of narratives about Muslim women. It won several prizes, shocking and impressing its audiences by its disclosures about North African culture. Bouraoui was only twenty-four when *La Voyeuse interdite* was published; hers is the account of an Algerian teenager, locked up by her father in their Algiers apartment, forced to live according to two gospels, two chronologies—the world of her father who lives in "the year 1380 of the Hegirian calendar" and her own— "for us, it was the very beginning of the seventies."[2] The underlying message of the novel could read as a proverb from Kabylia: *A girl is brought up for somebody else's house.* The novel's heroine, the eponymous "voyeuse," unwittingly uses her melancholy as a cure that will turn her scandalous seclusion into cohesion and rebirth. Bouraoui presents two very different, but equally violent sides of melancholy. The grief-stricken adolescent, prisoner in her own home, whose depression is in no way abstract, and the resourceful woman of sorrows who manages to escape from her world of grief through a complicated machination that I will call creative pain, and which constitutes an acute example of therapeutic melancholy.

2. Nina Bouraoui, *La Voyeuse interdite* (Paris: Folio, 1991), 22. All references to this novel come from this edition, followed in the text by page numbers only. The translations are my own. *La Voyeuse interdite* has been translated into English by K. Melissa Marcus as *Forbidden Vision* (Barrytown, N.Y.: Station Hill Press, 1995).

This is a book that has all the ingredients of the sociological potboiler: politically charged, graphic as far as the condition of Muslim women goes, it never shies away from dramatic content. There is no dearth of shocking episodes—the mother hurls her baby girl out of a window, too ashamed to admit to her husband that she has failed again to produce a son. Told entirely from the perspective of the narrator, also an unwanted daughter, the story is endowed with tremendous pathos. The tale is reported by one who would have been better off dead, and who hints that any trace of her existence is considered sinful, an insult to her father, a reminder that she will never be the boy who will carry on the family name.

The novel confronts us with a disturbing issue. Could there be such a thing as an instinctual desire to mourn for its own sake? Bouraoui seems to offer a singularly self-governing theory of melancholy, one generated by a deliberate distancing from the world, not traceable to a peculiar event, but rather to a preconscious time, where there seemed to be no disjunction between desire and fulfillment. What is so striking about a melancholy that seems to mourn an idyllic, never-experienced state, is that it bases all future experience on this perfectly predictable grid. Like Flaubert's sentence, which exists as the replica of another perfect sentence, now erased, but ever figuring as a tyrannical forerunner, the melancholic perceives present and future experiences as pale imitations of a flawless past. In terms of Freud's theory of melancholy, this tyranny stems from the generic need to situate all events against a perfect moment that has been irretrievably lost, a moment that is now forgotten, but that *must* have occurred. If Bouraoui's novel seems so urgent and yet so timeless, it is because it suggests that melancholy places itself somewhere between disaster and the idyllic.

Bouraoui's silent *voyeuse* painstakingly recounts her sufferings. Paradoxically, the more she attaches herself to them, the more she is able to strengthen the very identity denied to her by her father. Why would the ego perform a masochistic ritual (recounting intolerable memories) that appears to act against the self's best interest? According to Freud, this is a mechanism that recreates unity within the self. The wholeness we crave will be destroyed, or at least betrayed, if the self continues to find new attachments in the present. Whenever we attach ourselves to a new interest, a new object of desire, we are undermining the presumable integrity of our person. Living in the past, albeit a traumatic one, protects the ego from its desire to wander. Fundamentally unfaithful, all too capable of losing its "primary" self in future odysseys, it will be frozen in time, an icon to itself. Mourning is greatly reassuring in that it dispels the doubt that we might not be able to remain unified beyond death. Her mourning provides the external proof that her primary self is unscathed. As Adam Phillips puts it, mourning is "immensely reassuring because it convinces us of something we might otherwise easily doubt: our attachment to others. The protracted painfulness of mourning confirms something that psychoanalysis had put into question: how intransigently devoted we are to the people we love and hate. Despite the evidence of our dreams, our capacity for infinite substitution is meager."[3] Phillips stresses the importance of continuity. The ability to remain faithful to one's pain provides a gratifying sense of permanence, a renewed confidence that everything is not about to disappear through the aggressive agency of the present. Bouraoui's narrator is never destroyed by her opponents—specifically, her father—because her devotion to the pain he inflicts upon her stands for continuity. Even though his cruelty reminds her of what she has lost, the way in which she chooses to remember it makes it a positive weapon, one that enhances her sense of selfhood, or as Melanie Klein would put it, serves ultimately to consolidate her ego.

A paradox is at work here: with the increased awareness that mourning is indeed a willful act, and not strictly a passive reaction to loss, emerges a sense of comfort. The vigilant practice of anamnesis, of remembrance for its own sake, brings forth a powerful sense of being; in some ways, the fact of focusing so intensely on the wound compensates for what has been lost.[4] It is this compensatory activity that makes Bouraoui's fiction so compelling. While forgetting indicates both the emergent agency of a new self and the fickle dissolution of our "I" into a new identity, remembering is also a circuitous way of paying a sickly homage to an association that we hate, but cannot seem to shake off. Like the artistic process, melancholy always harks back to a first draft, an earlier rendering of a self that becomes constitutive of a preferred identity. To some, equating art with melancholy (as Freud and Kristeva do) amounts to the desire for a unified self, one that stands firm in the face of change. To others, like Adam Phillips, it might be generated by the "fantasy of purity," an intense loyalty to the self: "This version of the self, inspired by fantasies of purity, becomes the enemy of free association;

3. Adam Phillips, *Terror and Experts* (Cambridge, Mass.: Harvard University Press, 1996), 78.

4. This could be put in Marxist terms: "the wound can be healed only by the spear which made it" (*die Wunde schliesst der Speer nur, der sie schlug*). These are the words Wagner puts in Parsifal's mouth; quoted in Slavoj Žižek, *The Sublime Object of Ideology* (London: Verso, 1989), 3.

terrorized by exchange, its project is to define and sustain the idea of a real thing, to keep the self true."[5] Bouraoui's "real thing" is the reassuring recalcitrance of her pain; her real lover is loss itself, and she cannot afford to lose it.

The only cure for such annihilating feelings is to turn them into writing: fiction, whether one reads or writes it, is an effective way of managing endless stretches of solitary confinement. Creating an internal weapon to address a situation that is imposed from without enables Bouraoui's *voyeuse* to experience a form of euthanasia, a private way of dying in order to live.[6] It is at this juncture that the connection between writing and melancholy becomes particularly meaningful. If the point of writing is to describe the impossibility of living, then the very act of putting words to paper stands in direct opposition to this impossibility since it is actively grappling with it. Writing, then, means taking an active stance, but a paradoxical one in the sense that it reenacts, repeats, goes over the life sentence that the narrator received at birth. So why does Bouraoui's narrator dwell indefatigably upon this intolerable persecution? Why instigate rebirth through language if this rebirth is rooted in the abject? In her world, framed by the following Kabyle proverb, birth is death, and presence is absence.

> A new member of the family is born
> With it, I will not fill the house
> With it, I will not fight my enemies.

The birth of a daughter amounts to a stillbirth. She has no place, no function, and no concrete presence. The only way she will make a mark is to reinvent for herself a place in the written world. The book she produces will have to function as her history, enacted retroactively. It is the book that will give her life, not her life that will provide the book's material.

In psychoanalytical terms, this inversion corresponds to the relationship between a symptom and the trauma that caused it. According to La-

---

5. Phillips, *Terror and Experts*, 85.

6. The *voyeuse* functions very much like the little boy in Freud's *Beyond the Pleasure Principle*; he is so attached to his mother (the cathected object) that the only way to accept her comings and goings is to stage them on his own terms. The famous fort-da game consists in reenacting or anticipating her departure so that he can gain control over the situation. It is thus the replay of a negative desire that makes an intolerable situation bearable. Rather than being the passive *object* of this temporary loss, the little boy becomes its stage director; in the play-scenario of his own mind, it is he who orders her out of the house, taking a masterful revenge against her autonomy. Freud, *Standard Edition* 18:14–15.

can, the symptom "initially appears to us as a trace . . . which will continue not to be understood until the analysis has got quite a long way,
and until we have realized its meaning."[7] In the same way that analysis
symbolizes parts of the unconscious, turning the inchoate into a near-
coherent narrative, writing is essentially an organizing activity. It is per-
formative because it produces meaning as it goes along. Bouraoui's narrator starts believing her story as she writes it. She might think she is
transcribing facts, laying down symptoms, when in reality she is mistak-
ing the cause for the effect. Žižek constructs part of his *The Sublime Object
of Ideology* around this postulate. Symptoms, he argues, "are meaningless
traces, their meaning is not discovered . . . but constructed retroactively—
the analysis produces the truth; that is, the signifying frame which gives
the symptoms their symbolic place and meaning."[8] This is not to say that
Bouraoui's heroine invents her story, but "in working through the symptom," in excavating traces from her past, she produces an authenticated
version of past traumatic events. Writing is *de facto* a second chance, the
foundation stone that will revamp her fragmented and forgotten identity
and make it something complete. The analogy between writing and rebirth can be extended to melancholy: like writing, melancholy makes the
inchoate oddly coherent. Even though it is shot with despair and dejec-
tion, it naturally organizes itself around the subject's consciousness,
restoring some kind of unity. Kristeva makes a similar point when she explains affect in terms of a survival strategy: "The *depressive affect* can be
interpreted as a defense against parceling. Indeed, sadness reconstitutes
an affective cohesion of the self, which restores its unity within the framework of the affect. The depressive mood constitutes itself as a narcissistic
support, negative to be sure."[9] Against all odds, it is the sadness itself that
compensates for the intolerable loss: were I not sad, I would permanently
sever this existential umbilical cord, the last link to my irretrievable loss.
In Bouraoui's novel, Kristeva's archaic Thing is remembered as an instance where the subject and the world are one;[10] it is the memory of having once been part of a euphonious environment that produces the
disconcerting instability of being: the self now wavers permanently between escapism and nostalgia. The telling of the story coincides with the

7. Jacques Lacan, *Seminar 1: Freud's Papers on Technique, 1953–1954,* ed. Jacques-Alain
Miller, trans. John Forrester (Cambridge: Cambridge University Press, 1988), 159.
8. Žižek, *Sublime Object of Ideology,* 56–57.
9. Julia Kristeva, *Black Sun: Depression and Melancholy,* trans. Leon Roudiez (New York:
Columbia University Press, 1989), 19.
10. Kristeva borrows the concept of the "Thing" (das Ding) from Lacan's *Seminar 7.*

gathering of specifically chosen traces that will eventually shape a new identity-perception.[11] The power of Bouraoui's book comes from the dual aspect of this identity, from the way she intermingles two sets of concerns: the relationship between writing and mourning, and politically charged issues such as the future of the Muslim woman. Does this novel aestheticize politics, brushing off the communal tragedy of the sequestered woman with idyllic reminiscences? To the rhetorical question of whether this book has a message, the narrator answers: "A message? Sure. Get down from your hideouts, let's not waste our time or theirs, let's boldly sidestep the course of tradition, our customs, their values, let's tear the curtains and veils to unite our bodies" (14). The narrator is telling her fellow captives that it is time to strategize: disorient the enemies by putting them off guard. Substitute voyeurism for a vocal relationship with the world, one in which the veiled identity will make way for a fully fledged one. Bouraoui continuously balances her narrative between heartwrenching "hymns to communal pain," pleas for "our gangrene-ridden souls," and lyrical outbursts that refer to a nonworld, the *anti-monde* she eventually adopts as her true home. Her self-description is bloodcurdling: "I am a jointed scarecrow, a female with rotten genitals that must be ignored at all cost, if divine condemnation is to be avoided" (31). This scarecrow-narrator produces an astonishing *tour de force*: she is aware that her message will be more powerful if it remains abstract and timeless. Absence and unsayability, then, will transmit her plight.

La Voyeuse interdite is a narration of exile: the first-person teenage narrator has always been confined to her parents' house—she is exiled from the world, struck down by the codes assigned to the Muslim woman, banned from any right to an autonomous self. Any study of melancholy presents the melancholic subject as one whose odd fortune is to be able to escape from the primary affect of sadness into an even more profound and willful isolation. The melancholic, for all his or her passive demeanor, is the most active opponent of the present, of current events. In fact, the melancholic is immune, even uncannily impervious, to the present, since

11. This attempt to recover her "essence" is similar to Lacan's definition of the unconscious as the censored chapter of a book. He argues that its contents must be sought in traces—in the idiosyncratic use of grammar, in the way certain much-repeated stories help make up our identity, in our fashioning the heroic legends of other authors; in short, "in the traces . . . the meaning of which will surface through my exegesis." Jacques Lacan, *Ecrits I* (1966; Paris: Seuil, 1970), 137; my translation. The traces that Bouraoui's heroine is after are based on her desire to believe the tales of the servant Ourdhia. According to Lacan's scheme, her ability to endow Ourdhia's narration with meaning corresponds to a preexisting desire.

everything is necessarily refracted through memories of a better world. So the melancholic, by remaining outside of the constraints and the contingencies of time, is capable of generating an autonomous, purely abstracted zone. Bouraoui's narrative is a meditation on this escapism, raising the possibility that while it is describing oppression and psychological torture, the very act of writing, the translation of experience into words, becomes the unexpected tool of liberation. "Sadness gives me a great deal of words and worries, I touch her with the tips of my fingers, sometimes grabbing her, I drink from her chalice and she covers me with her inhumanly wide wings" (17).

This flight toward a grotesquely human sadness is at the core of the novel. Such fond reference to *tristesse* testifies to its redeeming function. Indeed, what else could you possibly conquer, locked up in a cell, burned with cigarette butts anytime you raise your voice? Like so many chronicles of melancholy, *La Voyeuse interdite* is about the redemption of the real through the imaginary; it chronicles the construction of an inalterable zone of beauty, a prelinguistic Beautiful, that affords not only a respite from the intolerable, but an advantageous compensation. To attain the Beautiful, however, a radical break from mimesis is required. There is much relinquishing to be done—one's own physical world must be evacuated in order to recover what Freud and Kristeva identify as the lost place, the original site of plenitude. This precious place, so radically different from anything that will follow, is the lost Eden in which we have buried all our hopes, the witness to our mourning-drive. Kristeva sees this exemplary scene as the presymbolic realm of language, which she develops in her famous distinction between the semiotic and the symbolic.[12] She points out that a "lack" is necessary for the *sign* to emerge: the child produces or uses objects that are the *symbolic* equivalents of what is lacking. Later, and beginning with Melanie Klein's so-called depressive position, the child attempts to signify the sadness that overwhelms it by producing, within its own self, elements alien to the outer; we are then faced with *symbols*, properly speaking, no longer with equiv-

12. "We understand the term 'semiotic' in its Greek sense . . . distinctive mark, trace, index, precursory sign, imprint, trace, figuration. . . . This modality is the one Freudian psychoanalysis points to in postulating not only the *facilitation* and the structuring *disposition* of drives, but also the so-called primary processes which displace and condense both energies and their inscription" (Julia Kristeva, *Revolution in Poetic Language,* trans. Margaret Waller [New York: Columbia University Press, 1988], 25). "On the other hand, the *symbolic* is identified with judgment and the grammatical sentence: We shall distinguish the semiotic (drives and their articulation) from the realm of signification, which is always that of a proposition or judgment, in other words, a realm of *positions*" (ibid., 43).

alencies.[13] The child has to acknowledge the end of its unmediated and oceanic oneness with the world and go forward. The melancholic acknowledges this sense of an ending, but places it at the center of all future experiences; in fact, the melancholic's dominant reflex is to blame every unhappiness on this break with the prelinguistic.

In the novel, the heroine's access to prelinguistic oneness occurs through Ourdhia, the faithful servant, who cannot or chooses not to speak: "Having been forced into our home, Ourdhia seemed deaf and dumb to everything, but I soon realized that her muteness was foreign to ours" (51). Unlike ordinary expressions of silence, usually passive and imposed from outside, the servant's is intentional. "Foreign to ours" suggests the uncanny in the sense of Freud's *Unheimlich;* it pretends to be the slave when it is really the master, uniquely capable of mediating other people's desires, and carving for itself an impregnable realm. Ourdhia and her silence are like the Greek *daimon,* the intermediary between the physical and the spiritual realm. As the book develops, it become[s] increasingly clear that her restraint will provide a model for the narrator, eventually demonstrating how the real and the suprasensible can be bridged: "Thanks to her, I was about to enter an unreal but soothing world: the imaginary world . . . the curious story of the desert" (52). The melancholic tries at all cost to relive the oceanic moment outside of language; it is a moment of pure denial, a forgetfulness that enables the subject to block out the world. Melancholy, although instigated by the imperfections of life, is a perfect antidote to life—it is what Sartre called, apropos Flaubert, *un trucage existentiel,* an existential act of trickery, that is, when one refrains from acting only to be able to revel in one's own passivity.[14] Imagine the heroine of Bouraoui: she is a *voyeuse,* prisoner of one room pierced by a single window, witnessing repression all around her, and beholding the fate of her neighbors all reduced, like her, to the same state of impotent bystanders peering out through a crack in the wall, craving romanticized lives that will never materialize.

Bouraoui divides her tale into two narrative threads. In the first, the *voyeuse* is a schizoid observer, torn between outside and inside. Her father orders her to follow the path that will take her from birth to marriage; Bouraoui describes this as a funeral rite, where the young girl waits in her

---

13. Kristeva, *Black Sun,* 23.

14. Marthe Robert disagrees with Sartre's reading of Flaubert as one who exonerates himself from action to enjoy "painfully" his passivity. She takes issue with *L'Idiot de la famille,* vols. 1 and 2. Marthe Robert, *En haine du roman: Étude sur Flaubert* (Paris: Balland, 1982), 18; my translation.

room until the mysterious unknown husband, much the figure of death, will be announced and will sweep her away, forcing her into the very same wretchedly familiar gestures that she saw performed by her mother. The second narrative thread, altogether more abstract, essentially converts the phenomenal into the noumenal, the explicit into a wholly individuated reconstruction of the real.

We have already mentioned Ourdhia, the mute servant; with her mystical sign language, she has devised an incorruptible form of disclosure that can never be co-opted. Placed between language and unsaying, she performs a seminal role for the narrator's salvation. She serves the purpose of transporting the *voyeuse* into an idyllic realm, that very space that will occupy the melancholic mind. Witness how the Ténéré, both Arcadian hallucination and region of absolute emptiness, can be filled with any blissful hankering. Here, it is the servant's revelation that is being described: "Led by the stars, she had reached the most barren of lands, unadorned beauty, the very essence of the sublime: the Ténéré. Void of voids, absolute of absolutes, center of the earth, epicenter of nothingness, this place at last crowned the nomad's disciplined steps, there, she encountered Truth" (54). Note the leitmotif of centrality: Ourdhia has found the essence of experience in the absolute center of the world, which coincides with the center of nothingness. The figure of the middle is crucial in that it has a gathering effect; like a magnet, the center of the universe provides reunification with the absolute; it counteracts the unwavering commands personified in the paternal figure.

Ourdhia manages to abstract herself from the real, thereby providing a model for the narrator, who will later apply it to her narration. As Kristeva elaborates in *Black Sun,* the experience of perfect reconstruction, of renewed communion with a lost center, can occur only through art. It is art, indeed, that secures "for the artist and the connoisseur a sublimatory hold over the lost Thing . . . by means of the polyvalence of sign and symbol [and that] affords the subject a chance to imagine the non-meaning, or the true meaning, of the Thing."[15] By means of its ability to decompose and recompose signs, the "poetic form . . . is the sole 'container' seemingly able to secure an uncertain but adequate hold over the Thing."[16] Beauty emerges as a most unexpected trade-off: as with "feminine finery concealing stubborn depressions, beauty emerges as the admirable face of loss, transforming it in order to make it live."[17] In *La Voyeuse interdite,*

15. Kristeva, *Black Sun,* 14.
16. Ibid.
17. Ibid., 99.

this metamorphosis is the mental escape from the prisoner's cell to the pages of the book. To quote Marthe Robert again, putting pen to paper is indeed the best way to turn shackles into powerful instruments of control. "Art is a tremendous means of domination . . . with it, we satisfy all needs, we accomplish everything, we become king and servant at once, active and passive, victim and priest. It is without limit."[18] With extraordinary restraint, Bouraoui combines this sense of power and the shockingly graphic episodes of the novel—for example, the father raping his wife on the kitchen floor. The language of art-making, the eulogizing of the Ténéré desert, is utterly antithetical to the non-metaphorical language of oppression. However, it is the juxtaposition of the two vocabularies, of the two worlds that makes Bouraoui's canvas so stirring. The only thing that saves the narrator from despair and provides a cure for the incurable is to have access to this mystical language of unsayability, to this apophatic realm.

This notion of apophatic art is central to Bouraoui's case study about the survival of identity in extreme situations. Is Bouraoui trying to demonstrate that art, or some kind of narrative reconfiguration of the real, is the only way to rescue her subject from isolation? And how could this occur through this curious flirtation with mysticism and unsayability? If one looks closely at some of the passages describing this mythical desert, the nucleus of the melancholic imagination, it becomes clear that part of its appeal is that it represents absolute absence. The narrator speaks of "absolute void—void of voids, absolute of absolutes, the epicenter of nothingness" (54–55). It cannot be described, it cannot be contaminated by symbolic appropriation, it is a monument only to what it is, to some ecstatic immutability that can be captured only if the self loses itself by shutting off the present. Michael Sells describes very convincingly the workings of this self-generated mysticism: "The source of emanation is not a supreme being, not a being or entity at all . . . it is nothing. . . . At the heart of that unsaying is a radical dialectic of transcendence and immanence. That which is utterly 'beyond' is revealed or reveals itself as most intimately 'within': within the 'just act' . . . within the act of love. . . . When the transcendent realizes itself as the immanent, the subject of the act is neither divine nor human, neither self nor other. The removal of linguistic dualism: beyond translation."[19] This passage underscores the connection between freedom and the unnarratable. Nobody can rob the

18. Robert, *En haine du roman*, 144.
19. Michael A. Sells, *Mystical Languages of Unsaying* (Chicago: University of Chicago Press, 1994), 71.

narrator of a space that is purely mental. By letting nothingness ("that which is utterly 'beyond'") occupy such a crucial place in her narrative, she removes the shackles of her own historicity. She manages to achieve autonomy, even if she does so via a negative perception of her identity, by cutting herself off, by carving out a space that is neither historical recollection nor projection into the future. This is truly a "radical dialectic of transcendence," a self-mythologizing realm that becomes a refuge because it has never been previously appropriated. It is an ekphrasis of the Maghreb itself: as Abdelkebir Khatibi puts it, it is "a gap directed toward the thought of difference, let us call it the Maghreb."[20] In Bouraoui's narrative, the mere attempt to separate oneself through abstract thought, to grasp both the terms and the inexorable quality of one's estrangement, is the only way to tame history. So much depends on finding a strictly individual window out of which the world can be viewed, be it daydreaming, myth, or poetry.

Melancholy floats somewhere between these categories, and the melancholic is a shrewd operator, one who has learned how to spy, to eavesdrop, and yet to shun any unmediated contact with the world. Such techniques of retreat turn the psyche into an impregnable fortress from which one can see but not be seen. Bouraoui's heroine, after all, is a *voyeuse*; behind her glass window, she is safe: her self-portrait is that of "a clandestine spectator positioned above the city . . . she risks nothing" (21). Because of the extraordinary state of suspension she has achieved, she describes herself as a *Doppelgänger*, a distant sister to Baudelaire's *Héautontimorouménos* who proudly proclaims:

> I am the wound and the knife!
> I am the slap and the cheek!
> I am the limbs and the spinning wheel,
> And the victim and the tormenter![21]

Here the *voyeuse* incarnates pawn and player, subject and object: "I manage to duplicate myself: I am the pawn and the player in one" (61). Victim and aggressor, she is simultaneously passive and active; passive because, like Dürer's famous allegorized figure of Melancholy, her eyes appear to be cast inward, her body slouched toward the ground; active,

20. Abdelkebir Khatibi, "Présentation," *Les Temps Modernes* 33, no. 375 bis (October 1977): 5.
21. Charles Baudelaire, *Les Fleurs du mal*, in *Œuvres complètes*, ed. C. Pichois (Paris: Pléiade, 1961), 74. "Je suis la plaie et le couteau! / Je suis le soufflet et la joue! / Je suis les membres et la roue, / Et la victime et le bourreau!"

because it is her decision to take to its extreme consequences the principle of dispossession.

This double position brings us to another dimension of melancholy, one so vividly explored by Giorgio Agamben in *Stanzas:* it has to do with the connection between creation and self-denial. Agamben writes: "The condition of success of this sacrificial task is that the artist should take to its extreme consequences the principle of loss and self-dispossession . . . the redemption of objects is impossible except by virtue of becoming an object . . . so the . . . artist must become a living corpse, constantly tending toward an other, a creature essentially non-human and antihuman."[22] Bouraoui's protagonist constructs herself as this corpse. She is one of Algeria's living dead, a shadow looking out of a window to a world that never reciprocates the glance. Writing, then, becomes the ultimate form of bracketing, the only way of rising above the silence to dispel the absence of reciprocity: to write means to reappropriate word and world. The narrator describes herself as a metonymy: never integrated into a whole, she is the single eye that absorbs the world—"an eye . . . veiled, I'm left with a single eye. . . . At the center of the event, I made my way in the night, one-eyed, resigned, toward the instrument of death" (143).

Bouraoui's *voyeuse* synthesizes experience so that it will never exceed the story she wants to tell and retell. Melancholy is the state that begins this process, and curiously, it is also the path to absolute liberation: it takes her back exactly to the place where she feels most at home—herself. No wonder Kierkegaard pairs the melancholic with Narcissus: "I have only one friend, and that is echo. Why is it my friend? Because I love my sorrow, and echo does not take it away from me. I have only one confidant, and that is the silence of night. Why is it my confidant? Because it remains silent."[23] Kierkegaard's narrator has reduced his contact with the world to his own reflection. An echo of himself is all he wants, as it is the only interaction that will not interfere with the production of his own mental images. He loves his sorrow because it binds him to the only thing that cannot be taken away from him, his self. Likewise, Bouraoui's *voyeuse* carefully preserves the space of her childhood. Her bedroom assumes tremendous symbolic importance as it coincides with a mythical as well as personal past that she aims to regain at all cost. When in the last scene, the heroine forgoes "her maiden's room," she is relinquishing a crucially

22. Giorgio Agamben, *Stanzas: Word and Phantasm in Western Culture*, trans. Ronald L. Martinez (Minneapolis: University of Minnesota Press, 1993), 50.

23. Søren Kierkegaard, "Diapsalmata," in *Either/Or*, pt. 1, ed. and trans. Howard V. Hong and Edna H. Hong (Princeton: Princeton University Press, 1987), 33.

reinvented space, one revamped with all kinds of survival strategies. Her room, very much like Des Esseintes' in *A Rebours,* is a closed world, a book that can be endlessly reread and reinterpreted, always retaining a basically recognizable structure. *La Voyeuse interdite* is about the creation of a space that is simultaneously inalterable and infinitely reworkable, in the sense that it is the host of memories that are being continuously reprocessed. This theme of a given (whether it is linguistic, social, or spatial) that locks the character in an inescapable situation seems to be a formative theme in a great number of exilic novels. Narratives as radically different from one another as Katia Rubinstein's *Mémoire illettrée,* Ben Jelloun's *Les Yeux baissés,* or Leïla Sebbar's *Schéhérazade* cycle document how characters extricate themselves from unhappy situations by recasting themselves somewhere on the fringes of both the host language and their language of origin. Knowing how to absorb not one, but two traditions seems to be the lot and the luck of these characters.

Even if Bouraoui's novel is about failure—sent to the slaughterhouse of marriage, the protagonist fails to get the better of tradition—it is failure on her own terms. She remains shielded by her voyeurism. Even as a wife, married to a stranger flung upon her by her father, her ability to become her own double, to be the witness as well as the actress of her own drama, protects her from passively accepting somebody else's decision. What turns out to be a melancholic elegy, the mourning of a blissful encounter with the desert, a farewell to this brief brush with freedom, also traces a possible path toward autonomy. Bouraoui's rebel is always observing. Never entangled in a single situation, she is able to describe it almost as it is occurring: "Focusing on objects, on my own actions and thoughts, I was becoming my own witness, and reflecting, I saw myself embracing adventure. . . . I was present and participating in a joyous funeral: my own. I was burying my childhood to live beyond it, myself, and the familiar" (124). Her vision corrects the catastrophe of her circumstances, engaging her in a bemused interaction with her own fate. She has objectified herself to the point of becoming somebody else, somebody who can laugh at that other person. This slanted gaze exchanges mimesis for poiesis, imagining rather than simply imitating the world, and producing a vision that ends up bypassing the window. This window, indeed, even though it passes itself off as the novel's central framing device, allows the narrator to meditate on a broader reality, one that bursts out of the confines of any realistic project. The liberation promised by what lies on the other side of the open window, the rush of freedom coming up from the streets, are, to say the least, a set of deceptions: a small girl run over by a bus, young women being carted off to unknown husbands—on the whole, nothing much different from what occurs in her own apartment. As in traditional representations of melancholy, the window quickly turns into a strangely distorting mirror, part real, part mythical. The window blocks out the outside, and rather than letting in the light, it does little more than reflect back the self.

Even though we owe a number of our theories of melancholy to Aristotle, and not to Plato, it is nonetheless the Platonic model that is reflected by Bouraoui's melancholic mirrors. The only way to achieve some form of spiritual reciprocity is to seek an unshakable reality, not the prosaic reflection thrown back to us from tarnished mirrors. The only tolerable mirrors are those that bypass the present, reflecting another dimension, a reality that emerges from the void, very much like the Ténéré, the desert summoned by the servant. So the window is turned into a mirror, and the mirror is turned into a prism, one that refracts an unfaithful reality: "I misrepresented my memories, and all that I had condemned gathers together in an immediate cluster of emotions" (138). "The lack of importance of an objective representation is clear in the two descriptions of the heroine's bedroom. It is first described as "a blood-spattered death chamber, in utter disarray, walls and cushions, head and body, lost in the most abject sentences!" (88). The room is likened to a cell filled with the abject, the bloody, and the chaotic. The narrator's relationship to her room, with its enshrouding effect, is that of the monk, who, full of loathing for his cell, still cannot leave it. Bouraoui, meditating once again on the melancholic's dependency on pain, feels at once the horror of the place and the panic at having to relinquish it. Agamben analyzes this mechanism as a form of *amour de loin,* love of the inaccessible, where "[the monk] sighs and moans that his spirit will produce no fruit so long as he remains where he is. . . . He plunges into exaggerated praise of distant and absent monasteries and evokes the places where he could be healthy and happy. . . . [E]verything that he has within reach seems harsh and difficult to obtain without effort."[24] But naturally, when it comes time to leave it, both the monk and the *voyeuse* turn their revolt into yearning, becoming nostalgic exiles, always doomed to love what they have lost. The narrator's cell-like child's room is metamorphosed into a paradise lost: "I had to leave my nursery. Dragged along by the future, torn to pieces by tradition and repetition, already overcome with regrets! These moments of unrest. . . . It all comes back so methodically, with such yearning for my

24. Agamben, *Stanzas,* 4.

enemies!" (138). Is the only way to survive trauma to cultivate it until it becomes one's own? Starobinski identifies this appropriation as the melancholic's unique ability to turn externally inflicted pain into self-imposed torture; commenting on Baudelaire, he notes the following reversal: "In a clever construction, [Baudelaire] transforms aggression directed toward others into aggression directed toward himself. He demonstrates . . . the precedence of sadistic aggression over that of masochism. This self-inflicted torture derives from the very energy by which the other is struck."[25] Melancholics, Starobinski implies, manage to convince themselves that under the guise of enslavement they are absolute masters over at least one thing: their own pain. Taking somebody else's sadistic energy—that of the father—and converting it into her own (where it becomes energy directed against the self) explains why the narrator fluctuates between pleasure and pain, love and hate.

As Khatibi once noted, the *problématique* of North African novels written in French stems from this dialectic. Identity, he argues, can arise only from the clash of two systems, of two languages. To crystallize his point, he quotes Deleuze: "It is perhaps between two languages that thought is possible to us today . . . the possession of several systems, each one of which would be self-sufficient."[26] Here one could argue that it is between two moments, a historical time and a mythical time, neither of which is ever allowed to congeal, that Bouraoui constructs her narrative. The use of such tension is a central device in her book; it paints a rather predictable portrait of the Algerian woman, but casts it in an utterly de-familiarizing framework, glossing it with seemingly inappropriate lyrical brushstrokes. By shunning a mimetic relationship to the real, at times even turning the intolerable into a dreamy abstraction, Bouraoui achieves Robert Musil's deep belief that "whoever seizes the greatest unreality will shape the greatest reality."[27] *La Voyeuse interdite* is just that: it writes itself out of the most unrelenting violence by turning blood into ink.

25. Jean Starobinski, *La Mélancolie au miroir: Trois lectures de Baudelaire* (Paris: Julliard, 1989), 30.

26. Gilles Deleuze and Claire Parnet, *Dialogues* (Paris: Flammarion, 1977), 11.

27. Toward the end of Robert Musil's *The Man without Qualities*, Ulrich, parroting Dostoevsky's Underground Man, concedes that reality as such is never desirable. What we are longing for is the desiring activity, not the result. Reality will always pale in comparison to our imaginings: "All desires, and not just love, are sad after they are fulfilled; but in the moment in which the activity *for* the desire fully takes the place of the desire, it is canceled out in an ingenious way, for now the inexhaustible system of means and obstacles takes the place of the goal. In this system, even a monomaniac does not live monotonously, but constantly has new things to do." Robert Musil, *The Man without Qualities*, trans. Burton Pike (New York: Vintage, 1995), 1495–96.

9 Voyeuristic Monomania

Sophie Calle's Rituals

In order to convert the boredom of the everyday into art . . .
Sophie Calle has spent the last twenty years
metamorphosing her life into strange rituals . . . .
Transfiguring the passing of time . . . [she] creates protocols,
imagines stories that end up being the fictional
representations of a . . . displaced life: her art is this
audacious ritual that exorcises and replaces life.

Jean-Michele Ribettes, "C comme Calle"

Sophie Calle is certainly the most resourceful, entertaining, and controversial figure in this book. Unlike our previous protagonists, often destroyed by their extremist worldviews, she is monomania's great success story, the only one to have turned obsession per se into a thriving way of life. A French artist known for her risk-prone artworks, she has let a continuous flow of idées fixes control the course of her creation. But while Flaubert, Baudelaire and Canetti dwell on the misanthropic rewards of obsession, Calle takes her obsession into the public realm, letting it spill dangerously into the lives of the innocent bystander. Her career, as controversial as it is successful, has reveled in the deliberate blurring between public and private, art and life. Often building her installations around taboos and transgressions, she has gleefully trampled on some of our most basic preconceptions to take her current obsession to its bitter end. She gets married to a near-stranger just to be able to film her sexless cross-country honeymoon; she takes a job as a chambermaid in Venice just so she can rummage through the guests' belongings and rob them of their intimacy with her camera; she performs nude in a Parisian striptease until she gets beaten up by one of her fellow strippers. Calle attaches herself compulsively to pursuits that allow her simultaneously to shape and showcase her own destiny. Inscribed in her *œuvre* is the desire to take on one of the great challenges of modernity, namely, to find out how one can use art to protect oneself, and yet to make sense of the bombardment of choices that assaults one at every turn. Can making art become an internalized source of authority, a superego of sorts that gives definition to a life that otherwise could become dangerously free-floating?

If everything is allowed, if neither religion nor censorship (artistic or societal) provides a convenient foil, then the individual can only turn within for authority; he or she will have to invent rules and regulations, surrender to self-imposed tasks. All our monomaniacs use some sort of scaffolding as the resting place for their anxieties; whether in the limpidity of a perfect sentence, the geometry of a library, or the unbending codes of a sanatorium, they find inexorable structures to help them curtail their *horror vacui*. With Calle, who moves so freely between worlds and people, obsessions cannot so easily attach themselves to such structures. This is why she keeps changing the rules of her own obsessive games. As long as her new aesthetic enterprises promise to swallow up her old self and give birth to the new, she will persist in her endeavors with the will of Flaubert's Saint Anthony.

But far from Flaubert's cushy writer's cave, Calle's migrating studios are not places of sedation; they are not havens against life, but curiosity shops from which spring veritable antidotes to the sluggishness of a life passively withstood. Her art takes into account the indigestible rhythms of the present, while folding them into a thrilling narrative. Calle uses art as escape, but it is a different type of release from that used by her feuilleton-prone predecessors. Balzac suspended his readers' lives by the thin thread of alluring characters, but remained hidden and protected from his audience's demands and desires. Calle does just the opposite. Her art is an adventure in risk taking; not only can she not hide behind it, it is precisely what gives her a face, a recognizable identity. The obsessive quality of her endeavors plays, as the obsessions in this book always do, a double role. While it injects her world with a highly charged sense of drama, keeping it safe from tedium or repetition, it also acts as the tyrannical master who forces her into one form or another of acute deprivation.

As the previous chapters have demonstrated, monomania is an identity-forming, identity-destroying affliction. Many of our cases hid behind their affliction in order to present themselves to the world as consequential beings. It was precisely by doing so that they ended up alienating their fellow humans. In Calle's case, it is not so much distinction she is after. Rather, she is mesmerized by the very disunity that lies all around her. Propelled by this discordant spectacle, her art reproduces it, only to readjust it to her singular vision; unlike her forerunners, she is not out to escape from the painful fragmentation that comes with modern life, but rather builds her work around the very consequences of this inconsistency. Calle's enterprise, more proactively than any of my previous cases, lays bare a world where fragmentation and the irresistible drive for order are twin disorders that call for a single treatment.

Among the most successful experiments involving this ordering appetite are: the installation of unopened gifts—a result of decades of birthday-present boycott; her yearly anonymous *envoi* to a fellow she fancied but found appallingly dressed. Only after she had outfitted him from head to toe could they perhaps get to know one another (all the articles of clothing are featured); her meticulously organized diet—each day is color coded and only foods of a certain color are allowed.

Through these carefully elaborated schemes, Calle the artist has managed to live life at a distance, these rituals limiting her role to observer and architect, rather than inhabitant of her own domestic space. She makes it clear that opening her *cadeaux d'anniversaire* would immediately destroy their momentousness, canceling for good their symbolic power. This is why the birthday ceremony had to be made into a very different, and ultimately more powerful type of ritual, one marked by the tenacity of absence rather than the rewards of presence. "Thou shalt not open these gifts" is the indomitable command that leaves the bounty intact—the unsealed wine bottles will never be sampled, always upright in their glass vials. Had they been drained of their precious contents, they would now be forgotten, gone without a trace; now, they will always stand for Sophie's birthday.

All the wrapped testimonies are lined up, each a small part of a lost year, resurrected in the very act of self-denial. Not only does Calle's dogged disallowance give rise to an impressive storehouse of goods, all intact in their individually polished cases, but they have been saved from the frittering away of time and annihilative consumption. To have reached that point, to have become the Proustian collection of aged objects that reflect a whole life, while remaining forever unexplored, demands an unprecedented degree of self-control on the part of their recipient. Control, as we have seen earlier, is of the essence. It turns out to be a rather Machiavellian way to preserve what, for the rest of us, would long have been forgotten or spent. The birthday gift, like so many other of Calle's aesthetic hobbyhorses, becomes precious because kept at bay. This notion is all too well understood by her bridegroom, who, when agreeing to embark on a purely experimental marriage, announces that the only way to keep Sophie was to resist her, to deny her what she thought she might really want—sex. "Being with Sophie" explains Greg Shephard, the husband-filmmaker, "means being willing to become subject matter because there is no separation between her work and her life. Her art is how she invents her life. It was a choice I had to make—to give up control."[1] But since her desires will dull as soon as they are satisfied, Shephard soon understands that he should restrain from indulging them. "Desire is the most important thing for Sophie," he says, describing Calle's obsessive nature. As a result, he decides to fuel her desire by "not being available."[2] Her honeymoon, and this is the genius of "No Sex Last Night," is a staged double-deferral. Shephard was about to break off the relationship when Calle convinced him that were they to get married, they could make a movie of their honeymoon. It is the promise of art that defers the failure of the couple, now given a second chance. But to this initial deferral Shephard juxtaposes his dogged resistance to her sexual advances. Calle wakes up every morning and says to the camera—"no sex last night," activating instead a whole process that perpetually defers the idée fixe of having sex.

Calle's obsessive hold on objects follows the most basic law of Brechtian anti-narrative. Only when it is estranged from its function can an object retain its power. But this power must then be redirected and used as a shield against the arbitrary. What happens once a bottle of wine is gulped down is of little aesthetic interest, but to keep it untouched is to maintain its Platonic hold over the imagination. Likewise—and crucial to the monomaniacal imperative—only when it has been severed from its everyday use does the object become an ally, a reassuringly malleable proof of one's control and power. Calle is beholden to nobody except to her own exigencies; her birthday presents will never be burdened with thank-you notes and Maussian pacts; they are abstractions that can be endlessly reconfigured; they are owned by Calle, forever under her yoke.[3]

---

1. Greg Shephard; quoted in Ginger Danto, "Sophie, the Spy," *Art News* 92, no. 5 (May 1993): 103.

2. Ibid.

3. There is an interesting essay to be written on Calle and Marcel Mauss. As Mauss identifies in his famous "The Gift" ("Essai sur le don. Forme et raison de l'echange dans les sociétés archaïques," 1923–1924), gift-giving is a competitive and highly strategic transaction. The giver may appear to be paying homage to the recipient, but he or she inevitably expects

Double Game is full of such instances. In her piece about eating, Calle devises a "chromatic regimen that consists in restricting herself to foods of a single color for any given day." Becoming the Rimbaud of nutrition—*lundi bleu, mardi rouge, mercredi blanc*—she orders her eating habits around a diet that not only becomes the authoritarian guide to her gastronomical life, but a therapeutic prison that controls her while liberating her from the anxiety of disorder and chance.[4] Come Sunday, she invites all her friends to sample all the color-coded dishes together. While it restricts, limits, and seriously cramps her freedom, this regimen forces her to comply with an order that produces an exquisite work of art, reining in the fear that the formless could take over her world.

One of the most telling examples of her finessing everyday encounters is her meeting with "the most intelligent man I have ever known."

One day he called to invite me to lunch, and proposed we meet the following week. Somehow the idea of the pleasure I would have from listening to him was countered by a malaise: the fear of not being up to it. So, to ready myself I asked him what we would talk about. It was an exercise that I knew was silly as it was vain, but one that would comfort me. D. chose a theme instantly: 'What makes you get up in the morning?' I prepared myself all week, accumulating all kinds of answers. When the day came, I asked him for his opinion on the matter and he said: 'The smell of coffee.' That was it. Then we changed the subject. At the end of the meal, after the coffee was served, I stole a cup as a memory of our lunch together.[5]

Of all Calle's superstitious precautions, the story of the coffee cup seems to convey the most straightforwardly the root cause of aesthetic monomania. Note how her anticipation of pleasure is conjoined with that of malaise. If we go back to Janet's diagnosis of compulsive reflexes, we can recall that this vague feeling of flotation could only be dispelled by another emotion, this time violent and overwhelming. Anticipation, even

something in return. A gift always carries with it an obligation. Forever marked by the identity of its giver, it will never be entirely free of its previous history. Calle decontextualizes her *presents*, thereby dissociating them from their giver, turning them into her own creatures. Cast out of the give-and-take loop, the giver loses the power to coerce or to blackmail. The gift becomes the mirror of Calle's present endeavor and not of somebody else's past.

4. Her "inflexible obedience to inhuman duties commands her whole life: the succession of days, her artistic trips, her alimentary diet, her social behavior, her loves, including marriage and divorce" (Ribettes, "C comme Calle," *Beaux arts magazine*, no. 172 (September 1998): 49); my translation.

5. Sophie Calle, *La Visite guidée* (Rotterdam: Museum Boymans-van Beuningen, 1996), n.p.

when it is pleasurable, is a form of anxiety. This may be why almost all of Calle's experiments are designed to blunt this waiting time, to anticipate an event rather than letting it unfold on its own. History should be planned, not endured.

Calle's work comes with an intense need to map out reality before it spirals out of control. What seems to motivate her curious conversational preparations is the fear that the much-awaited rendezvous might take its own course; the chat might start to ramble, run circles around her, and eventually expose her as unprepared, eventually irrelevant. Art—in this respect her week-long preparation qualifies as such—is a terrific shield against the volatility of words. If this fear of formlessness is at the root of the aesthetic experience (after all, art is always a form of alchemy, transforming one substance, one conception, into something else), the willfulness of Calle's transaction provides us with a perverse type of escapism. Why indeed would you choose to escape from one prosaic reality just to fall into another? If reality is indeed so intolerable, why not subvert it entirely and retreat into a Mondrian-like universe of Platonic essentialism?

The reason Calle provides such a striking contrast to our previous monomaniacs, with their zealous quest for tyrannical absolutes, is because rather than fighting the real with the unreal, she takes the real head-on, treating it not as an enemy, but as a rival. Her competitive nature leads her right to the weakness that characterizes the world she is competing with—life is messy; it cannot settle on one form, one structure, remaining pathetically *informe*. So the solution to this sloppy world is to fix it with the kind of art that manages to present life as it is, while at the same time redesigning it as it should be. Her lists and tireless tasks do the astonishing work of internalizing life's disorderliness, taking it as a fait accompli, while bringing to it a different kind of randomness—that of her arbitrary obsessions. Life, it turns out, can be reclaimed by random acts of art, and year after year, Calle's installations, her photographs, do just that. They graft a meticulous understanding of the detail, of the texture, of the slight crease in the perfectly starched sheet, onto a universe that, for the duration of a snapshot, will cease to be simply itself, becoming radically changed by her willful artifice.

Recall how Pierre Janet attempted to cure his patients' obsessions by making them more aware, more sensually receptive, to the texture of everyday life. Even though they all seemed to yearn for an alternate world, one where the only tenable refuge smacked of domination and control, Janet managed to return them to simpler tasks, mechanical gestures that would be so physically engrossing that they would blunt the appeal of the ideal. Calle's relationship to such all-consuming physicality is no longer of the order of the mechanical, but of the investigative. Armed with her camera, she infiltrates herself into hotel rooms, where, disguised as a chambermaid, she lets herself be both witness to and actor of other people's lives.[6] What a change from our nineteenth-century heroines, who could endure their own lives only if they immersed themselves in the adventures of fictional heroines! Calle becomes the real-life protagonist of a story that begins as somebody else's, but ends up as her own. The unwitting Venetian tourists have no idea that they are living in a ménage à trois, the third being the all-seeing eye, who remembers them by the trash they produce and turns their waste into meaning.

Even though Calle is the first to court the capricious, braving great dangers to bring risk into her world, she is remarkably timid when it comes to absorbing alien textures and unpremeditated transactions. The coffee cup sketch, despite its lightness, takes us back to the great efforts made by *Middlemarch*'s Dorothea to impress her carbuncle-ridden Casaubon. But the great difference between the two women is that the former might proceed by frantically memorizing Pascal's *Pensées,* while the latter serenades with her random and yet highly stylized interventions. What is hilarious and poignant at the same time is her double urge to master circumstances and then to turn them into the most trivial and down-to-earth of moments. What she rehearses for a whole week before the encounter are the possible answers to a ridiculously simple question: What makes you get up in the morning? She has no time, alas, to tell us about her planned comebacks; she is trumped by *"l'homme le plus intelligent,"* who produces a disarmingly straightforward response. What makes him get up in the morning? Well, the smell of coffee, of course. His flip answer both kills the game and preserves it. As it breaks the ice, robbing her of her scripted scenario, it also enables her to preserve the experience through the stolen coffee cup and the written rendition of the episode. So the stolen coffee cup, like the birthday gifts, will forever memorialize the surprising fact that preparing for life is a useless exercise—the smartest of men will undoubtedly come up with the most prosaic of answers, thereby saving the day.

Considering Calle's incessant courting of chance encounters and for-

6. See Katie Clifford, "Scopophilia, Exhibitionism, and the Art of Sophie Calle," *Art Criticism* 10, no. 1 (1994): 59–65. "In more moderate terms . . . voyeurism, also referred to as scopophilia, and exhibitionism have been considered integral to the artistic process . . . bounding scopophilia must be balanced with an assertive exhibitionism . . . in that exhibitionism is the willingness to show what one has created, seen and/or learned," 59.

tuitous trysts, her careful building of fortifications around her life can seem surprising. But not if we go back to Janet's theory about the double side of ritual. Obsession can stem from the desire to control a world that contains two adversarial realities—the random and the immutable. Both are daunting unless tamed, brought down to size. Through her work, Calle seems to keep those opposites in constant balance, reminding us that when we think we have grasped the one, the other surfaces and undermines our confidence in any stable conception of the real. So rather than unifying her selfhood, Calle taps into her successive monomanias to generate new possibilities of self-making. She flees from her own self by reinventing herself for each art project. In *Suite Vénitienne* (1980), "she dresses in a blond wig, dark glasses, and raincoat" pursuing a man with whom she was casually acquainted. For *La Filature* she paid a private eye to follow her. Those who have read Paul Auster's *Leviathan* (1992) remember that in the novel's acknowledgments, he thanks the French artist Sophie Calle for letting him borrow episodes from her life to create a fictitious character named Maria. Auster was mesmerized by Calle's obsessive and single-minded impersonations and made his heroine Maria live the way Sophie practices art. When Calle, a good friend of Auster, read *Leviathan*, she took her own "game" one step further: "I decided to go by the book. . . . I followed [Auster's] instructions." So, modeling herself after her own fictionalized self, Calle takes the rituals of Auster's character Maria and resurrects them in her exhibition *Double Game*. Rituals shape both Maria's and Sophie's lives. They are dangerous situations involving strangers, foreign places, and potentially destructive gambles that smack of Loyolan flagellation. Some of the disciplinarian exercises she inflicts on herself are indeed reminiscent of monastic rituals that have lost their ultimate purpose—to please God and to help purify the body of sin. Calle is wed to such exacting rites, submitting willingly, perhaps even gratefully, to an aesthetic that flirts dangerously with the agonizing pleasure of a disciplined life.[7]

Another great rift between Calle and her monomaniacal forerunners is her ability to provoke situations that challenge the double standards of a public, which would be repelled to find in life what is so enticing in art. As one critic notes, what "makes Calle's work so precious (being indiscrete, voyeurism, daring, rudeness) would be legitimately hateful in our

---

7. Ribettes comments on the masochism involved in Calle's production: "The artist condemns herself to a life of acquiescent obedience. . . . [S]he creates an aggregate of terrible laws that she forces herself to submit to . . . gratuitously surrendering to artistic servitude." Ribettes, 50; my translation.

next door neighbor, or at least utterly devoid of the fascination that her art manages to confer on these mythical images."[8] Why should art not unsettle, infuriate, and shake the world? How can we convince people that it is even more powerful than the everyday? What might be expected in a novel (a character spying or relentlessly pursuing a stranger) becomes shocking, even scandalous, when carried out in reality. So why not blur the boundaries between life and art? Why not confuse viewers who will no longer be able to assume what is reality and what is fiction? This destabilization principle, a good estrangement technique, will infuse art back into the quotidian and vice versa. The results can be surprising.

In the summer of 1983, the French newspaper *Libération* came out with a daily column that would soon become a *succès de scandale*. "Putting a serious dent in the circulation of *Le Monde* . . . that summer Calle was a latter-day Dickens."[9] It all began when Calle, at the time an already well-known performance artist, picks up a lost address book on the streets of Paris. With her trademark tenacity, she decides to reconstruct the owner's personality by phoning and questioning each of the names in the book. From *A* to *Z*, Calle religiously contacts the scribbled names and numbers, compiling information about the man who became known, that fateful summer, as Pierre D. Each conversation was written up in a special column that *Libération* devoted to the strange exercise. Not unlike nineteenth-century serialized novels, readers soon became addicted to the voyeuristic supplement in their daily news. By the time she reached letter *Z*, Calle had not only hoped to reconstruct his identity, but had proved that she had been able to play God, turning ink blotches into human beings, not only actively interfering in their lives, but rekindling lost friendships and extracting from the narratives juicy tidbits about Pierre's life that would have remained hidden without her divine intervention. Pierre D., still nowhere to be found or heard from, had become the topic of highbrow dinner conversations. Speculations flew about his character, his looks, etc. Stripping him of his privacy provided Calle with the double thrill of transgressing against somebody's life in private (the phone conversations) and in public (bringing it to the public through the newspaper). When Pierre D. finally returned from his long trip to Norway (coincidentally, he was a photographer and a journalist, passionately attached to his privacy), one can only imagine his horror: he was the talk

8. Didier Semin, "Sophie Calle: La limite comme expérience," *Art Press*, no. 138 (July–August 1989): 30.

9. Yve-Alain Bois, "Character Study: Sophie Calle," *Artforum* 38, no. 8 (April 2000): 130.

of the *tout Paris*, his life was an open book, he was known to all, and could do nothing to stop this demonic process. His revenge, which hardly qualifies as such considering Calle's propensity to exhibitionism, was to send a picture of her in the nude to *Libération:*

Pierre Baudry returned from northern Norway [discovering] that he had been "exposed," that so many facts of his life and traits of his character—including his repugnance toward any form of publicity—had been revealed to a wide audience. . . . His outrage was an informed one, and his retaliation thus all the more to the point: he published a photo of Calle in the nude (without naming her, however). . . . He wrote that when he filmed he always worked *with* his subjects so that "they are not the objects, the victims, the prey of an inquiry" whose "model is that of police surveillance and of spying."[10]

Gripping about this episode is not only the nineteenth-century feuilleton techniques that Calle so brilliantly uses—she lets her readers "hang" from one day to the next—but her meticulous desire to associate the random (a found phone book, contacting all the people in it, hounding information out of them) with the orderly. Indeed, her *exercice de style* manages to reorder a lost world of scattered people into a series of neat and interlocking stories, analyzable narratives that promise in the end an Aristotelian catharsis. Reconstructing Pierre D.'s profile, sniffing out his personality, and finally tossing her discoveries onto the laps of millions of readers, endowed Calle's pieces with great power. Not only had she turned around the lives of countless people, but out of this chance encounter, she had made herself into the historian, the secretary, and impresario of this anonymous man's life; she had, overnight, converted him into a celebrity and alleviated the famous boredom of French holidays with a piquant, irresistible flavor that suffused excitement into her and her readers' lives.

The most shocking factor in Calle's project is perhaps the abandon with which she simply decides to turn other people's fates, not just her own, into life-altering experiments. She is the antithesis of those patients of Pierre Janet's who passively endured their boredom. Boredom is the real persona non grata in Calle's world. It is impossible to be bored if you treat your life the way Pygmalion treated his sculpture. You recreate life, you make it happen despite taboos and bourgeois codes of good behavior. It is as though Calle had read Flaubert's letters, been seduced by his deification of the writing process, but had been frustrated by its being limited

10. Ibid., 129.

to the page. What about transcending the confines of the page or of the canvas, and having art violently alter the way the world unravels?

Playing God, however, is a risky activity. After the aforementioned trip where she shadowed a man in Venice (*Suite Vénitienne*), Calle suffered from what she called a strange loss of identity. Having spent days in disguise, following a man who would continue to remain a stranger, she felt like reconnecting to her own body, to her sense of self. Walking through the streets of Paris, she was overcome by a daunting sense of foreignness. Places and people passed before her eyes like ghosts, never sticking to her consciousness. Her anxious *flâneries* were not simply a function of her having lost a sense of purpose and of place; suddenly, everything was beginning to feel displaced and dislocated. Traces of the melancholy that we have found in all the monomaniacs in this book started to appear. The *informe,* the chaotic, was finally becoming threatening, no longer the exhilarating mass that could be shaped into infinite possibilities. It could no longer be made her own. She had lost her hold over the world, over her city.

So how did she defeat the languidly sprawling streets of Paris? By throwing herself into yet another borderline experiment, one that would bury her old worn-out identity and buy her a new skin: getting herself hired in a strip joint, Place Pigalle. As she had done with the telephone book, but this time with her own body, she took something seemingly worn out and actively turned it into an art form. Sophie Calle generated Calle the stripper who, aware of each bend in her body, was also conscious of her viewers' gaze, piercing enough that it took her out of her agonizing anonymity. The episode finished abruptly as one of Calle's co-strippers ended up attacking her. The attack itself (no moment is ever wasted) was turned into art, photographed by one of Calle's friends who happened to be watching.

The issue of control and its impact is something that mesmerized Calle from early on. In *Des Histoires vraies,* she shares a series of anecdotes that congeal around people's ability to shape their lives through the sheer force of will. She begins with her great-aunt: "My great-aunt was called Valentine. She was born on February 4, 1888. At the age of ninety-six, she felt tired of life. But she had set herself this one goal: to live to a hundred. A few days before her hundredth birthday, she was in agony, but came back to life to ask: 'How many more days?' There were six days left. She whispered: 'I'll make it. I'll make it.' She died on February 4, 1988."[11] This

---

11. Sophie Calle, *Des Histoires vraies* (Paris: Actes Sud, 1994), 40. My translation.

woman, Calle writes, had a ferocious (*farouche*) character. She had willed herself to stay alive until her birthday. Before dying, she had embroidered a pair of sheets with Sophie's initials. Her survival effort, as it were, had become an installation, a tribute to her great-niece's artistic identity.

Sophie's name, her signature, has a special agency in Calle's works. Two months after her wedding (as I mentioned briefly, it was not exactly a *mariage d'amour*), she pulled a letter out of her husband's typewriter. It was written to another woman and read: "I want to confess something to you; last night, I kissed your letter and your picture." The letter was addressed to H. "I erased the H. and replaced it with an S. This love letter became the one I never received."[12] Inscribing her initials and placing them on a sheet of paper that would never be sent is part of the subtle system of substitutions that keeps redirecting Calle's life. She wills herself to be the love letter's addressee, just as she had turned the lost address book into her own summer romance. Life, and this is the great revelation, is never a closed book but a rough draft always receptive to a fresh script. By substituting *S* for *H,* she imposes a new version on an unsatisfactory reality, permanently transfiguring it with her signature.

How remote is all of this from Esquirol's interpretation of monomania? Hadn't he, after all, been the first to find an intimate connection between obsession and the tireless nineteenth-century drive toward self-promotion? He had also argued that the obsessions that had made and unmade so many nineteenth-century minds and fates had everything to do with the bourgeois's new mobility, his will to reinvent himself. Esquirol was not merely referring to the self-made heroes and heroines of Balzac's novels—Goriot and his girls, Grandet and his gold—he was also alerting his readers to a particularly disturbing strain of modernity. Selfhood, that nebulous prerequisite of the post-romantic generation, was increasingly being equated with one single trait, one interest, or one all-consuming passion. The new self was becoming more and more single-minded as the pressure to make a mark on society increased by the day. The machinery of the self, Esquirol mourned, was being pumped up at the expense of the "proper workings" of society as a whole: "a single-mindedness of goal, a directedness, an intense and exclusive fixation on particular ends of striving, as opposed to a dedication to the spontaneous, diverse, and well-rounded good life."[13] These lines, if they fit nicely into the general

---

12. Ibid., 55.

13. See Jean Etienne Esquirol, "Monomanie," in *Dictionnaire des sciences médicales* (Paris: Pancoucke, 1819), 34:115.

direction of this book, look slightly out of place in terms of Calle's artistic production. Granted, her *œuvre* has been the immediate result of such goal-oriented projects, her fame growing directly out of her exclusive fixations. But where she differs from our previous cases, and where her monomania reflects a new relationship to the fabric of everyday life, is in the aggressive annexation of chance to her obsessive schemes. Not that she is dedicated to "the spontaneous, diverse, and well-rounded good life"; indeed, despite her inhabiting multiple incarnations and whimsical personas, she shares very little with the aesthetic libertarian. But although rituals are at the heart of her production, the weapon of choice in her quest to defeat a passively endured relationship to the real is chance itself. Molded and manipulated, it becomes the authoritative way of making sense of the senseless.

Sophie Calle's art is a call to arms against the preconceived notion that our lives are controlled from the outside. She brings control back into the slipshod accidents of routine by cooking up schemes that she will see right through to the end. And having become an expert at willfully organizing her life around a prevailing sense of pandemonium, she has, curiously, managed to render her universe reliably steadfast. The objects of her aesthetic desire, once captured by her willful gaze, are no longer the frustrating results of missed opportunities and all too brief encounters. They assist her in conveying that sense of precarious permanence (as in the untouched birthday presents) that has become her signature in time. Even though it is chance (the bête noire of all monomaniacs) that nourishes her idées fixes, it is a chance that she has made her own.

Conclusion

This book might have been called *Uses and Misuses of Obsession*.[1] One of its paradoxical conclusions is that compulsions have their own strange silver lining. The obsessive individual finds an order, a modus vivendi, that simulates the sheltering conditions of artistic production. The idée fixe, when it offers a life altogether wed to an idea, is a great way of escaping from reality. Fulfilling single-mindedly their absolutist quests, our monomaniacal figures have acted with staunch autonomy, reconfiguring the heterogeneous into a set of strictly-organized rituals, finding temporary solace behind the thick walls of their creed. But how can something as negative as a debilitating delusion furnish the subject with such potential power? And more generally, how do excessive modes of behavior provide a barrier against the mundane?

Monomania, that remarkable nineteenth-century invention, implied that you could have it both ways. The havoc caused by an obsessive illness could sometimes turn in your favor, providing radical immunity against a whole array of anxieties. By its intensity, the idée fixe blocked out the haphazard elements of everyday life, restoring focus and meaning.[2] To the hypochondriac, for example, life might have been made up of excessive prodding and symptom-searching, but at least this excess provided a rationale, a safety belt that came with its own therapeutic rewards. The hypochondriac, the melancholic, and even the anorexic all use their idées fixes to endow their objects of predilection with order and direction. But it is not the mere act of ordering life into neat and formulaic categories that is so arresting; it is the faith that rigidity will finally cure

---

1. Parts of the section on laziness appeared in my essay "The Importance of Being Lazy: Paul Lafargue's Indecent Proposal," *Cabinet* 11 (Summer 2003): 30–35.

2. See in particular how Charles Nodier conceived *monomanie* as the re-creation of a lost unity, perhaps our last chance to retrieve an ideal world. His work is built around the conviction that ideals, dreams, and any consummate "unreality" are imperative to fend off the meaninglessness of modern life.

the world of its complexity, bringing to a solacing standstill the inevitably changing landscapes of existence. We have seen that obsessive behavior can turn impotence into mastery: Casaubon, Kien, and even Flaubert relied on their routines to overcome their fear of asymmetry and confusion. Nothing was as frightening to them as disorder, nothing as disorienting as the sprawling and fluid quality of time. Letting themselves go, even for a moment, might reveal a life tragically devoid of meaning.

Might this explain why certain people are always occupied with something, always assuring us that they are busy, that they are working, that they are doing something imperative? They have frantically substituted countersloth for "sloth," overdirected activity for empty time, hoping that the sheer exercise of their will might mask the weak and confused person they might really be. In the dutiful nature of such gestures hides the great fear of living a life without an overarching meaning, of merely following one's trivial inclinations. It is certainly noteworthy that none of our characters ever indulges in the undirected pleasure of daydreaming, in what nineteenth-century writers refer to as the vaporous. Much can be gleaned from this panic about free time, this haunting anxiety in the face of leisure. What possible danger lies in the state of repose, what part of the self will be lost if alertness is relaxed, perhaps even lost? Is it the fear of being unproductive, even if one's productivity is inherently mechanical and unsatisfying? Could it be that we conflate downtime and laziness, idleness and transgression?

—⁂—

A look at our anxious relationship to laziness can teach us a great deal about our goal-oriented impulses, our fear of living a life devoid of a grand plan or an organizing principle. Few frown upon the immoderate hours put in by high-powered professionals; few would identify them as signs of an obsessive disorder. On the contrary, they are proof of commitment and civic responsibility. But on closer examination, are they not also marks of escapism, an exhausting, while paradoxically passive, resistance to introspection? Is it then so surprising that this same impeccable professional is legendarily inept at vacationing, hopelessly tormented about office politics or the untended yard? If activity appears to define us, then overactivity betrays our ongoing fear of reflection. We use our heavy schedules to prolong the illusion of our usefulness, while postponing indefinitely the turn inward.

Leisure, the contemplative life, and laziness do not fare well with those who identify work with worthiness, labor with virtue. As Nietzsche puts it, enjoyment for its own sake will always be frowned upon and unless it is turned into something useful, even medically legitimate, it becomes a blemish on our character. "More and more, *work* enlists all good conscience on its side: the desire for joy already calls itself a 'need to recuperate' and is beginning to be ashamed of itself. 'One owes it to one's health'"—that is what people say when they are caught on an excursion into the country. Soon we may well reach the point where people can no longer give in to the desire for a *vita contemplativa* (that is, taking a walk with ideas and friends) without self-contempt and a bad conscience. Well, formerly, it was the other way around, it was work that was afflicted with the bad conscience."[3] It is worth digressing for a moment to consider one of the keenest analysts of this "work pathology." Karl Marx's son-in-law Paul Lafargue, the relatively little-known author of *The Right to Laziness*, wrote a remarkable pamphlet that denounced compulsive workers (workaholics *avant la lettre*) as dangerous monomaniacs, victims of a pathology embraced with equal ardor by economists, intellectuals, and the clergy. Like Charles Fourier and his utopia-driven critique of work, Lafargue balked at the disingenuousness with which the work ethic was being masqueraded as a healthy appetite, a fundamental human urge that should be inflamed and rewarded. He notes with disgust that the vocabulary traditionally applied to desire or leisure had suddenly come to flaunt the glories of labor, slyly passing itself off as virtue and high morals. Work was being used as a didactic tool that was slowly eroding the individual's ability to be contemplative. Lafargue saw the onslaught of the work ethic everywhere: he quotes Napoleon, who had already figured out that "the more I make my people work, the fewer vices they will have. . . . I would be willing to establish that Sundays, after church, shops will be reopened and the workers will resume their work."[4]

Lafargue's critique of work is an indirect commentary on our attachment to compulsive activities that manage our lives *for us.* He is one of the first to note how any obsessive surrender—whether to work or to religion—can blunt a rich relationship to the world and blames his contemporaries for letting their puritanical cogito—I work, therefore I am—get the better of them. He would beg them to remember that the root of *travail* is *trepalium*, a sinister instrument of torture. But this particular torture,

---

3. Friedrich Nietzsche, *The Gay Science*, bk. 4, no. 329, trans. Walter Kaufmann (New York: Vintage, 1974), 259–260.

4. Paul Lafargue, *Le Droit à la paresse* (Pantin, France: Le Temps des Cerises, 1996), 48. All quotations come from this edition, followed in the text by page numbers only. All translations are mine.

with its way of compressing the day into strained but regular motions, has a devious analgesic quality; it desensitizes by replacing thought with activity. Here is not the place to question Lafargue's quixotic portrayal of the "leisurely" worker, but rather to give him credit for having located a drive that would increasingly take on a life of its own. The great twist in Lafargue's critique is the plan to resurrect the forgotten virtues of *paresse* (laziness). By doing this, he forces us to pay closer attention to the drive to let work dominate one's life and to wonder what makes us be attached to work for its own sake—a substitute, perhaps, for the examined life. With his typical wit, he reminds his overzealous readers that the God of *Genesis* "gave his adorers the supreme example of ideal laziness; after six days of work, he rested for eternity" (45). So what holds these same readers back, he asks, and why not "proclaim the right to laziness, a thousand times nobler and more sacred than the diseased Rights of Man?" (59).

Lafargue's attacks, addressed to the great philosophers of his time and of time past, are certainly not outdated today. From the Situationists' scrutiny of everyday life to Giorgio Agamben's attack (in his *Homo Sacer*) on the corrupting "ethics" of work in Nazi concentration camps, Lafargue seems to be asking one fundamental question: why is work endowed with such an aura? And what real benefits do we expect from it—that is, when it is carried to an excess, performed far beyond its economic use? He points his finger at the first person who made us believe that fulfillment and humanity derive from work, not from repose. Work, even if it is traditionally viewed as part of our fallen human condition, should be grasped first and foremost as a punishment. But by placing it on such a pedestal, Lafargue argues, we have accepted to turn punishment into our highest aim.

Lafargue is toying with one of the questions central to Aristotle's *Ethics:* which activity is most humanizing (or dehumanizing)—work or leisure? Lafargue reminds us that Aristotle looks down at work because per se it did not nourish our higher faculties. Hannah Arendt would echo this point in her chapters on work and labor in *The Human Condition*. It is leisure, or at least Aristotle's understanding of leisure as a mode of philosophizing, that actually valorizes humans as such. Work, as practiced by Lafargue's contemporaries, had become an automatic reflex, a conspiracy, a sinister ploy to dull our critical faculties. He is not far from Schopenhauer's discussion on leisure in *The World as Will and Representation*. Leisure, Schopenhauer contends, actually terrifies us. This might explain why so many people secretly hate Sundays. Sunday is a day of forced rest. It fills us with panic, with *horror vacui*. The characters in this book are all Sunday-haters. The day of rest fills them with feelings of incompetence and restlessness. They do not know what to do with themselves when they are not rehashing their obsessions.

To denounce work is one thing, but to promote *paresse* is another. How does Lafargue plan to sell his slothful vision and in what way would it help our own practitioners of the idée fixe? If we go back to Aristotle's notion of leisure—the time that a free man (as opposed to a slave) devotes to learning something that has no social or utilitarian use—we can begin to grasp Lafargue's wishful idleness. It is this type of gratuitous leisure that will best promote genuine social progress. But Lafargue also focuses on the saintly idleness that Christ preaches in his Sermon on the Mount: "Consider the lilies of the field, how they grow; they neither toil nor spin; yet I tell you, even Solomon in all his glory was not arrayed like one of these" (Matt. 6:28–29).

The frenzy for work has made it impossible to relish the slow process of living. Lafargue is identifying the sly fear of everyday life. His unhappy case studies come awfully close to the standard definition of the obsessive-compulsive—where the living of life itself becomes work, where everything is measured in terms of productivity and motion.

Lafargue evokes rather bitterly the famous water mill that the poet Antipatros had predicted would liberate women from menial tasks in ancient Greece. Why did it fail to do so? Because "the blind passion for work, perverted and homicidal, ended up turning the liberating machine into shackles: its productivity impoverishes free men" (60). The terrible irony is that instead of being saved by the blessed machine, instead of letting it do his or her work, "the worker, instead of extending his or her repose . . . multiplies activities, as though competing with the machine. O absurd and lethal rivalry" (61). This lust for work has killed some of our more endearing characteristics; our ability to be gluttons, for instance, has vanished; work has shrunk our gargantuan stomachs; it has debilitated our minds and limited our spirits. Much wiser to bask in philosophical *paresse*—that is, to engage in the type of work that only entails enjoying the immediate fruits of one's labor. Like Arendt, some sixty years later, Lafargue locates in the work ethic the misery of a nation that does not even know what to do with its free time. If the benefits of the machine do not include training the individual to higher and spiritually richer activities, then what is the point of having gained this freedom in the first place? What Lafargue makes clear is that work is becoming an all-powerful de-ity, all the more insidious for having turned into an auto-pilot mechanism. Work ultimately makes for more work. As in Arendt's scheme, work has become its own teleology. "This madness is the love of work, the moribund passion for work, stretching the individual's vital forces until breaking point. Instead of reacting against this mental aberration, priests, economists, and moralists have sanctified work . . . they have tried to rehabilitate what God had cursed" (43).

Compare this "madness" to the drives we have been following throughout this book. It is a similar need to drown oneself in a larger scheme, into an activity that claims to endow the self with value, when in fact it absorbs the self to the point of dissolution. Lafargue's attack on work gives fresh meaning to a defense of the misused quotidian.

The quotidian is on the one hand the realm of routine, repetition, reiteration: the space/time where constraints and boredom are produced. . . . Even at its most degraded, however, the everyday harbors the possibility of its own transformation; it gives rise, in other words, to desires which cannot be satisfied within a weekly cycle of production/consumption. . . . It is in the midst of the utterly ordinary, in the space where the dominant relations of production are tirelessly and relentlessly reproduced, that we must look for utopian and political aspirations to crystallize. . . . To read everyday life, what Hegel called "the prose of the world," is therefore to become engaged in the act of *poiesis*. . . . It means . . . that we understand *poiesis* in the sense of a transformative or creative act.[5]

The gravest problem for Lafargue is that the work ethic—and, I would add, any dogmatic ethic—is keeping us from *poiesis*, from a genuinely elastic relationship to the real. It involves us so thoroughly in a relentlessly repetitive present that we can never hope to transform it into something else. In an interview aptly titled "Osons être paresseux" ("Let's dare to be lazy"), Roland Barthes mourns his own inability to be lazy. His daily routine is poisoned by nagging feelings of guilt; any interruption of productive work—from the innocent act of getting a glass of water to the sacrilegious answering of a social call—fills him with depression. To find time for laziness would signify a break from the self-serving world of recognizable accomplishments; it would be the victory of creative chaos, of unpredictability, over ritualized and comforting work habits.

5. Alice Kaplan and Kristin Ross, "Introduction to Everyday Life," *Yale French Studies* 73 (1987): 1–4; quoted in Ben Highmore, *The Everyday Life Reader* (London: Routledge, 2002), 78–79.

I might be tempted to say that I make no place for laziness in my life and that that is my mistake. I feel it as a lack, and a wrong. I often place myself in a situation to struggle to do things. When I don't do them, or at least during the time when I can't manage to do these things—because I do end up doing them in the long run—it's more a question of an idleness that is imposed upon me rather than a laziness of my choosing, and imposing myself upon it.[6]

These thoughts may well have been inspired by *Le Droit à la paresse*. And even though Lafargue was no Schopenhauer, his manifesto, no *Oblomov*, and his recipes for laziness somewhat lacking in metaphysical savoir faire, he still managed to sound the alarm that the curse of work is upon us and unless we cultivate the right to laziness, we will turn into the sickly outgrowths of our own relentless producing. Lafargue's words, aimed at the nineteenth-century French working class, resonate with anybody afflicted with the curious puritanical shame about idleness. Besides providing us with fresh excuses for dozing off in libraries and procrastinating in the remainder section of bookstores, he demands the same lucidity as Nietzsche, another debunker of the religion of work. Both men share an antipathy to a work ethic that barely could conceal its ends: to police human emotions, to provide a flow of activity so relentless that it would finally allow us not to think, let alone to feel:

In the glorification of "work" and the never-ceasing talk about the "blessing of labour," I see the same secret *arrière-pensée* as I do in the praise bestowed on impersonal acts of a general interest, viz. a fear of everything individual. For at the sight of work—that is to say, severe toil from morning till night—we have the feeling that it is the best police, viz. that it holds every one in check and effectively hinders the development of reason, of greed, and of desire for independence. For work uses up an extraordinary proportion of nervous force, withdrawing it from reflection, meditation, dreams, cares, love, and hatred.[7]

In our frenetic lives, napping is looked down upon as a fatal flaw, while exercising is a sure sign of strength and character. Reading is decadent unless we can contribute our newly-found knowledge to a future enlightening conversation. In sum, appearing to be doing nothing makes others intensely uncomfortable. In our previous chapters, we have been dwelling on obsession as the counterpoison to such uneasiness. Engaging compulsively in any activity keeps us clear from the demon of en-

6. "Osons être paresseux," *Le Monde*, September 16, 1979; my translation.

7. Friedrich Nietzsche, *Daybreak*, bk. 3, no. 173, trans. R. J. Hollingdale (Cambridge: Cambridge University Press, 1982), 105.

nui and the anxieties of self-examination. Goals keep us out of trouble, while indolent daydreams, like slow heartburn, invade our whole being, hinting at parallel lives, filling us with dangerous doubts. But what if, as Nietzsche is suggesting, these doubts are an integral part of our thinking selves and doing away with them is the smug way of taking ourselves off the hook, putting to sleep our bad conscience? Let's get to work fast! One more minute of procrastination might push us off the edge and throw in our faces the painful questions that we have been too busy to ask!

Max Weber addressed this relationship between asceticism and work, tracking the change in attitude between a suffering and a proud relationship to work. This transformation is at the core of the monomaniacal imagination. The daunting fear of "wasted time" that plagues the characters in this book (as if time were a commodity that we choose either to waste, to spend, or to save) is converted into a highly-organized sense of redeeming temporality. In the various manifestations of the idée fixe, the world falls into place because it is guided by a work plan, a rigid timetable, a firm and meaningful teleology. What Lafargue describes as an empty workaholic impulse is a therapeutic solution to loss; it is a way of counteracting chaos with directed motion, a way of relieving the mourner's nostalgia for metaphysical plenitude.

—ɯ—

With the exception perhaps of Nodier's visionary Jean-François, this book has not presented obsession as a happy solution to life's travails. Granted, monomania has protected its victims from senselessness, from insignificance, but one would be hard pressed to call it salutary. Before I bring this book to a close, I need to ponder one more question, and I will take Don Quixote along with me to find my answer. What is the link between obsession and delusion? What is it about the latter that actively helps us get through life's most troublesome spots? Whether we read about it or succumb to it ourselves, delusion has often served us well. While we are being duped by love, politics, or bad novels, we seem to walk more steadily, with less hesitation. Our absolutist delusions coat the world's acerbity, protecting us from the debilitating gray zone that demands that we take a stance and stick to a responsible choice. Don Quixote, and there lies his strength, never had to make choices; he knew immediately what was just and who was wrong. Casting aside the dreariness of hesitation, he embraced instead a radicalism that shaped him and propelled him along an unwavering course. Only he could enjoy the blissful accord between action and thought, dream and reality.

It is this blissful symmetry that Cervantes' readers have been mar-
veling at for generations. Don Quixote's monomaniacal ideals provide a
sense of closure that we can only dream about. Don Quixote's idée fixe is
an action carried out to its bitter end, bearing with it an unflagging logic.
We cannot help being hypnotically attracted to a drive that fulfills *itself* so
inexorably, while affording such personal fulfillment. We follow Don
Quixote as he enacts two roles at once—master and slave of his own delusion. He has managed to obliterate his old self while making his new
identity coincide with the idée fixe of chivalry. By doing so, he duplicates
the principle of creation begotten by his own author. Cervantes, indeed,
creates a fictional world that follows its own rules (of which there is more
than one version), its own logic, and that ends up replacing the very reality it is representing. The reader, analogously, is also absorbed by this
fiction, gladly forsaking his or her reality for Don Quixote's delusions. So
by inventing a character immune to doubt and skepticism, Cervantes has
accomplished the double feat of creating a character who overcomes his
reality and, in the process, enables his readers to escape their own. Skepticism, that enlightened quality that has turned us into cautious thinkers,
will continue to protect us from Quixotic fundamentalism. But in the
process, it has robbed from us the deadly bliss of absolute belief.

If Cervantes' reader's and protagonist's overlapping achievements
have been so successful, it is because they have effortlessly trickled out of
the knight's undeviating conviction. It is this same untarnished ideal that
will help readers overcome their own sense of limits, while gently docu-
menting (and mocking) their endless ability to con themselves out of despair, to write and read themselves out of the mediocrity of life. By
following one idea, by emulating one model of chivalry, Don Quixote
leaves behind his past commonplaceness, taking our own with him. His
almighty idea of knighthood acts as the transforming force that converts
impotence into supremacy. Don Quixote had to kill his worldly identity
to be reborn as a figure whose extravagant visions could dispel disappointment and humiliation.[8] His faith in this alternate life resembles the

8. It is worth rereading Marthe Robert's *Roman des origines et origines du roman* (Paris:
Gallimard, 1972). Don Quixote, she writes, "exists only by the suicide of the very individual
he has himself invented; he is born of a death and this death remains law, ghost swallowed
by the void . . . Don Quixote kills Don Quixada without ever taking on a real substance, remaining, thereby, the true incarnation of pure imagination (*l'imaginaire pur*), one that is radically released from the pressures of thought" (190). Robert reads Don Quixote as the great
success story of desire; by staging and acting out his fantasies, he has regressed to a blissful
state of infancy, using stories to alleviate the failures and humiliations of everyday life. Not
only has Don Quixote engendered himself, but he uses his new identity to erase the failures

naïvely beautiful hopes Hyacinth Robinson voices in Henry James's *The Princess Casamassima:* what if literature could carry you "to some brighter, happier vision," leaving behind the mediocrity of the empirical world?

—𝔪—

I will argue, as a conclusion to this book, that the moment of artistic creation, in its simultaneous embrace and rejection of the empirical, mimics Don Quixote's crystallized bliss. Despite the tyrannical nature of creation, despite the way it mocks its "chosen ones" by conjuring up visions, words, or sounds that seem impossible to get right or to duplicate, the drive to produce a work of art is uncannily congruent with the logic of obsession. It is those who are so eager to use this "art-making moment" as a corrective that are most relevant to this study. Like Don Quixote, they suffer from an unbearable ontological brittleness. Only by masking this weakness under the hard shell of a belief, a self-imposed order, can they turn fragility into strength. But like a frozen plant that easily snaps off its stem, this brittle self can become unbending, turning its artfully structured patterns into the monomania that is both the disease and its cure. These studies on obsession have sought to illustrate how certain idées fixes help make the world appear more manageable, a simple by-product of one's own act of volition. The production of art has often been a particularly efficient means to this end. Its self-contained nature can indeed promote unparalleled feelings of mastery and influence.[9]

Storytelling is a bold step against impotence and frustration, because it actively disturbs and distorts the status quo, allowing both its maker and its reader to redirect the flow of history. Telling a story is always a retelling; accordingly, any type of artistic production will use this retelling, this retooling, to re-ascertain its influence over the passing of time. The time of writing, for instance, stands in victorious contrast to the time that passes us by. The passive surrender to flux, to the seemingly insignificant tasks of the everyday, robs us of a sense of agency, often provoking in us the desire to turn the accidental into the intentional, the fortuitous into the premeditated. Writing, painting, or indeed any cre-

of the past. "The enchanter, who enchants himself to cure his injured vanity . . . has of course the great privilege of being able to erase everything he has learned . . . during those fifty mediocre past years, embittered by the resentment of bruised self-love" (193). My translation.

9. See again Janet Beizer's analysis of Flaubert's letters to Louise Colet: Flaubert is constantly admonishing his lover to tighten up her style, to give it musculature, to stop letting herself go. Writing is about control, not the loss thereof. Janet Beizer, *Ventriloquized Bodies: Narratives of Hysteria in Nineteenth-Century France* (Ithaca: Cornell University Press, 1994).

ative gesture rooted in an urgent sense of purpose brings time back under our control. Seated in the driver's seat, the artist afflicted by the fear of unstoppable motion hopes to reconnect to a world that has now been endowed with meaning.

This total absorption in the static, in the self's familiar ruminations, cannot survive the piercing nature of dialogue. Casaubon could resist Dorothea's petulance only by making her subservient to his grand project, to his own deadly rhythms. Kien, likewise, could not maintain his system once it had been disturbed by one who had her own mad methods, her own obsessive relationship to life. In most of the cases I have examined, what lies behind the nervous activity is a profound fear of discovering that once you scratch the veneer of the quotidian, there is nothing but emptiness. The advantage of obsession is that it is essentially preservationist, protecting us from our more or less explicit aversion for the everyday. Nodier's Jean-François les bas-bleus only makes sense of language when asked about the loftiest of abstractions, when he can be guaranteed that nothing will corrupt his own train of thought. He suddenly takes on the persona of a specialist, discussing constellations and higher mathematics, for only then is his language secure and precise. But when asked about the weather, his speech breaks down, deteriorating into babble and non-sequiturs. Jean-François goes mad when the world returns to its prosaic state, when it can no longer liberate his spirit from the limits of the body. Functioning only through abstract hypotheses, such mundanity-adverse individuals manage to escape the tyranny of communication, turning the language of words, music, or art into a peaceful space of solitary confinement. As a medicinal counterpoison, this space excludes any alien presence. But many of the cases we have examined couple this isolation with the disturbing urge to command or surrender to authority. Witness both Mondrian's visceral horror of anything that might resist the "purification" of painting and his not so secret affection for authority. It is curious, though, that the retreat back into a private realm, while it seems to contradict this hunger for authority, is in fact a way of turning it back against the self, a subtle source of self-disciplining and censoring.

When Flaubert and Mondrian use art as their solitary workshop, they are simultaneously placing their skills (writing, painting) at the center of the world, while at the same time using them to obliterate their individuality. Flaubert's godlike omniscience has eyes for everything except himself. The order he imposes on his creatures is so intensely impartial that it keeps out the painfully autobiographical. Such an ordering principle cuts out any form of self-examination, offering instead a convenient blindfold. We return to the question: so what indeed is so frightening about the self that it needs so mercilessly to be cut out? Shapiro has argued that the rigid individual tends to associate any activity that is not blatantly useful (in a civic sense) with decadence and self-indulgence. Such natures understand very precisely Plato's admonition against the teary, softening quality of certain poetic works. With these misgivings comes the fear that if we stop working, producing, creating useful things, we might become fatally attracted to leisure. Leisure is dangerous because it makes us porous to the unstructured nature of time itself. This pervious quality might lead us to the very self that obsession managed to conceal. This perilous formlessness might well bring to the surface a potentially abhorrent side of our nature, a nature better concealed by the steel fist of a willed task.

Much can be read in this panic of recreation. There is a haunting feeling of anxiety in a stillness that could well generate a loss of the very self we are trying to shape and to structure into a palpable entity. What brings about dread is not being able to give an explanation for the shape of our life. How else to explain the dutiful quality with which the writer, the scholar, or the artist retreats behind the closed doors of his or her atelier? Behind the deliberateness of such blatantly isolating gestures lies the great fear of being mistaken for somebody frivolous, wasteful, who squanders life.[10] There has to be a higher duty, a greater goal, that these solitary hours are working toward. Time must be used, not wasted. The compulsion, the idée fixe, stands for this business, turning it into a valuable venture. All the more so for obsession, the most authoritarian form of private thinking, a compulsion that protects by enslaving its victim to the blissful blindness of a single idea.

While the whirlwind quality of life mirrors our own wavering identities, our anxious place in the world, the act of making something permanent (it can be art, but also education, a relationship, a political speech) provides ballast to this floating sensation. Firming up the lack of our existential contours is exactly the function of the compulsive gestures that I have been identifying throughout this study: they too are antidotes, more or less successful shields against existential dysphoria and dis-

10. Shapiro describes this in terms of the compulsive individual's "identification of himself with the regime of dutiful work and purpose." This identification "transforms the subjective meaning of autonomy from being free to follow one's own wishes" to a "state of continuous tension between will and underlying inclination. Even innocuous interests (like watching television) may become antagonists of superior purpose . . . and may be experienced as weakness or laziness." David Shapiro, *Autonomy and Rigid Character* (New York: Basic Books, 1981), 86.

placement. Being a collector, focusing one's entire energy on possessing a person or an object, single-mindedly mastering a craft or promoting an ideology—all these impulses have the astonishing power of buffering the self against unpredictable life changes.

All these attempts to simplify and to unify protect the self from the intolerable pressure of being cast out in a realm where division reigns. Retreating into one's solipsistic world provides a simultaneous sense of autonomy and subordination. It is the balance between these two opposite states that makes monomania such an enthralling condition. The practitioners of brutally rigid rituals seem, on the one hand, to be entirely masters of their time, while, on the other hand, the servants of sustaining and defining routines. This makes one wonder what type of connection exists between art, obsession, and dictatorship. Does art (or obsession) keep us from life or does it provide a home within it? Kierkegaard answers this very question in terms of melancholy when he talks about depression as a shelter against the predatory intrusions of the world. He describes the melancholic perched in his aerial castle, master of his desire and appetites. This mastery, however, is hollow, because, like Narcissus, melancholic monomaniacs have only learned to tolerate what is themselves; like Echo, they can only become what they already are, their own reflection, forever blind to what is other.

Appendix*

—m—m—m—

Introduction

Page 16, n. 30: "La vie est une chose tellement hideuse que le seul moyen de la supporter, c'est de l'éviter. Et on l'évite en vivant dans l'Art, dans la recherche incessante du Vrai rendu par le Beau." Flaubert to George Sand, April 3, 1876. Gustave Flaubert, *Préface à la vie d'écrivain*, ed. Geneviève Bollème (Paris: Seuil, 1963), 271.

Chapter 2

Page 42, n. 2 : "Vous me demandez comment je me suis guéri des hallucinations nerveuses que je subissais autrefois? Par deux moyens: 1. en les étudiant scientifiquement, c'est-à-dire en tâchant de m'en rendre compte, et 2. par la force de la volonté. J'ai souvent senti la folie me venir. C'était dans ma pauvre cervelle un tourbillon d'idées et d'images où il me semble que ma conscience, que mon moi, sombrait comme un vaisseau sous la tempête. Mais je me cramponnais à ma raison. . . . L'humanité est ainsi, il ne s'agit pas de la changer, mais de la connaître." Flaubert to Mademoiselle Leroyer de Chantepie, May 18, 1857, *Œuvres*, 2:716.

Page 49, n. 19: "Il faut s'habituer à ne voir dans les gens qui nous entourent que des livres. L'homme de sens les étudie, les compare et fait de tout cela une synthèse à son usage. Le monde n'est qu'un clavecin pour le véritable artiste. A lui d'en tirer des sons qui ravissent ou qui glacent d'effroi." Flaubert to Ernest Chevalier, February 24, 1842, *Œuvres*, 1:96.

---

*This appendix makes available only those texts that would lose considerably in translation or that have not been translated at all. Since the Baudelaire quotes are very short, I have transcribed "Mademoiselle Bistouri" in its entirety.

Pages 49–50, n. 20: "Je me demande si un livre, indépendamment de ce qu'il dit, ne peut pas produire le même effet. Dans la précision des assemblages, la rareté des éléments, le poli de la surface, l'harmonie de l'ensemble, n'y a-t-il pas une vertu intrinsèque, une espèce de forme divine, quelque chose d'éternel comme un principe? (je parle en platonicien) . . . la loi des nombres gouverne donc les sentiments et les images, et ce qui paraît être extérieur est tout bonnement là-dedans." Flaubert to George Sand, April 3, 1876, *Préface,* 271.

Page 50, n. 21: "La vie est une chose tellement hideuse que le seul moyen de la supporter, c'est de l'éviter. Et on l'évite en vivant dans l'Art, dans la recherche incessante du Vrai rendu par le Beau. Lisez les grands maîtres en tâchant de saisir leur procédé, de vous rapprocher de leur âme, et vous sortirez de cette étude avec des éblouissements qui vous rendront joyeuse. Vous serez comme Moïse en descendant du Sinaï. Il avait des rayons autour de la face, pour avoir contemplé Dieu." Flaubert to Mademoiselle Leroyer de Chantepie, May 18, 1857, *Œuvres,* 2:717.

Page 51, n. 22: "Il y a un sentiment ou plutôt une habitude dont vous me semblez manquer, à savoir l'amour de la contemplation. Prenez la vie, les passions et vous-même comme un sujet à exercices intellectuels . . . Prenez un plan d'études, qu'il soit rigoureux. . . . Astreignez-vous à un travail régulier et fatigant." Flaubert to Mademoiselle Leroyer de Chantepie, *Œuvres,* 2:716–17; italics in original.

Page 51, n. 24: "Quant à l'amour, ç'a été le grand sujet de réflexion de toute ma vie. Ce que je n'ai pas donné à l'art pur, au métier en soi, a été là; et le cœur que j'étudiais, c'était le mien." Flaubert to Louise Colet, July 5, 1852, *Œuvres,* 2:124.

Page 51, n. 25: "Comment donc tirer profit de tout cela [les découvertes de la Renaissance], pour la beauté? . . . en étudiant quelle forme, quelle couleur convient à telle personne, dans telle circonstance donnée. Il y a là un rapport de tons et de lignes qu'il faut saisir. Les grandes coquettes s'y entendent et, pas plus que les vrais dandys, elles ne s'habillent d'après le journal de modes. . . . De quoi cet effet-là dépend-il? D'un rapport exact, qui vous échappe, entre les traits et l'expression du visage et l'accoutrement." Flaubert to Louise Colet, January 29, 1854, *Œuvres,* 2:519; italics in original.

Page 52, n. 26: "Ce que je redoute étant la passion, le mouvement, je crois, si le bonheur est quelque part, qu'il est dans la stagnation." Flaubert to Ernest Chevalier, August 13, 1845, *Œuvres*, 1:249.

Page 52, n. 27: "Fais comme moi: romps avec l'extérieur, vis comme un ours—un ours blanc—envoie faire foutre tout." Flaubert to Alfred Le Poittevin, September 16, 1845, *Œuvres*, 1:251.

Page 52, n. 28: "Je vis absolument comme une huître. Mon roman est le rocher qui m'attache et je ne sais rien de ce qui se passe dans le monde." Flaubert to George Sand, September 9, 1868, *Œuvres*, 3:797.

Page 52, n. 30: "J'écris pour moi, pour moi seul, comme je fume et comme je dors. C'est une fonction presque animale, tant elle est personnelle et intime . . . il me semble que mon œuvre perdrait même tout à être publiée. Il y a des animaux qui vivent dans la terre et des plantes que l'on ne peut pas cueillir et que l'on ignore. Il y a peut-être des esprits crées pour les coins inabordables. A quoi servent-ils? A rien! Ne serais-je pas de cette famille?" Flaubert to Louise Colet, August 16, 1847, *Œuvres*, 1:467.

Page 53, n. 32: "J'éprouve une répulsion invincible à mettre sur le papier quelque chose de mon cœur. . . . Est-ce que Dieu l'a jamais dite son opinion? Voilà pourquoi j'ai pas mal de choses qui m'étouffent, que je voudrais cracher et que je ravale. A quoi bon les dire en effet." Flaubert to George Sand, December 5, 1866, *Œuvres*, 3:575.

Page 55, n. 35: "Homère, Shakespeare, Goethe, tous les fils aînés de Dieu (comme dit Michelet) se sont bien gardés de faire toute autre chose que représenter." October 23, 1863, *Œuvres*, 3:353.

Page 56, n. 37: "Il faut se renfermer et continuer la tête baissée dans son œuvre comme une taupe." Flaubert to Louise Colet, September 22, 1853, *Œuvres*, 2:437.

Page 56, n. 38: "L'homme n'est rien, l'œuvre est tout. . . . Je recherche avant tout la beauté. . . . Des phrases me font pâmer, qui leur paraissent fort ordinaires. Goncourt est très heureux quand il a saisi dans la rue un mot qu'il peut coller dans un livre, et moi très satisfait quand j'ai écrit une page sans assonances ou répétitions . . . c'est bien écrire qui est mon but, je ne le cache pas." Flaubert to George Sand, December 1875, *Œuvres*, 4:1000.

Page 57, n. 39: "Je mène une vie âpre, déserte, de toute joie extérieure, et où je n'ai rien pour me soutenir qu'une espèce de rage permanente. . . . J'aime mon travail d'un amour frénétique et perverti, comme un ascète le cilice qui lui gratte le ventre." Flaubert to Louise Colet, April 24, 1852, *Œuvres,* 2:75.

Page 57, n. 40: "Ce qui me semble beau, ce que je voudrais faire, c'est un livre sur rien, un livre sans attaches extérieures, qui se tiendrait de lui-même par la force interne de son style, comme la terre sans être soutenue se tient en l'air. . . . Les œuvres les plus belles sont celles où il y a le moins de matière. . . . Je crois que l'avenir de l'Art est dans ces voies. . . . C'est pour cela qu'il n'y a ni beaux ni vilains sujets et qu'on pourrait presque établir comme axiome, en se posant au point de vue de l'Art pur, qu'il n'y en a aucun, le style étant à lui tout seul une manière absolue de voir les choses." Flaubert to Louise Colet, January 16, 1852, *Œuvres,* 2:31.

Page 59, n. 41: "tâche de l'aimer d'un amour exclusif, ardent, dévoué. Cela ne te faillira pas. L'Idée seule est éternelle et nécessaire." Flaubert to Louise Colet, August 8–9, 1846, *Œuvres,* 1:283.

Page 59, n. 42: "Les femmes, qui ont le cœur trop ardent et l'esprit trop exclusif, ne comprennent pas cette religion de la beauté, abstraction faite du sentiment. Il leur faut toujours une cause, un but." Flaubert to Louise Colet, August 6–7, 1846, *Œuvres,* 1:278.

Page 59, n. 43: "Ce que j'aime par-dessus tout, c'est la forme, pourvu qu'elle soit belle, et rien au-delà. . . . Il n'y a pour moi dans le monde que les beaux vers, les phrases bien tournées, harmonieuses, chantantes. . . . Au delà, rien." Flaubert to Louise Colet, August 8, 1846, *Œuvres,* 1:278.

Page 59, n. 44: "Non! la Littérature n'est pas ce que j'aime le plus au monde. Je me suis mal expliqué. . . . Je vous parlais de distraction. . . . Je ne suis pas si cuistre que de préférer des phrases à des Êtres." Flaubert to George Sand, March 3, 1872, *Œuvres,* 4:491.

Page 59, n. 45: "Je me grise avec de l'encre comme d'autres avec du vin. Mais c'est si difficile d'écrire que parfois je suis brisé de fatigue." Flaubert to Mademoiselle Leroyer de Chantepie, December 18, 1859, *Œuvres,* 3:65.

Page 59, n. 46: "Le moyen de vivre avec sérénité . . . c'est de se fixer sur une pyramide quelconque, n'importe laquelle, pourvu qu'elle soit élevée et la base solide." Flaubert to Louise Colet, May 30, 1852, *Œuvres*, 2:100.

Page 60, n. 47: "Voilà pourquoi j'aime l'art. C'est que là, au moins, tout est liberté dans ce monde des fictions.—On y assouvit tout, on y fait tout, on est à la fois son roi et son peuple, actif et passif, victime et prêtre. Pas de limites. . . . Je me suis ainsi bien vengé de l'existence." Flaubert to Louise Colet, May 23, 1852, *Œuvres*, 2:91.

Chapter 3

Page 62, second epigraph: "C'est pourquoi je préfère considérer cette condition anormale de l'esprit comme une véritable grâce, comme un miroir magique où l'homme est invité à se voir en beau, c'est-à-dire tel qu'il devrait et pourrait être, une espèce d'excitation angélique, un rappel à l'ordre sous une forme complimenteuse." Baudelaire, "Le Poème du haschisch," in *Œuvres complètes, Paradis artificiels* (Paris: Gallimard, édition de la Pléiade, 1961), 348.

Page 63, n. 6: "La monomanie s'est divisée naturellement en monomanie explicite, mais inoffensive, c'est l'affaire du médecin; et en monomanie militante, c'est l'affaire du jury. . . . Je me suis avisé, moi, de vous entretenir un moment d'une espèce de monomanie qui échappe à tous les deux parce qu'elle n'agit que d'une manière intime, individuelle, grième et poignante pour l'infortuné seul auquel elle s'est attachée, et j'ai pris la liberté grande de l'appeler monomanie réflective, aucun philosophe à ma connaissance n'ayant songé à lui donner un nom. Elle est cependant fort commune, surtout chez les peuples dont la civilisation s'use à force de prétendus perfectionnements. C'est celle qui se dénoue ordinairement par le suicide." Charles Nodier, "Rêverie psychologique de la monomanie réflective," in *L'Amateur de livres*, ed. Jean-Luc Steinmetz (Paris: Castor Astral, 1993), 48–49.

Page 64, n. 7: "Il existe dans les hommes bien organisés un doux état de pensée où elle s'isole à plaisir de toutes les réalités de la vie; où elle peut se déposséder, sans rien perdre, du passé, du présent, de l'avenir, et même de l'espérance, pour se former un monde à son choix, sur lequel elle ex-

erce avec un souverain empire tous les attributs de la puissance de Dieu."
Nodier, "Rêverie psychologique de la monomanie réflective," 50.

Page 66, n. 10: "Je n'écrirai de ma vie une histoire fantastique, on peut
m'en croire, que si je n'ai en elle une foi aussi sincère . . . que dans les faits
journaliers de mon existence; et je ne crois pas pour ceci rien devoir en intelligence et en raison aux esprits forts qui nient absolument le fantastique.
. . . Je diffère d'eux . . . par une certaine manière de voir, de sentir et de
juger." From Nodier's introduction to "Jean-François les bas-bleus," in
Smarra, Trilby, et autres contes, ed. Jean-Luc Steinmetz (Paris: Garnier Flammarion, 1980), 415.

Page 66, n. 12: "Tout ce que la vie a de positive est mauvais. Tout ce qu'elle
a de bon est imaginaire." Nodier, *La Fée aux miettes,* in *Smarra, Trilby, et
autres contes,* ed. Steinmetz.

Page 68, n. 15: "Une des particularités les plus remarquables de la folie de
ce bon jeune homme, c'est qu'elle n'était sensible que dans les conversations sans importance, où l'esprit s'exerce sur des choses familières. Si on
l'abordait pour lui parler de la pluie, du beau temps . . . du journal . . . les
paroles qui affluaient sur ses lèvres se pressaient si tumultueusement
qu'elles se confondaient avant la fin de la première période en je ne sais
quel galimatias inextricable. . . . Il continuait cependant, de plus en plus
inintelligible, et substituant de plus en plus à . . . la phrase naturelle et
logique de l'homme simple le babillage de l'enfant qui ne sait pas la
valeur des mots, ou le radotage du vieillard qui l'a oublié." Nodier, "Jean-
François les bas-bleus," 418.

Page 69, n. 16: "Les problèmes les plus difficiles des sciences exactes . . .
n'étaient pour lui rien qu'un jeu. . . . Il n'en était pas de même quand
l'entretien se résumait avec précision en une question morale ou
scientifique de quelque intérêt. Alors les rayons si divergents, si
éparpillés de cette intelligence malade se resserraient tout à coup en
faisceau . . . et prêtaient tant d'éclat . . . à son discours, qu'il est permis
de douter que Jean-François ait jamais été, plus savant . . . dans l'en-
tière jouissance de la raison." Nodier, "Jean-François les bas-bleus,"
416.

Page 70, n. 19: "vaste désert de pensée où s'égare un monde déchu qui se précipite vers le néant, [comme un] . . . doute affreux entre le faux et le vrai." Preface to *La Fée aux miettes*.

Page 71, n. 21: "Quelle paix sans mélange à goûter dans cette région limpide qui n'est jamais agitée, qui n'est jamais privée du jour du soleil, et qui rit, lumineuse et paisible, au-dessus de nos ouragans comme au-dessus de nos misères." Nodier, "Jean-François les bas-bleus," 423.

Page 72, n. 25: "C'était toute une âme qu'il fallait á . . . la mienne, une âme tendre, une âme sœur et cependant souveraine, qui m'enveloppât, qui me confondît et m'absorbât dans sa volonté, qui m'enlevât tout ce qui était pour moi pour le faire elle, qui fût autre chose que moi, un million de fois plus que moi, et qui cependant fût moi. Oh! cela ne peut se dire." Nodier, *La Fée aux miettes*, 335.

Page 73, n. 27: "L'habitude des fascinations en pâlit le prestige; le retour obstiné des désabusements l'éteint tout à fait; il s'évanouit et disparaît comme une bulle de savon de nos écoliers. . . . Comme elle a vérifié par expérience que son bonheur idéal n'était que mensonge, elle se saisit avec un dépit cruel des rigueurs de la vie positive . . . sûre qu'elle est du moins que la réalité ne manquera plus à ses espérances." Nodier, "Rêverie psychologique," 51.

Page 74, n. 28: "Cette joie immense, accablante, indéfinissable, qui me manquait, et qui manque probablement à la plupart des hommes, j'en avais amassé, tous les rayons au portrait de Belkiss." Nodier, *La Fée aux miettes*, 335.

Page 75, n. 31: "Si je refaisais jamais une histoire fantastique, je la ferais autrement. Je la ferais seulement pour les gens qui ont l'inappréciable bonheur de croire, les honnêtes paysans de mon village, les aimables et sages enfants qui n'ont pas profité de l'enseignement mutuel, et les poètes de pensée et de cœur qui ne sont pas de l'Académie!" Nodier, *La Fée aux miettes*, 225.

Page 76, n. 34: "Je vous ai dit qu'il s'était formé, entre son portrait et moi une espèce d'intelligence merveilleuse qui suppléait . . . la parole, avec plus de mouvement, de rapidité, d'entraînement peut-être, comme si la plus légère des impressions de ma pensée allait se refléter, par je ne sais quelle puissance, dans ces linéaments immobiles, dans ces couleurs fixées par le pinceau." Nodier, *La Fée aux miettes*, 295.

Page 77, n. 35: "Funeste instinct qui ouvrit . . . à Ève les portes de la mort, à Pandore la boîte où dormiraient encore toutes les misères de l'human-ité . . . depuis ce moment-là . . . je n'interrogeais presque plus. Je pris ma vie comme elle était." Nodier, *La Fée aux miettes*, 349.

Chapter 4

"Mademoiselle Bistouri," by Baudelaire

Comme j'arrivais à l'extrémité du faubourg, sous les éclairs du gaz, je sentis un bras qui se coulait doucement sous le mien, et j'entendis une voix qui me disait à l'oreille: «Vous êtes médecin, monsieur?»

Je regardai; c'était une grande fille, robuste, aux yeux très-ouverts, légèrement fardée, les cheveux flottant au vent avec les brides de son bon-net.

«—Non; je ne suis pas médecin. Laissez-moi passer.

—Oh! si! vous êtes médecin. Je le vois bien. Venez chez moi. Vous serez bien content de moi, allez!

—Sans doute, j'irai vous voir, mais plus tard, *après le médecin,* que dia-ble!—Ah! ah! —fit-elle, toujours suspendue à mon bras, et en éclatant de rire, —vous êtes un médecin farceur, j'en ai connu plusieurs dans ce genre-là. Venez.»

J'aime passionnément le mystère, parce que j'ai toujours l'espoir de le débrouiller. Je me laissai donc entraîner par cette compagne, ou plutôt par cette énigme inespérée.

J'omets la description du taudis; on peut la trouver dans plusieurs vieux poètes français bien connus. Seulement, détail non aperçu par Rég-nier, deux ou trois portraits de docteurs célèbres étaient suspendus aux murs.

Comme je fus dorloté! Grand feu, vin chaud, cigares; et en m'offrant ces bonnes choses et en allumant elle-même un cigare, la bouffonne créa-ture me disait: «Faites comme chez vous, mon ami, mettez-vous à l'aise. Ça vous rappellera l'hôpital et le bon temps de la jeunesse.

—Ah çà! où donc avez-vous gagné ces cheveux blancs? Vous n'étiez pas ainsi, il n'y a pas encore bien longtemps; quand vous étiez interne de

L. . . . Je me souviens que c'était vous qui l'assistiez dans les opérations graves. En voilà un homme, qui aime couper, tailler et rogner! C'était vous qui lui tendiez les instruments, les fils et les éponges. —Et comme, l'opération faite, il disait fièrement, en regardant sa montre: «Cinq minutes, messieurs!» —Oh! moi, je vais partout. Je connais bien ces Messieurs.»

Quelques instants plus tard, me tutoyant, elle reprenait son antienne, et me disait: «Tu es médecin, n'est-ce pas, mon chat?»

Cet inintelligible refrain me fit sauter sur mes jambes. «Non! criai-je furieux.

—Chirurgien, alors?

—Non! non! à moins que ce ne soit pour te couper la tête! S . . . s . . . c . . . de s . . . m . . . !

—Attends, reprit-elle, tu vas voir.»

Et elle tira d'une armoire une liasse de papiers, qui n'était autre chose que la collection des portraits des médecins illustres de ce temps, lithographiés par Maurin, qu'on a pu voir étalée pendant plusieurs années sur le quai Voltaire.

«Tiens! le reconnais-tu celui-ci?

—Oui! c'est X. Le nom est au bas d'ailleurs; mais je le connais personnellement.

—Je savais bien! Tiens! voilà Z., celui qui disait à son cours, en parlant de X.: «Ce monstre qui porte sur son visage la noirceur de son âme!» Tout cela, parce que l'autre n'était pas de son avis dans la même affaire! Comme on riait de ça à l'École, dans le temps! Tu t'en souviens? —Tiens, voilà K., celui qui dénonçait au gouvernement les insurgés qu'il soignait à son hôpital. C'était le temps des émeutes. Comment est-ce possible qu'un si bel homme ait si peu de cœur? —Voici maintenant W., un fameux médecin anglais; je l'ai attrapé à son voyage à Paris. Il a l'air d'une demoiselle, n'est-ce pas?»

Et comme je touchais à un paquet ficelé, posé aussi sur le guéridon: «Attends un peu, dit-elle; -ça, c'est les internes, et ce paquet-ci, c'est les externes.»

Et elle déploya en éventail une masse d'images photographiques, représentant des physionomies beaucoup plus jeunes.

«Quand nous nous reverrons, tu me donneras ton portrait, n'est-ce pas, chéri?

—Mais, lui dis-je, suivant à mon tour, moi aussi, mon idée fixe, — pourquoi me crois-tu médecin?

—C'est que tu es si gentil et si bon pour les femmes!

—Singulière logique! me dis-je à moi-même.

—Oh! je ne m'y trompe guère; j'en ai connu un bon nombre. J'aime tant ces messieurs, que, bien que je ne sois pas malade, je vais quelquefois les voir, rien que pour les voir. Il y en a qui me disent froidement: «Vous n'êtes pas malade du tout!» Mais il y en a d'autres qui me comprennent, parce que je leur fais des mines.

—Et quand ils ne te comprennent pas . . . ?

—Dame! comme je les ai dérangés *inutilement,* je laisse dix francs sur la cheminée. —C'est si bon et si doux, ces hommes-là! —J'ai découvert à la Pitié un petit interne, qui est joli comme un ange, et qui est poli! et qui travaille, le pauvre garçon! Ses camarades m'ont dit qu'il n'avait pas le sou, parce que ses parents sont des pauvres qui ne peuvent rien lui envoyer. Cela m'a donné confiance. Après tout, je suis assez belle femme, quoique pas trop jeune. Je lui ai dit: «Viens me voir, viens me voir souvent. Et avec moi, ne te gêne pas; je n'ai pas besoin d'argent.» Mais tu comprends que je lui ai fait entendre ça par une foule de façons; je ne le lui ai pas dit tout crûment; j'avais si peur de l'humilier, ce cher enfant! —Eh bien! croirais-tu que j'ai une drôle d'envie que je n'ose pas lui dire? —Je voudrais qu'il vînt me voir avec sa trousse et son tablier, même avec un peu de sang dessus!»

Elle dit cela d'un air fort candide, comme un homme sensible dirait à une comédienne qu'il aimerait: «Je veux vous voir vêtue du costume que vous portiez dans ce fameux rôle que vous avez créé.»

Moi, m'obstinant, je repris: «Peux-tu te souvenir de l'époque et de l'occasion où est née en toi cette passion si particulière?»

Difficilement je me fis comprendre; enfin j'y parvins. Mais alors elle me répondit d'un air très-triste, et même, autant que je peux me souvenir, en détournant les yeux: «Je ne sais pas . . . je ne me souviens pas.»

Quelles bizarreries ne trouve-t-on pas dans une grande ville, quand on sait se promener et regarder? La vie fourmille de monstres innocents. — Seigneur, mon Dieu! vous, le Créateur, vous, le Maître; vous qui avez fait la Loi et la Liberté; vous, le souverain qui laissez faire, vous, le juge qui pardonnez; vous qui êtes plein de motifs et de causes, et qui avez peut-être mis dans mon esprit le goût de l'horreur pour convertir mon coeur, comme la guérison au bout d'une lame; Seigneur, ayez pitié, ayez pitié des fous et des folles! Ô Créateur! peut-il exister des monstres aux yeux de Celui-là seul qui sait pourquoi ils existent, comment ils *se sont faits* et comment ils auraient pu *ne pas se faire?*

Chapter 5

Page 109, n. 13: "Quand le monde extérieur vous dégoûte, vous alanguit, vous corrompt, vous abrutit, les gens honnêtes et délicats sont forcés à chercher en eux-mêmes quelque part un lieu plus propre pour y vivre." Flaubert to Louise Colet, September 4, 1852, *Œuvres complètes*, 2:151.

Chapter 6

Quotations are from Thomas Mann, *Gesammelte Werke*, vol. 2, *Der Zauberberg* (Berlin: Aufbau-Verlag, 1955).

Page 130: "Höchst ärgerlich . . . ist das und beinahe peinlich. Erkältungen, muß du wissen, sind hier nicht *reçus*, man leugnet sie, sie kommen offiziell bei der großen Lufttrockenheit nicht vor. . . . Aber bei dir ist es ja etwas anderes, du hast am Ende das Recht dazu . . . hier aber, ich zweifle, ob man sich hier genügend dafür interessieren wird." (165)

Page 131: "Ein schwerer Schnupfen schien im Anzuge, er saß ihm in der Stirnhöhle und drückte, das Zäpfchen im Halse war weh und wund, die Luft ging ihm nicht wie sonst durch den von der Natur hierzu vorgesehenen Kanal . . . seine Stimme hatte über Nacht die Klangfarbe eines dumpfen und wie von starken Getränken verbrannten Basses angenommen." (165)

Page 131: "unmißverständlich und streng persönlich zu *ihm* herübergeblickt . . . als wollte sie sagen: "Nun? Est ist Zeit. Wirst du gehen?" (denn nur die Augen sprechen, geht ja die Rede per Du . . .). Wußte sie denn, daß er sich auf zwei Uhr zur Untersuchung hatte bestellen lassen?" (176)

Page 131: "Ich habe Sie auf dem Strich gehabt, Castorp, nun kann ich's Ihnen ja sagen,—von vornherein, schon seit ich zuerst die unverdiente Auszeichnung hatte, Sie kennenzulernen,—und ziemlich sicher vermutet, daß Sie im stillen ein Hiesiger wären." (180)

Page 132: "Da drohten sie ihm mit den Zeigefingern, —es war sehr sonderbar. Sie wurden schelmisch, legten den Kopf auf die Seite, kniffen ein Auge zu und rührten die Zeigefinger in Höhe des Ohres, als kämen

kecke, pikante Dinge an den Tag von einem, der den Unschuldigen ge-
spielt hatte." (172)

Page 133: "Messen Sie sich etwa überhaupt nie?"
     "Doch, Frau Oberin. Wenn ich Fieber habe."
     "Menschenkind, man mißt sich in erster Linie, um zu sehen, *ob* man
Fieber hat." (166)

Page 134: "Er nahm lächelnd das rote Etui vom Tisch und öffnete es.
Schmuck wie ein Geschmeide lag das gläserne Gerät in die genau nach
seiner Figur ausgesparte Vertiefung der roten Samtpolsterung gebettet.
Die ganzen Grade waren mit roten, die Zehntelgrade mit schwarzen
Strichen markiert. Die Bezifferung war rot, der untere, mit spiegelig glän-
zendem Quecksilber gefüllt." (167)

Page 134: "Aber ich habe mich nicht zu bemühen brauchen, es ist mir von
selbst in den Schoß gefallen." (168)

Page 135: "Er nahm das zierliche Gerät aus dem Futteral, betrachtete es.
. . . Sein Herz klopfte rasch und stark." (168)

Page 138: "Nein, nein", sagte er, "Sie irren sich, mein Fall ist der denkbar
harmloseste, ich habe Schnupfen, Sie sehen: die Augen gehen mir über,
meine Brust ist verstockt, ich huste die halbe Nacht, es ist unangenehm
genug." (172)

Chapter 7

Quotations are from Elias Canetti, *Die Blendung* (Vienna: Herbert Reichner Verlag, 1935).

Page 146: "Kleine Knaben müßten in einer bedeutenden Privatbibliothek
aufwachsen. Der tägliche Umgang mit nur ernsten Geistern, die kluge,
dunkle, gedämpfte Atmosphäre, eine hartnäckige Gewöhnung an pein-
lichste Ordnung, im Raum wie in der Zeit." (12)

Page 147: "Kien verabscheute die Lüge; von klein auf hielt er sich an die
Wahrheit. . . . . Wissenschaft und Wahrheit waren für ihn identische Be-

griffe. Man näherte sich der Wahrheit, indem man sich von den Menschen abschloß. . . . *Er* legte seinen Ehrgeiz in eine Hartnäckigkeit des Wesens. Nicht bloß einen Monat, nicht ein Jahr, sein ganzes Leben blieb er sich gleich." (15–16)

Page 149: "Es war, als hätte sich jemand gegen die Erde verbarrikadiert; gegen alles bloß materielle Beziehungswesen, gegen alles nur Planetarische eine Kabine erbaut . . . so groß, daß sie für das wenige ausreichte, welches an der Erde und mehr als der Staub ist, zu dem das Leben wieder zerfällt, sie dicht verschlossen und mit diesem Wenigen erfüllt." (67)

Pages 149–150: "Man lernt sich in allerlei Menschen einfühlen. Am vielen Hin und Her gewinnt man Geschmack. Man löst sich in die Figuren auf, die einem gefallen. Jeder Standpunkt wird begreiflich. Willig überläßt man sich fremden Zielen und verliert für länger die eigenen aus dem Auge. . . . Romane müßten von Staats wegen verboten sein." (42)

Page 150: "Memoiren sind uninteressant. . . . Du bist neugierig, ich nicht. Du hörst täglich neue Geschichten und möchtest heute wieder eine zur Abwechslung von mir. Ich verzichte auf Geschichten. . . . Du lebst von deinen Irren, ich von meinen Büchern. Was ist anständiger? Ich könnte in einem Loch hausen, meine Bücher hab' ich im Kopf, du brauchst eine ganze Irrenanstalt. . . . Eigentlich bist du eine Frau. Du bestehst aus Sensationen." (436)

Pages 154–155: "So wie du, bis zur vollendeten Selbstlosigkeit, bis zur Arbeit um der Arbeit und der Pflicht um der Pflicht willen, wie sie Immanuel Kant und lange vor allem Konfuzius fordert, werde ich es freilich nie bringen. Ich fürchte, ich bin zu schwach dazu." (427)

Page 155: "Um eine Kleinigkeit hervorzusuchen, die er ohnehin auswendig wußte, um einer bloßen Bestätigung willen. . . . Dreißig Blätter las er. . . . Gedrucktes oder Geschriebenes, worauf sein Auge einmal fiel, konnte er nicht übergehen." (31)

Pages 155–156: "Gelehrter mit Bibliothek von ungewöhnlicher Größe sucht verantwortungsbewußte Haushälterin. Nur charaktervollste Persönlichkeiten wollen sich melden. Gesindel fliegt die Treppe hinunter. Gehalt Nebensache." (26)

Page 156: "Er ist ein Mann, was hat jetzt zu geschehen? Geschehen? Das geht zu weit. Erst sei festgestellt, wann es zu geschehen hat." (57)

Pages 156–157: "Ein furchtbarer Haß steigt langsam hoch: das hat sie gewagt. Die Bücher! . . . Kien stürzt in langen Sätzen aus dem Zimmer, sperrt sich ins Klosett, dem einzigen bücherfreien Raum der Wohnung ein, zieht sich an diesem Ort mechanisch die Hosen herunter, setzt sich aufs Brett und weint wie ein Kind." (57)

Page 157: "Von nun an werde ich die Türen zu deinen Zimmern geschlossen halten. Ich verbiete dir, diesen Raum zu betreten, solang ich drin bin. . . . Er schnappte nach Schweigen wie andere nach Luft." (66)

Page 158: "Da brauchte er ein Buch, er hob sich und holte es. Bevor er es noch hatte, drängte sich das verdammte Bett in seinen Kopf. Er zerriß den straffen Zusammenhang, es entfernte ihn um Meilen von seinem Wild." (68)

Page 158: "Sehr müde . . . legte sich Kien aufs Bett und sehnte sich nach seiner Bibliothek, wie er sie bald wieder haben würde: vier hohe Räume, die Wände von oben bis unten mit Büchern ausgekleidet. . . . Arbeit, Arbeit, Gedanken, China, wissenschaftliche Kontroversen, Meinung gegen Meinung." (382)

Page 158: "Die Übung im Blindgehen machte aus ihm einen Meister. Drei, vier Wochen verstrichen, und er fand in kürzester Zeit, was er wollte." (71)

Page 158: "Blindheit ist eine Waffe, gegen Zeit und Raum; unser Dasein eine einzige, ungeheuerliche Blindheit, bis auf das wenige, das wir durch unsere kleinlichen Sinne—kleinlich ihrem Wesen wie ihrer Reichweite nach—erfahren. Das herrschende Prinzip im Kosmos ist die Blindheit. Sie ermöglicht ein Nebeneinander von Dingen, die unmöglich wären, wenn sie einander sähen. Sie gestattet das Abreißen der Zeit dort, wo man ihr nicht gewachsen wäre." (71)

Page 159: "Ihr liebster Buchstabe war das O. Im O-Schreiben hatte sie noch eine Übung von der Schule her. (Die O müßt ihr so brav schließen wie die Therese, hat die Lehrerin immer gesagt. Die Therese machte die schönsten O. . . . Die restlichen Stunden der Nacht war sie damit beschäftigt, die Summen, die sie erben würde, durch ihre Geschicklichkeit im O-Schreiben zu steigern." (116, 127)

Page 160: "Sie seien alle zu Hause. Sie hätten Charakter. Er liebe sie . . . je länger die abgeschrittene Reihe wurde, je unversehrter und geschlossener die alte Bibliothek sich erhob, um so lächerlicher erschienen ihm die Feinde. Wie konnten sie es wagen, einen Leib, ein Leben durch Türen zu zerstückeln?" (89)

Page 160: "Aber wer hatte denn je die Fühllosigkeit des Anorganischen wirklich bewiesen, wer weiß, ob ein Buch sich nicht nach anderen sehnt, mit denen es lange beisammen war, auf eine Art, die uns fremd ist und die wir darum übersehen?" (67)

Page 162: "Aus der ersten Zeile löst sich ein Stab und schlägt ihm eine um die Ohren. Blei. Das tut weh. Schlag! Schlag! . . . Eine Fußnote tritt ihn mit Füßen. Immer mehr. Er taumelt. Zeilen und ganze Seiten, alles fällt über ihn her." (463)

Page 163: "Buchstaben klappern im Buch. Sind gefangen und können nicht heraus. Blutig haben sie ihn geschlagen. Er droht ihnen mit dem Feuertod. So rächt er sich an allen Feinden! Vor dem Schreibtisch der Teppich brennt lichterloh. Er geht in die Kammer neben der Küche und schleppt die alten Zeitungen sämtlich heraus. Er blättert sie auf und zerknüllt sie, ballt sie und wirft sie in alle Ecken. Er stellt die Leiter in die Mitte des Zimmers, wo sie früher stand. Er steigt auf die sechste Stufe, bewacht das Feuer und wartet. Als ihn die Flammen endlich erreichen, lacht er so laut, wie er in seinem ganzen Leben nie gelacht hat." (464)

Chapter 8

Quotations are from Nina Bouraoui, *La Voyeuse interdite* (Paris: Gallimard, 1991).

Page 168: "Il est né un membre de plus à la famille
  Avec, je ne remplirai pas la maison
  Avec, je ne combattrai pas mes ennemis."

Page 170: "Un message? Oui. Descendez dans vos tanières, ne perdons plus notre temps et le leur, désorientons avec courage le cours de la tradition, nos mœurs et leurs valeurs, arrachons rideaux et voiles pour joindre nos corps." (14)

Page 170: "Je suis un épouvantail articulé, une femelle au sexe pourri qu'il faut absolument ignorer afin d'échapper à la condamnation divine." (31)

Page 171: "La tristesse me donne bien des mots et des maux, je la touche du bout des doigts et l'empoigne parfois, je bois dans sa coupe et elle me couvre de ses ailes à l'envergure inhumaine." (17)

Page 172: "Etant imposée dans notre maison, Ourdhia semblait à son tour sourde et muette, mais je m' aperçus vite que son mutisme était étranger au nôtre." (51)

Page 172: "Grâce à elle j'allais pénétrer dans un monde irréel mais bienfaisant: le monde de l'imaginaire . . . le curieux récit du désert." (52)

Page 173: "Guidée par les étoiles, elle avait atteint la région la plus nue, la beauté sans apparat, l'essence même du sublime: le Ténéré. Vide du vide, absolu de l'absolu, centre de la terre, épicentre du néant, ce lieu couronnait enfin la marche disciplinée de la nomade, là, elle communiait avec la vérité." (54)

Page 175: "spectatrice clandestine suspendue au-dessus de la ville . . . elle ne risque rien." (21)

Page 175: "J'arrive à me dédoubler: je suis pion et joueuse à la fois." (61)

Page 176: "un œil . . . voilée, il ne me reste qu'un œil. . . . Au centre de l'événement, je m'avançai dans la nuit, borgne et résignée vers le véhicule de la mort." (143)

Page 177: "Concentrée sur les choses, sur mes gestes et sur toutes mes pensées, je devenais mon propre témoin, et par un effort réflexif, je me regardais étreindre l'aventure . . . j'assistais et participais à de joyeuses funérailles: les miennes. J'enterrais mon enfance pour aller vivre au-delà d'elle, de moi et du connu." (124)

Page 178: "Je falsifiais mes souvenirs, et tout ce que j'avais maudit se groupait dans l'instant présent en un bloc d'émotions." (138)

Page 178: "une cellule mortuaire où les sangs mêlés, les sens sans dessus dessous et les sentences les plus abjectes abasourdissent murs et coussins, tête et corps!" (88)

Page 178: "Je devais quitter ma chambre d'enfant. Tirée par l'avenir, écartelée par le répétitif et la tradition, je gisais déjà là dans les regrets! Ces heures d'ennui . . . tout revenait méthodiquement et je pleurais déjà mes ennemis!" (138)

Conclusion

Quotations are from Paul Lafargue, *Le Droit à la paresse* (Pantin, France: Le Temps des Cerises, 1996).

Page 195: "Plus mes peuples travailleront, moins il y aura de vices . . . je serais disposé à ordonner que les dimanches, passé l'heure des offices, les boutiques fussent ouvertes et les ouvriers rendus à leur travail. (48)

Page 196: "donna à ses adorateurs le suprême exemple de la paresse idéale; après six jours de travail, il se reposa pour l'éternité." (45)

Page 196: "proclame le droit à la paresse, mille et mille fois plus noble et plus sacré que les phtisiques Droits de l'homme." (59)

Page 197: "La passion aveugle, perverse et homicide du travail transforme la machine libératrice en instrument d'asservissement des hommes libres: sa productivité les appauvrit." (60)

Page 197: "L'ouvrier, au lieu de prolonger son repos . . . redouble d'ardeur, comme s'il voulait rivaliser avec la machine. O concurrence absurde et meurtrière." (61)

Page 198: "Cette folie est l'amour du travail, la passion moribonde du travail, poussée jusqu'à l'épuisement des forces vitales de l'individu. . . . Au lieu de réagir contre cette aberration mentale, les prêtres, les économistes, les moralistes, ont sacro-sanctifié le travail . . . ils ont voulu réhabiliter ce que leur Dieu avait maudit." (43)

Selected Bibliography

Abraham, Karl. *Selected Papers*. Vol. 1. New York: Basic Books, 1953.

Agamben, Giorgio. *Stanzas: Word and Phantasm in Western Culture.* Translated by Ronald L. Martinez. Minneapolis: University of Minnesota Press, 1993.

Anzieu, Didier. *Le Moi-peau*. Paris: Dunod, 1995.

Baudelaire, Charles. *Œuvres complètes*. Vol. 2. Paris: Pléiade, 1976.

———. *The Parisian Prowler: Petits Poèmes en Prose*. Translated by Edward K. Kaplan. Athens: University of Georgia Press, 1977.

Baur, Susan. *Hypochondria: Woeful Imaginings*. Berkeley: University of California Press, 1988.

Beizer, Janet. *Ventriloquized Bodies: Narratives of Hysteria in Nineteenth-Century France*. Ithaca: Cornell University Press, 1994.

Bidaud, Éric. *Anorexie mentale, ascèse, mystique: Une approche psychanalytique*. Paris: Denoël, 1997.

Bois, Yve-Alain. "Character Study: Sophie Calle." *Artforum* 38, no. 8 (April 2000).

Bonnefoy, Yves. *The Lure and the Truth of Painting: Selected Essays on Art*. Edited by Richard Stamelman. Chicago: University of Chicago Press, 1995.

Borch-Jacobsen, Mikkel. *Lacan: Le maître absolu*. Paris: Flammarion, 1995.

———. *Lacan: The Absolute Master*. Translated by Douglas Brick. Stanford: Stanford University Press, 1990.

Bouraoui, Nina. *Forbidden Vision*. Translated by K. Melissa Marcus. Barrytown, N.Y.: Station Hill, 1995.

———. *La Voyeuse interdite*. Paris: Gallimard, 1991.

Brown, Peter. *The Body and Society: Men, Women, and Sexual Renunciation in Early Christianity*. New York: Columbia University Press, 1988.

Calle, Sophie. *Double Game*. London: Violette Editions, 1999.

———. *Douleur exquise*. Arles: Actes Sud, 2003.

———. *Des Histoires vraies*. Paris: Actes Sud, 1994.

———. *La Visite guidée*. Rotterdam: Museum Boymans-van Beuningen, 1996.

Canetti, Elias. *Auto-da-Fé*. Translated by C. V. Wedgewood. 1935. New York: Farrar, Straus, and Giroux, 1984.

———. *Die Blendung*. Vienna: Herbert Reichner Verlag, 1935.

——. *Earwitness: Fifty Characters*. Translated by Joachim Neugroshel. 1974. London: André Deutsch, 1979.

——. *The Play of the Eyes*. Translated by R. Manheim. New York: Farrar, Straus and Giroux, 1986./

Cavell, Stanley. *Disowning Knowledge in Six Shakespeare Plays*. Cambridge: Cambridge University Press, 1987.

Clément, Catherine. *La Folle et le saint*. Paris: Seuil, 1993.

David, Christian. *L'État amoureux*. Paris: Payot, 2002.

Du Plessix Gray, Francine. *Rage and Fire: A Life of Louise Colet, Pioneer Feminist, Literary Star, Flaubert's Muse*. New York: Simon and Schuster, 1995.

Ehrenberg, Alain. *La Fatigue d'être soi: Dépression et société*. Paris: Odile Jacob, 1998.

Eliot, George. *Middlemarch*. Edited by W. J. Harvey. New York: Penguin, 1965.

Fédida, Pierre. "Une parole qui ne remplit rien." *Nouvelle revue de la psychanalyse* 11 (1975): 91–103.

Flaubert, Gustave. *Œuvres complètes*. Edited by Jean Bruneau. 4 vols. Paris: Pléiade, 1973–98.

——. *Préface à la vie d'écrivain*. Edited by Geneviève Bollème. Paris: Seuil, 1963.

Goldstein, Jan. *Console and Classify*. Cambridge: Cambridge University Press, 1987.

——. "The Uses of Male Hysteria: Medical and Literary Discourse in Nineteenth-Century France." *Representations* 34 (Spring 1991): 134–65.

Gordon, Rae Beth. *Ornament, Fantasy, and Desire in Nineteenth-Century French Literature*. Princeton: Princeton University Press, 1992.

Green, André. "Obsessions et psychonévroses obsessionnelles." *Encyclopédie médico-chirurgicale: Psychiatrie*. Paris: Editions techniques, 1965, 3:37370.

——. *On Private Madness*. Madison, Conn.: International Universities Press, 1993.

Gros, Frédéric. *Création et folie: Une histoire du jugement psychiatrique*. Paris: PUF, 1997.

Guillaumin, Jean. *Le Moi sublimé: Psychanalyse de la créativité*. Paris: Dunod, 1998.

Harpham, Geoffrey G. *The Ascetic Imperative in Culture and Criticism*. Chicago: University of Chicago Press, 1987.

Highmore, Ben, ed. *The Everyday Life Reader*. London: Routledge, 2002.

Hulse, Michael, trans. *Essays in Honor of Elias Canetti*. New York: Farrar, Straus and Giroux, 1987.

Jamison, Kay Redfield. *Touched with Fire: Manic-Depressive Illness and the Artistic Temperament*. New York: Free Press, 1994.

Janet, Pierre. *L'Amour et la haine*. Paris: Editions Medicales Norbert Maloine, 1932.

——. *De L'Angoisse à l'extase*. Vol. 1. 1926. Paris: Alcan, 1975.

Janet, Pierre, and Fulgence Raymond. *Les obsessions et la psychasthénie*. Vol. 2. 1903. New York: Arno Press, 1976.

Jaspers, Karl. *Strindberg et Van Gogh*. 1922. Paris: Minuit, 1953.

Kant, Immanuel. *Anthropology from a Pragmatic Point of View*. Translated by Victor Lyle Dowdell. Carbondale, Ill.: Southern Illinois University Press, 1978.

Kaplan, Alice, and Kristin Ross, eds. *Everyday Life*. Special issue, *Yale French Studies* 73 (1987).

Kaplan, Edward K. *Baudelaire's Prose Poems: The Esthetic, the Ethical, and the Religious in "The Parisian Prowler."* Athens: University of Georgia Press, 1990.

Klein, Richard. *Cigarettes Are Sublime*. Durham, N.C.: Duke University Press, 1993.

Kofman, Sarah. *The Childhood of Art*. Translated by Winifred Woodhull. New York: Columbia Univesity Press, 1988.

——. *L'Enfance de l'art: Une interprétation de l'esthétique freudienne*. Paris: Galilée, 1985.

Kramer, Peter D. *Listening to Prozac*. New York: Penguin, 1997.

Kristeva. Julia. *Black Sun: Depression and Melancholy*. Translated by Leon Roudiez. New York: Columbia University Press, 1989.

——. *Soleil noir: Dépression et mélancolie*. Paris, Gallimard, 1987.

Lafargue, Paul. *Le droit à la paresse*. Pantin, France: Le Temps des Cerises, 1996.

Lebrun, J.-P. *Un monde sans limites*. Paris: Érès, 1997.

Löwy, Michael, and Robert Sayre. *Révolte et mélancolie: Le romantisme à contrecourant de la modernité*. Paris: Payot, 1992.

——. *Romanticism against the Tide of Modernity*. Translated by Catherine Porter. Durham, N.C.: Duke University Press, 2002.

Lyotard, Jean-François. *L'Inhumain, causeries sur le temps*. Paris: Galilée, 1988.

——. *The Inhuman*. Translated by Geoffrey Bennington and Rachel Bowlby. Stanford: Stanford University Press, 1991.

Mann, Thomas. *Gesammelte Werke*. Vol. 2. *Der Zauberberg* Berlin: Aufbau-Verlag, 1955.

——. *The Magic Mountain*. Translated by H. T. Lowe-Porter. 1928. London: Penguin, 1969.

Marder, Elissa. *Dead Time: Temporal Disorders in the Wake of Modernity (Baudelaire and Flaubert)*. Stanford: Stanford University Press, 2001.

Melman, Charles. *L'homme sans gravité: Jouir à tout prix*. Paris: Denoël, 2002.

M'Uzan, Michel de. *De l'art à la mort*. Paris: Gallimard, 1977.

Nancy, Jean Luc. *La communauté désœuvrée*. Paris: Christian Bourgois, 1986.

Nodier, Charles. *De quelques phénomènes du sommeil*. Edited by E. Dazin. Bègles, France: Le Castor Astral, 1996.

——. *L'Amateur de livres: Précédé du bibliomane, de bibliographie des fous et de la monomanie réflective*. Edited by J. L. Steinmetz. Pantin, France: Castor Astral, 1993.

——. *La Fée aux miettes: Précédé de Smarra et de Trilby*. Paris: Gallimard, 1982.

Pareyson, Luigi. *Conversations sur l'esthétique*. Translated by Gilles Tiberghien. Paris: Gallimard, 1992.

Paulson, William, ed. "Les genres de l'hénaurme siècle." In *Papers from the Four-teenth Annual Colloquium in Nineteenth-Century French Studies*. Ann Arbor: University of Michigan, Department of Romance Languages, 1989.

Phillips, Adam. *On Flirtation: Essays on the Uncommitted Life*. Cambridge, Mass.: Harvard University Press, 1994.

———. *On Kissing, Tickling, and Being Bored: Psychoanalytic Essays on the Unexam-ined Life*. Cambridge, Mass.: Harvard University Press, 1993.

Porter, Roy, ed. *The Faber Book of Madness*. London: Faber and Faber, 1991.

Rambures, J. L. *Comment travaillent les écrivains*. Paris: Flammarion, 1978.

Robert, Marthe. *En haine du roman: Étude sur Flaubert*. Paris: Balland, 1982.

———. *Roman des origines et origines du roman*. Paris: Gallimard, 1972.

Sass, Louis. *Madness and Modernism: Insanity in the Light of Modern Art, Literature, and Thought*. Cambridge, Mass.: Harvard University Press, 1994.

Schaeffer, Jean-Marie. *Art of the Modern Age: Philosophy of Art from Kant to Hei-degger*. Princeton: Princeton University Press, 2000.

———. *L'Art de l'âge moderne: L'esthétique et la philosophie de l'art du XVIIIème siècle à nos jours*. Paris: Gallimard, 1992.

Shapiro, David. *Autonomy and Rigid Character*. New York: Basic Books, 1981.

Stein, J. D., and Michael Stone, eds. *Essential Papers on Obsessive-Compulsive Dis-order*. New York: New York University Press, 1997.

Swain, Gladys. *Dialogue avec l'insensé: Essais d'histoire de la psychiatrie*. Paris: Gal-limard, 1994.

Worringer, Wilhelm. *Abstraction and Empathy: A Contribution to the Psychology of Style*. Translated by Michael Bullock. New York: International Universities Press, 1967.

Yalisove, Daniel, ed. *The Essential Papers on Addiction*. New York: New York Uni-versity Press, 1997.

Index

absolutism: art and, 5n.10; and identity,
107–8; monomania as longing for, 5–6
Abraham, Karl, 6, 147n.84, 157
absence, 75, 114, 116, 118, 168
abstraction: empathy vs., 17–18, 101–8,
116–19; Flaubert and, 57–58; *horror
vacui* as cause of, 104; and identity,
106–8, 175; and marriage, 117–18;
nature vs., 1–2; Nodier and, 71–72,
81; as ontological weakness, 29; quotidian vs., 203; rigid characters and,
162n.37; scholarship as, 104–5. *See
also* scholarship
Abstraction and Empathy (Worringer),
17–18, 102–3
abstract space, 111–14, 113n.18, 147
adaptability, obsession and, 34
aesthetics: and *dispositio*, 155;
hypochondria as principle in, 122–23;
melancholy and, 123; of the Unreal,
66–67; verification and, 94
Agamben, Giorgio, 79n.40, 176, 178, 196
agoraphobia, 5
alienation, 60, 86n.9, 87
ambiguity, 34, 85–87. *See also* disorder
amour de loin, 178
anal phase, 157
anamnesis, 167
anorexia, 122, 122nn.4–5, 124–25, 193
*Anthropology from a Pragmatic Point of
View* (Kant), 117
anticipation, as anxiety, 184–85
anti-decadence, in Germany, 150n.18
anti-elitism, 75–76, 76n.32
anti-monde, 170
anti-narrative, 183
Antipatros, 197
Anzieu, Didier, 42, 43, 80
apophatic art, 174
arabesque, 6, 34, 45

A Rebours (Huysmans), 177
Arendt, Hannah, 196, 197–98
Aristotle, 178, 196
art: and absolutism, 5n.10; abstract, 66,
71; apophatic, 174; autonomous,
72n.23; and disorderliness, 8–9,
9n.15, 42, 42n.3, 47; as escapism, 59,
181, 185; and impermanence, 163; as
impersonality, 6–7; life as, 142–44,
187–91; melancholy and, 165, 168–71;
mimesis vs., 57; as monomania, 44–
47; as montage, 67; nature vs., 1–2,
1n.3, 46, 59–60, 119; and otherworldliness, 73; and perfectionism, 46, 57;
plastic, 46n.13; *rapport exact* and,
55–56; as reconstruction, 75; as risk-
taking, 181; and stasis, 52–53, 202–3;
therapeutic benefits of, 88, 143–44,
202–5; therapeutic space provided
by, 46–47; unopened birthday gifts
as, 182–83. *See also* art and identity;
art as control; art as substitute for
life; writing
art and identity: in *Auto-da-Fé*, 44, 142–
44, 151–52, 154–55, 157–58, 160–63;
Calle and, 190, 191–92
art as control: and anonymity, 54–55;
Bouraoui and, 173–74; Calle and,
180–81, 182–83, 190–92; Canetti and,
143–44, 161; as dual process, 43–44;
Flaubert and, 43–44, 43–44n.7, 54,
143–44, 202n.14; therapeutic benefits
of, 45–47, 143–44, 202–5
art as substitute for life: Flaubert and,
16, 43n.6, 48–52, 48nn.16–17, 59–61,
62, 78–79; as idée fixe, 5; as monomania, 44–45; Nodier and, 62–63, 63n.4;
as Romantic theme, 78
art collecting, as obsession, 138, 138n.10
asceticism: in *Auto-da-Fé*, 150–51; em-